This is number two hundred and fifteen in the
second numbered series of the
Miegunyah Volumes
made possible by the
Miegunyah Fund
established by bequests
under the wills of
Sir Russell and Lady Grimwade.

'Miegunyah' was Russell Grimwade's home
from 1911 to 1955
and Mab Grimwade's home
from 1911 to 1973.

INNER SONG

INNER SONG

A Biography of Margaret Sutherland

JILLIAN GRAHAM

THE MIEGUNYAH PRESS

To my husband Peter, my son Olivier and daughter Freya,
and to all women who dare to challenge dominant paradigms.

THE MIEGUNYAH PRESS
An imprint of Melbourne University Publishing Limited
Level 1, 715 Swanston Street, Carlton, Victoria 3053, Australia
mup-contact@unimelb.edu.au
www.mup.com.au

First published 2023

Cover design by Pfisterer + Freeman
Cover image: source unknown
Text design and typesetting by Cannon Typesetting
Printed in China by 1010 Printing Asia Ltd

NATIONAL LIBRARY OF AUSTRALIA
A catalogue record for this book is available from the National Library of Australia

9780522878233 (hardback)
9780522878240 (ebook)

CONTENTS

ACKNOWLEDGEMENTS

I AM DELIGHTED TO offer sincere thanks to those who have contributed variously to this project. Since I embarked on my MMus thesis research on Margaret in the 1990s, her grandson and custodian of her estate, Anthony Bunney, has been consistently helpful and generous in sharing his collection of Margaret's papers. I could not have wished for a more supportive Sutherland family member. Thanks also to Anthony and his siblings, Michael and Kirsten, and to Barbara Taylor and Astrid Dahl for their willingness to share their memories of Margaret and the wider family.

To others who have spared time for conversations and email exchanges, I extend my deep appreciation. These include those whom I interviewed for my MMus thesis in the 1990s: Valerie Cohen, Margaret Schofield, Elizabeth Von Rompaey (all deceased), Pamela Bloom, Jane Bunney, Helen Gifford and Maureen White. More recently they include Katy Abbott, Elizabeth Campbell, Vicki Fairfax, Beryl Kimber Leske, Zoe Knighton, Diane Langmore, Stephen McIntyre, Suzanne McWha, Paul Mishura, Benjamin Northey, Karen Pack, Elizabeth Sellars, Claire Spencer AM and Professor John Spicer.

For their encouragement, support of the project and suggestions I thank Associate Professor Fay Anderson, Professor Warren Bebbington,

Dr Ian Burk, Elena Kats-Chernin, Professor Linda Kouvaras, Dr Sandra McComb, Professor Kerry Murphy, Dr Suzanne Robinson and Associate Professor Janice Stockigt.

This biography could not have been written without access to resources at the State Library Victoria, National Archives of Australia (Sydney), Public Records Office Victoria, Australian Dictionary of Biography, Australian Music Centre and the National Library of Australia, including the invaluable Trove online collection of newspapers and journals. I also thank Darren Capon at the Supreme Court of Victoria, Dr Jennifer Hill, Curator of the University of Melbourne's Rare Music Collection, Dr Heather Gaunt, Curator at the Grainger Museum, and Dr Elizabeth Kertesz at the Melbourne Conservatorium of Music.

The award of the 2018 Redmond Barry Fellowship enabled me to devote more time to research. It also conferred value on the project, as did my being shortlisted for the Hazel Rowley Literary Fellowship in 2018 and 2021. I am extremely grateful to the selection panels for their encouragement.

There were many useful texts, but three authors stand out. I frequently consulted Dr David Symons' monograph, *The Music of Margaret Sutherland*, and thank him for his support of my research. Associate Professor Stuart Rosewarne's willingness to share his draft of the Sutherland family history is acknowledged. Dr Cherie Watters-Cowan's PhD dissertation, 'Reconstructing the Creative Life of Australian Composer Margaret Sutherland: the Evidence of Primary Source Documents', was a crucial resource, particularly her comprehensive catalogue of Sutherland's works included as an Appendix.

The following have kindly granted permission for use of materials: Anthony Bunney (Sutherland archives in his private collection); Australian Broadcasting Corporation (radio program recordings); Australian Dictionary of Biography; Australian Music Centre (James Murdoch photograph); Australian Performing Arts Collection, Arts Centre Melbourne (Margaret Sutherland material and George Fairfax photograph); National Archives of Australia (ABC archives); Robert Glass (Mollie Turner Shaw material); Kalli Rolfe Contemporary Art

(Athol Shmith photograph); HarperCollins Publishers Australia (Judith Wright poem); Meredith McKinney (Judith Wright quote); Jane Sinclair (John Sinclair quotes); Dr Shane Simpson (James Murdoch archives, NLA); *The Age* and The Aaron Copland Fund for Music (Copland material); The Catalysts (Catalysts archives); The Diggers Foundation (Heronswood image); The Lyceum Club (Lyceum archives, SLV and photograph of portrait of Sutherland by Rupert Bunny). I also thank Lyceum Art Advisory member Dinny Birrell for her assistance with the Bunny portrait.

To Emeritus Professor Desley Deacon, I offer my heartfelt thanks for reading draft chapters, asking astute questions, making practical suggestions, and for her interest in the topic. For guidance offered by Nathan Hollier (CEO) and Louise Stirling (Senior Editor) at Melbourne University Publishing, and copy editor Sarina Rowell, I am also most grateful.

To friends—Mandy Beattie, Ros Braham, Nancy Calo, Helen Rommelaar and Kathrin Schmieder, and to my son and daughter, Olivier and Freya Miller, thank you for acting as sympathetic sounding boards.

Finally, my profound appreciation goes to my husband, Peter Garnick, who could not have been more supportive, long-suffering and patient. He listened regularly to my 'Margaret monologues', read my work and provided an essential 'once-removed' perspective.

PRELUDE

For many years, the 'grand old man' of Australian music has been a woman—Margaret Sutherland.[1]

UNDETERRED BY THE baking heat on 6 November 1982, hordes of people lined the streets of inner-city Melbourne, expectantly awaiting the parade. With a pied piper in the lead, bands and floats set off from the State Library of Victoria past Flinders Street Station and over the Princes Bridge. This was not in honour of the famous Melbourne Cup that pervades the city annually at this time. Instead, it marked the beginning of the celebrations for the opening of Melbourne's new concert hall in St Kilda Road, on the banks of the Yarra River.

The festivities continued throughout the day, and in the evening a glittering gala took place in the new auditorium. Official guests arrived on a tram decorated by French-born Australian artist Mirka Mora. The usual types of speeches were delivered, and music followed. Maestro Hiroyuki Iwaki, chief conductor of the Melbourne Symphony Orchestra, led the orchestra, the Melbourne Chorale Occasional Choir and Australian concert pianist Geoffrey Tozer through an international program intended to reflect the magnitude of the occasion. For the grand finale, the audience was regaled with what *Herald* music critic John Sinclair pronounced to be the loudest performance of Respighi's *Pines of Rome* he had ever heard.[2]

In attendance that night was the 'grand old lady of Australian music', 84-year-old composer Margaret Sutherland. Thirty-nine years earlier, she had formed a lobby group, the Combined Arts Centre Movement (CACM), and fought tirelessly to have the forlorn Wirth's Park site protected from commercial interests and reserved for a centre the group considered essential to the survival of the arts in Melbourne.

There is no record of what the grand old lady—now wheelchair bound and nearly blind—thought as the formalities ended and a high-spirited audience took to the stage to dance. But she deserved to feel proud to witness the joyful culmination of her struggle for the Victorian Arts Centre (now Arts Centre Melbourne). Given Margaret's history of directly expressing her opinions, especially in advocating for Australian musicians and composers, she would also have been justified in feeling a little disgusted. Although the former premier of Victoria, the Honourable Sir Rupert Hamer, acknowledged that the 'great Australian musician, Margaret Sutherland', was present, none of her music—nor that by any Australian composer—was programmed. John Sinclair, shocked that Margaret's music was excluded, criticised the ill-chosen program. He added scathingly that 'the programme planners then proceeded to dispense their own inimitable blend of mediocrity, fatuity and carelessness'.[3]

Seven weeks after Margaret's death, this error of judgment was finally partially rectified. In October 1984, a memorial performance of her chamber compositions was given in the Concert Hall (now Hamer Hall) foyer, to acknowledge her contribution to the creation of Arts Centre Melbourne. Coincidentally, this concert occurred in the same month as the opening of the State Theatre.

Arts Centre Melbourne is one of the major legacies of an extraordinary life. But Margaret's most profound legacy was her music. Switching on the radio one morning in the late 1990s, I was captivated by her *Sonata for Violin and Piano*. To me, it sounded hauntingly lyrical, poignant and deeply expressive, with a restrained and dignified emotionalism. Its tonalities were unconventional for a work composed in 1925—they did not progress as expected.

Why had I not known about this composer? Having spent the first twenty years of my life in New Zealand couldn't explain this, because I had been in Australia for more than ten years. A performing musician myself, I had completed an undergraduate music degree at the University of Melbourne and embarked on postgraduate studies in the late 1990s. Like many others, I could name but few Australian women composers, let alone those of her calibre. I was seeking a thesis topic and resolved to discover more. My research stimulated an interest that has remained with me for two decades.

I learned that, consonant with her music, Margaret did not behave quite as expected. She was an innovative composer at a time when composers were mostly men, and in a country where sporting achievements were valued above the arts. For a woman with competing demands on her time, including two children and an unhappy marriage, she was musically productive, composing just over two hundred works in her lifetime. These were mostly chamber and vocal/choral works, but Margaret also wrote orchestral works, pieces for theatre and an opera. She loved the intimacy of chamber music, her defence of this preference pointing to the historically hierarchical and gendered nature of musical genres.

Margaret's early romantic style evolved into musical modernism. This diverse and innovative style challenged and reinterpreted musical conventions of harmony, melody, rhythm and sound. Related to changes in aesthetic worldviews reflected in modernism in art, the movement aimed to express the mood of the modern age at the turn of the nineteenth and twentieth centuries. Like any new movement, it was initially resisted by critics and audiences, particularly in early twentieth-century Australia.

Aspects of modernism appeared in Margaret's music early, when she employed what she referred to as 'slanting tonalities'.[4] Increasingly, she used idiosyncratic musical language that destabilised conventional tonality and attempted to redefine beauty in music. She was a pioneer in Australia, who struggled to gain acceptance of her surprising creative output. Matching her individual nature, she developed a distinctive compositional style, preferring to avoid being linked with any musical fashion or school.

Nevertheless, her credentials as a composer and as a fierce advocate for Australian music earned respect. Australian musicologist, critic and author Roger Covell, for example, claimed that 'it was a woman composer, Margaret Sutherland of Melbourne, who really naturalized the twentieth century in Australian music'. 'Probably no other person in Australia has worked, fought, lobbied and achieved so much for Australian music and the Australian composer', asserted James Murdoch, arts administrator, author and spokesman for Australian music.[5]

I was a mature-age student with two young children, and was intrigued that a woman—one a generation older than my mother—aspired to blend a creative career with parenthood. I was trying to achieve a workable balance between family and study, but that option was not available to my mother. She felt compelled to stop work when she married, experiencing more social constraints and having fewer alternative models.

I wondered what had shaped Margaret's life and who her models were. Historically, women were considered incapable of composing music—it was men who held the creative gift, as opposed to the generative powers of women's wombs.[6] Eighteenth-century French philosopher Jean-Jacques Rousseau exemplified this thinking:

> Women, in general, don't like any art, are not well versed in any, and have no talent for it. They can acquire knowledge … and all that can be acquired through hard work. But that celestial fire that emblazens and ignites the soul, that quality of genius that consumes and devours … those sublime ecstasies that reside in the depths of the heart—these will always be lacking in the writings of women.[7]

Instead, Rousseau instructed, a woman had a duty to a man to 'be pleasing in his sight, to win his respect and love, to train him in childhood, to tend him in manhood, to counsel and console, to make his life pleasant and happy'.[8]

With particular reference to music, American critic George Upton argued in 1880 that a woman could interpret but not create music, because to 'limit her emotions within the rigid laws of harmony and counterpoint, and to express them with arbitrary signs, is a cold-blooded operation, possible only to the sterner and more obdurate nature of man'.[9]

These attitudes, now fortunately outdated, were alive and well in early twentieth-century Australia when Margaret was establishing herself. I wondered what made her struggle against the weight of historical convictions. When she returned from Europe in 1925, resolved to be a composer in her homeland, there was barely any tradition of professional composition in Australia—particularly among women.

My research led me to master's and PhD dissertations about Australian women composers' experiences. My doctoral studies behind me, I had not finished with Margaret—her story deserves to extend beyond musical academia. There were scholarly publications about her and her music, but no overarching story of her life, and I took on the project with enthusiasm.

There are gaps in primary sources. Margaret did not keep a diary, except of her trip overseas in 1951—and it was a travelogue rather than an outlet for her innermost feelings, which found their release more in music than words. But she wrote well and was an accomplished public speaker. Consequently, there are autobiographical notes and articles, talks, opinion pieces, letters, musings, scrapbooks, photographs, and in-depth interviews that were rich sources of insight and information.

When mining these sources, I was mindful of the fickle nature of memory. As American psychiatrist Bessel van der Kolk eloquently summarises it:

> Such autobiographical memories are not precise reflections of reality; they are stories we tell to convey our personal take on our experience. Our autobiographical self creates connections among experiences and assembles them into a coherent story. Our narratives change with the telling, as our perspective changes and as we incorporate new input.[10]

I take the view that Margaret's words were reflections of her truth when she produced them. The opportunity to converse with family members, friends and acquaintances was invaluable, providing different insights and perspectives.

Loved by many and hated by some, Margaret's character was strong, her intellect sharp, her persistence and hope eternal. A natural leader who commanded respect, she was interested in people, compassionate, charming, nurturing, introspective and disarming. Not one to suffer fools, she could be abrasive, but usually in the service of music. She had a fighting spirit, essential in a life trajectory that was at odds with the traditional pathways for women. Existing in a rarefied atmosphere, she surrounded herself with influential men of music as well as high-achieving women, mostly members of Melbourne's Lyceum Club.

Writing a Woman's Life by Carolyn Heilbrun is one of several texts that inspired me. Heilbrun referred to the conventional 'marriage or erotic plot' that shaped a woman's life.[11] The ultimate destination was the safety and closure of marriage, in which a man, his career and their children were her principal focus. Unlike men, women could not be seen to strive openly towards their non-domestic ambitions, or to assume power over their lives.

The issue of gender is central to Margaret's story—being a woman affected her vocation. Over half her compositions remain unpublished. She was nearly forty when significant publication of her works occurred, and fewer than half have been recorded. She was sixty-nine when she received her first commission.

Historical disparities between women's and men's compositional expertise are now acknowledged as due more to inequalities in education and social expectations than to innate differences in ability.[12] In swimming against the tide of social expectations, Margaret was enabled by a supportive father and facilitated by her genteel alternative extended family, particularly on her father's side. They did not conform without question and valued education for both sexes. Money did not motivate them. Margaret's privilege, manifested through cultural rather than financial capital, was attained through growing up in one of the most creative, intellectual, liberal and prodigious families in Australian history.

As her life evolved, so too did Margaret's choice of genres and musical style—she always sought to be original. I don't provide detailed musicological analyses—this has been done admirably by David Symons and others. Nor do I indulge in speculation regarding contemporaneous expressions in her music of her mood or personal circumstances. Margaret's tendency not to provide exact dates for many of her compositions, together with the fact that various scores are missing, would render this task imprecise. Moreover, when she did intend her music to convey a particular meaning or influence, she said so, and is unlikely to have appreciated conjecture by others. I focus instead on works, performances and critiques that assist in conveying her story. I urge curious readers to listen to her music, glean from it what resonates for them, and decide to what extent they agree with critical opinion. I list available recordings in the References, to facilitate this process.

In a paper given to the Catalysts women's group in 1956, Margaret wrote of being at the mercy of 'ceaseless sound pictures' or 'floating ideas'. These she referred to as *le chant intérieur.* I hope to reveal something of that 'inner song' in the pages that follow.[13]

PART ONE

EARLY LIFE: 1897–1913

CHAPTER 1

THE GALA DAYS (1897–1901)

The creative musician—the composer—very often exhibits extraordinary precocity. Indeed, it will be found that if a student is going to write music of any quality, he will have been at it quietly by himself from an early age. For it is virtually impossible to start later without early trial and error.

Margaret Sutherland[1]

MELBOURNE, 1902. 'DUNROBIN' was an imposing Victorian mansion at the University of Melbourne, now known as University House. Margaret and her older sister Dorothy were staying there briefly with Uncle Alexander, registrar and acting professor of English, and Aunt Lizzie after their family's move to Melbourne. Arriving late one afternoon, they were welcomed into a cosy house with fires glowing and blinds drawn against the bleak winter evening outside. The floors were fashionably covered with varying shades of felt, and in the formal dining room, a large dark-wood table was set with glittering silver in readiness for a dinner party.[2]

Four-year-old Margaret was dressed for the occasion in her best cream delaine frock, sewn by a painstaking seamstress. Her long, fair hair was held back off her face and secured with a large bow, and on her feet were soft suede shoes of delicate pale green. She surveyed the scene, awestruck, but was whisked away with her sister and cousins to the nursery, appropriately separated from the 'grown-up' dinner party.[3]

The meal over, the guests retired to the parlour for port, and the youngsters were recalled from the nursery. Margaret's 13-year-old sister Dorothy, already an accomplished pianist, was asked to provide musical entertainment, and obliged with a difficult *Impromptu* by Franz Schubert. Not to be outshone, Margaret confidently climbed onto the piano stool, her feet not yet reaching the pedals. She played another Schubert *Impromptu,* one she had 'audaciously learned' by ear through listening to Dorothy practising.[4]

Margaret's memory of this event may be linked to an early portrait of herself painted in pastels by her aunt, Jane Sutherland. In it, she is about seven, seated on a stool, her long red-blonde hair drawn into a loose plait secured by a bow. It falls over her left shoulder against her cream frock, drawing the viewer's gaze to a straw hat on the floor. Margaret looks like a demure little girl just returned from church. In her own world, she gazes down at an object she is holding. Had she been looking at the viewer, we might have detected in her eyes the determination and drive that later helped her to stand out from the crowd.

Retelling this story much later, Margaret remarked that even a year afterwards, she would not have had the effrontery to perform at such a gathering. She mourned the loss of youthful courage, yearning for the 'brazenness' of childhood.[5] Effrontery aside, this early vignette reveals Margaret's precocious talent. That no one tried to prevent her performance is equally pertinent.

Although Margaret was talented and interested in music from the minute she was born, she did not regard herself as a 'musical prodigy'. In 1963, aged sixty-five, she addressed the Catalysts regarding this phenomenon:

> For all the innumerable crimes constantly committed against children, to my way of thinking, the conscious exploitation of the unusually gifted child is one of the most horrible ... The youngster, conditioned so rigidly and so tirelessly as to be utterly defenceless, is tragically alone ... The youngster with a special bent—the one who gives evidence, at an

> early stage, of unusual precocity in any one direction, will naturally drift into spending a great deal more time on the thing that grips him, and that he feels he particularly wants to explore … but always along with the natural maturing of his own personality and knowledge of life and living.[6]

These words constitute just one example of the strong opinions Margaret regularly expressed. They also encapsulate her own experience. She was that 'youngster with a special bent', who was 'at it quietly … from an early age', and not 'conditioned so rigidly and so tirelessly'.[7] Within the enabling and nurturing cocoon of her extended family, she was encouraged to develop and articulate opinions, and her talent was permitted to grow and flourish naturally.

Margaret Sutherland was born in 1897 into a liberal-thinking family that valued education and creative aspirations. Her grandparents, George and Jane Sutherland, had emigrated to Sydney from Dumbarton, Scotland, in 1864. Like most Scottish immigrants to Australia at this time, George was a skilled worker. He had followed his father's profession of carving ships' figureheads, a trade requiring both practical and artistic skills. Carvers were trained through apprenticeships and were typically not otherwise highly educated. George didn't attend university but read widely and educated himself. He was a competent draftsman, talented commercial artist, enthusiastic painter (though colour blind) and music teacher. Jane was an organiser with a strong personality, and was 'keen of intellect', encouraging her daughters to contribute to family debates. With their attitude to education, and relishing of robust discussions, interest in journalism and cultural contributions, the Sutherlands and their descendants upheld characteristics often attributed to Scottish immigrants.[8]

The discovery of gold in 1851 and a booming economy made Australia an increasingly popular destination for free settlers, but this was not the principal reason for George and Jane's decision to emigrate to Sydney. George's health was fragile, and the harsh Scottish climate's impact on him and the children was the strongest impetus. They were not alone in their move. Since the mid-eighteenth century, the Scots have emigrated more than most other European peoples, aside from Australia being a popular destination in the 1850s. In 1864, George, Jane and their first six children set sail for Sydney. Two more children were born before the family relocated to Melbourne in 1870. This move would prove a good decision. Melbourne had been in the grip of a land and property boom since the gold rush. Cable trams ferried people around, and the fashionable filled the footpaths and arcades of Collins Street. By the 1880s, 'Marvellous Melbourne' was considered one of the greatest cities in the world, demonstrating its sophistication with international exhibitions of industrial, scientific and artistic progress from all over the globe.[9]

After their arrival in Melbourne, the Sutherlands settled in Lytton Street, Carlton, overlooking the Melbourne General Cemetery. George gained employment as a drawing teacher and later as a wood block engraver, but found time for art, exhibiting several works at the Victorian Artists Society from 1875 to 1878. Two of his brothers—Alexander and John—soon joined him in Melbourne with their families. Like other family members, John was a keen artist, who exhibited at the Victorian Artists Society in the 1890s.[10]

In an ominous harbinger of the future, George's poor health culminated in his death from heart disease in 1885, aged fifty-six. All his sons would later suffer the same fate, dying one after another in or around their fifties. Probate documents list his legacy of £1284, all of which he bequeathed to his wife Jane. This equates to around $175 000 today, suggesting that the family was comfortable, but by no means wealthy. As he was a drawing teacher with a wife and eight children to support, this is hardly surprising.

Though they were not affluent, George and Jane's broad interests provided a rich environment for their children. George Junior (1855–1905), Margaret's father, was a historian, journalist and inventor with interests in music, art and photography. He attended the private

Presbyterian school of Scotch College. This choice was influenced by the school's Scottish heritage and the family's religion. Its educational values matched those of George and Jane, with its egalitarian, non-sectarian culture and its broadly based liberal curriculum in the arts, sciences and humanities.[11]

George Junior studied history and political economy at the University of Melbourne, where he earned a Bachelor of Arts in 1877 and a Master of Arts in 1879. In his first job following graduation, he taught humanities at Carlton College, which his older brother Alexander had established in 1877 on Royal Parade near the university.[12] The school reflected the family's progressive ideals, its mission being to instil curiosity and a love of learning. It became one of Melbourne's largest private schools, its ranks swollen by the Sutherland clan.

Carlton College's founding principles were akin to those of the breakaway Australian Church, a forward-thinking institution established in 1885. Margaret's family were Presbyterians, and attended church dutifully, but decided to switch their allegiance to this new church. Margaret attributed this to the 'irritating inconsistencies and glaringly outworn dogma' of the Presbyterian Church.[13] Her understanding of their decision hints at egalitarian and progressive attitudes inherited from her extended family.

George Junior's contributions to Australian society were significant, particularly in the fields of Australian history and journalism. During his graduate studies and his teaching at Carlton College, he and his brother were writing the widely read *History of Australia,* one of a series of schoolbooks first published in 1877.[14]

With his seven brothers and sisters, George Junior absorbed the stimulating and liberal-minded family environment. He enjoyed teaching but found it constricting. Fascinated by the gold rush, he resigned, intending to nurture his adventurous spirit, and left Melbourne to explore the goldfields. The stories he heard about the early prospectors' experiences inspired him to produce *Tales of the Goldfields* (1880). With this book, he aimed to inculcate in young readers the notion that, for hard workers, Australia was a land of progress and opportunity.[15]

Tales of the Goldfields launched his career as a journalist. His interest in the outback as a source of Australia's wealth and the basis of a uniquely Australian character led him to an influential trip down the Murray River to Adelaide. He became convinced that a more scientific approach to development was necessary.[16]

In Adelaide, *Register* editor John Harvey Finlayson offered him a journalism post. He accepted and embarked in 1881 on what he referred to as 'technological journalism'. He wrote about industrial innovations displayed at the 1880s international exhibitions, conducted experiments relating to modernisation of the newspaper industry, and designed improved printing processes. This culminated in the publication in 1901 of *Twentieth Century Inventions: A Forecast*.[17]

The decision to reside in South Australia was also influenced by developments in the arts, education and music. The Art Gallery of South Australia opened the year he arrived, and several art schools were established in the 1880s. George was keen to associate himself with the progressive University of Adelaide, which was the first to admit women and allow them to graduate with degrees.[18]

Music thrived in Adelaide in the 1880s and 1890s, due largely to the 1883 appointment of Governor Sir William Robinson, a powerful musical patron. In the same year, Australia's first professional music school, the Adelaide College of Music, was founded, and two years later, a chair of music was appointed at the University of Adelaide. In 1891, the first semi-professional orchestra was formed, and a bequest from Sir Thomas Elder led to the formal constitution of the Elder Conservatorium in 1898. As musical and dramatic evenings became regular features of Adelaide society, George's newspaper, the *Register*, became the major advertising forum for cultural events.[19]

At a Bach Society meeting, George met his future wife, Ada Bowen. They were married in 1882, when he was twenty-six and she eighteen. The Bowens were well established in Adelaide society's upper stratum, and through his marriage, George accessed this group and its cultural activities. Ada's sister's family, the Bullocks, resided at St Helen's in Prospect, the centre of family gatherings and cultural events. It was here that Ada's artist brother Tom introduced his children, nieces and nephews to art—a formative environment for his daughter, painter Stella Bowen.[20] Stella's story is told in her memoir, *Drawn from Life* (1941), and in Drusilla Modjeska's landmark biographical work *Stravinsky's Lunch* (1999).

George and Ada settled in Angas Street, Norwood. Their daughter Ruth was born in 1884, and two years later Douglas arrived, then Alfred in 1888 and Dorothy in 1889. Margaret was born at home on 20 November 1897, the youngest by eight years, which worked in her favour.

The family's artistic bent was matched by the high value placed on music. In George and Ada's social circles, young ladies were expected to supplement their education by piano playing or singing. Fond of music and accomplished at both, Ada ensured that Ruth and Dorothy learned piano from an early age.[21]

We know less about Ada than we do George. Margaret rarely mentioned her, except to say she was a wonderful mother who was 'only eighteen when she married and had no training to fall back on'. Like most women of her era, Ada was destined for domesticity. She was unselfish, lacked confidence, and was prone to depression. Her sister-in-law, Tom Bowen's wife and Stella's mother, similarly lacked opportunity beyond the domestic sphere. 'She lived entirely for us children', Stella said. 'Even her activities as secretary to the Mothers' Union were but an extension of her own parenthood.'[22] Despite Ada's restricted opportunities, she did not discourage her daughter's ambitions.

Margaret was born when women's rights were coming to the forefront. South Australian women had been actively seeking the vote since the 1880s. Morally conservative but politically radical organisations such as the Woman's Christian Temperance Union (WCTU) led this movement, believing that women's innate moral and spiritual superiority would protect the home from masculine vices such as drinking, gambling and sexual licentiousness. George and Ada supported women's enfranchisement and were pleased when South Australia became the first Australian colony to grant the vote to women, in 1894.[23]

Despite its emphasis on women's domestic roles, the suffrage movement provided role models of independent, outspoken women who made their mark on society.

For girls of Margaret's era, childhood was often the happiest and freest time, and this was true of her first four years in Adelaide. These were the 'gala days', when she enjoyed dedicated time with her father, and their close and loving relationship marked her for life. 'I had a tremendous feeling for my father', she later remarked. His paternal attention was unusual for the time, but George never felt compelled to conform to social conventions without question, and his dislike of idleness meant that, despite other commitments, he made time for his children. As the youngest, Margaret benefited, especially after her older siblings had left for school, as her father was home in the mornings before going to the *Register* around midday.[24]

Margaret recalled the Angas Street house as having 'an air of great peace and regularity'. A veranda ran along the front, and two tall Norfolk pines stood as sentinels on either side of the front garden. Between them ran a straight path from the front door to the garden gate, giving an impression of complete conformity. Each morning, Margaret perched on the gate, waving goodbye to her brothers as they crossed the parklands to Prince Alfred College, a private boys' school. While her sisters also went to school, it was the image of her brothers disappearing into the distance that remained. She would then retreat inside and 'strum' on the piano, inventing tunes and piecing together music she had heard her two sisters practising. Her father sometimes played to her, favouring movements from Beethoven's early sonatas. In the evenings, after Margaret had gone to bed, Ada sang Schubert lieder and other songs. Her 'sweet, plaintive voice' when singing Grieg's *Solveig's Song* was sometimes too much for one of Margaret's brothers: 'Please don't sing that song', he begged. 'It makes me sorry.'[25]

In Margaret's early 'placid enough life', there were inevitably ups and downs. One involved a family friend—a 'pseudo' aunt nicknamed Mrs Fodgins, her real name being difficult to pronounce. She dressed ominously in black and was 'stern and unyielding in all matters'.

An impending visit instilled such terror in Margaret that she would escape to a favourite hiding haven in the back garden. Beneath a large, spreading daisy bush, she was convinced that no one could find her as she made daisy chains, an activity that saw her 'patiently and loyally' through the 'dangerous periods' of her early life. Her older sister Dorothy was complicit, sounding an alarm at crucial moments to ensure Margaret remained undetected.[26]

Mrs Fodgins' disapproval of Margaret's piano playing elicited high indignation, especially as making music was already a 'routine affair' for her, as it was for all her family. But Mrs Fodgins believed the piano was 'a contraption for the playing of hymns' and thought there were too many 'strummers' in the family. Before one visit, the piano was locked so that Margaret couldn't play it and upset the unwelcome visitor. Horrified, Margaret retreated to her hiding place and her daisy chains.[27]

'Cedar Villa', an enchanting lean-to constructed by her father, was another refuge. Grown-ups were denied entry, but friends were welcome. She wanted to invite the children from a nearby orphanage but was unsuccessful. The orphans lived in a ramshackle building surrounded by an iron fence with broken bottles on top. Margaret pitied them, and was desperate to make friends, but her advances were met with poked-out tongues and stone throwing. She was too shy to ask anyone about this, but their rejection 'puzzled and troubled' her, presaging the social conscience that would manifest throughout her life.[28]

In 1901, after twenty years in Adelaide, George moved his family back to Melbourne, where he joined the *Age*'s editorial staff. The newspaper's political leanings at that time were towards the left, which may have attracted George, though the move was mostly for family reasons. His brother Alexander was back in Melbourne, having finished a short stint as the *Register*'s overseas correspondent. With both parents now dead and his sister Jane's health fragile, he felt the distance from family acutely. Family ties in the Sutherland clan were strong, not uncommonly for the era.[29]

Ada was initially unhappy about the move to Melbourne. She dreaded leaving her family, especially her sisters, to whom she was close.

The decision to leave their 15- and 13-year-old sons behind to complete the school term also saddened her. But the prospect of 17-year-old budding artist Ruth attending the National Gallery of Victoria Art School was in Melbourne's favour. With the family's involvement in music, an added stimulus was the city's active musical life, to which Professor George Marshall-Hall was making a significant contribution. At his private Melbourne Conservatorium of Music in Albert Street, East Melbourne, he was challenging previously narrow notions of tertiary music education through his dynamic approach to pedagogy. He had also established the Marshall-Hall Orchestra, and instigated regular concert series, including 'The People's Promenade Concerts' at the Royal Exhibition Building in Carlton. Other musical experiences were provided by the Royal Melbourne Philharmonic Choir and the Musical Society of Victoria, two liedertafel societies and a range of other amateur music groups.[30]

Among the hectic preparations for the family's departure from Adelaide, one thing in particular remained vivid for Margaret. She was given a topcoat with fur trimmings, the 'discarded grandeur' of her older cousin, Stella Bowen. Bearing this precious memento, Margaret left with her family for Melbourne. This was a pivotal event for the shy and sensitive yet self-possessed young girl, as she encountered the formative influences of her father's side of the family.[31]

CHAPTER 2

THE FIRST MEMORABLE JOLT (1901–1903)

A gradual, undefined realisation came to me which has stayed with me through all the endless ups and downs of a fairly choppy existence. It was the concept that true greatness is simplicity, and that simplicity is the essence of all greatness. And I know positively that it came to me through the opportunity that was mine to hear much lively discussion and see life lived in the fullest sense.

Margaret Sutherland[1]

SOON AFTER FOUR-YEAR-OLD Margaret's arrival in Melbourne, she was drawn into an extraordinary family that provided the foundation for her life course. While her parents searched for a house, they stayed in the large Victorian home at 2 Stawell Street, Kew, where the children's five unmarried uncles and aunts lived with their widowed mother. Over the next twelve years, the intelligent and talented occupants gave Margaret love, learning and role models.

The arrival at her relatives' home left a lasting impression on Margaret. A sprawling woodbine tree by the front gate exuded 'the most fragrant and heady aroma' she had ever experienced, which excited her senses. The precious time spent in the garden haven in Adelaide had ignited her lifelong appreciation of nature. An even lovelier surprise awaited her entry to the living room—a Blüthner grand piano that dwarfed everything around it. Margaret would soon become well acquainted with this 'strange and arresting object' through piano lessons with Aunt Julia.

Margaret was shy, but being in a house of grown-ups intrigued her, and she soon felt at home, enveloped in this extended family where intellectual and creative pursuits were part of life. Music, art, science and appreciation of nature pervaded the household. Her articulate, liberal-minded uncles and aunts participated equally in lively discussions on a range of topics, from the evolutionist theories of Charles Darwin and Thomas Huxley to the predicament of Australian Aboriginal people. Here Margaret learned to value the importance of thinking for herself. 'It was tremendous when they were together', she reflected. The house 'hummed' with interesting conversation:[2]

> There was no sign of awe-inspiring intellectualism in the Sutherland family. You might have called theirs a down-to-earth idealism. They were not in the clouds. But there was a spiritual quality about their agnosticism … Like so many people who are profoundly contented in their chosen fields of work they enjoyed life as it came, and with the modesty of the sincere agnostic pegged out no claim, one way or the other, for a future life.[3]

Margaret later observed that they were all 'more "Christian" than many a noted cleric'.[4]

In her determination to be a professional artist, Aunt Jane was a crucial role model for her niece, as a woman who pursued a career in a male-dominated domain. Margaret referred to her aunt's chosen field of endeavour as 'a calling' and identified with her resolve to follow a challenging path.[5] As Jane saw art, Margaret saw her composing as a calling.

Born in 1853, Jane was a serious artist at a time when women were usually the subjects of art rather than artists themselves. Most young women studying art were painting purely for pleasure, their real destinies lying in the domestic sphere.[6] Despite the determined struggle of first-wave feminists for women's emancipation in the 1880s and 1890s, it remained difficult for female artists to achieve fame, or to support themselves through their art.

One of the first students to enrol at the National Gallery Art School in Melbourne, Jane studied there for fourteen years. She gained respect in Melbourne's art world, exhibiting at prestigious venues such as the Victorian Academy of Arts, the Australian Artists' Association, and the Victorian Artists Society, where she was elected to the council in 1900. In 1894, she was one of the first women elected to the esteemed Buonarotti Club.[7] With her friend and peer Clara Southern, Jane set up a teaching studio in the 1880s in Grosvenor Chambers in Collins Street, Melbourne, where fellow Heidelberg School member Tom Roberts had his studio. The innovative Heidelberg School included renowned painters such as Arthur Streeton, Charles Conder, Walter Withers and Frederick McCubbin. Despite her being a leading woman artist in this group, Jane's works were not accepted for Tom Roberts' important *9 by 5 Impression Exhibition* in August 1889, demonstrating that women artists were not yet taken seriously.

Among her finest works, *Obstruction* (1887) is one of a number of Jane's paintings that show girls with paths blocked by obstacles, or who gaze wistfully at a world beyond. In *Obstruction*, a girl looks over a creek and a fence to a bull that returns her gaze. It is tempting to interpret these poignant works as metaphors for the barriers faced by girls and women in their life journeys—or, more specifically, for the paths that blocked women's full recognition as professional artists.[8] This could have been conscious or unconscious on the artist's part, but the bewilderment and powerlessness of these girls are palpable. These paintings could also refer to Jane's own delicate health, which hindered her success. In the early 1900s—the exact date is unknown—she suffered a stroke, which rendered her fragile until her death in 1928.

Jane's health eventually prevented her from painting large canvasses, and she sought subject matter in her immediate environment. Margaret, Dorothy and Aunts Julia and Jessie regularly obliged. Jane would sit at home with a box on her knee, painting pastels and watercolours. During her more active years, she had produced some sixty works, most of which are now in public galleries. Margaret greatly admired her aunt's approach to art, and respect for persistent trial and error in discovering new perspectives.[9]

Frederick McCubbin was a close friend of Jane's, and Margaret thought they might have married if circumstances had permitted.[10] Perhaps Jane's fragile health was an obstacle. One wonders why five out of the eight Sutherland siblings chose not to marry. In the booming city of Melbourne, where the population rose to half a million in the 1880s, there would not have been a shortage of eligible partners. Perhaps this close-knit group were happy in each other's company and didn't need to look outside for affection, intellectual stimulation or mutual support. There is little evidence that they ventured beyond their artistic and intellectual circles, suggesting self-contained contentment. Intent on their respective vocations, it may also have been difficult to find partners who were a match for their interests and talents.

Margaret adored her bachelor uncle William, who was an important influence. He played piano and violin, painted watercolours and read widely. He studied arts and science at the University of Melbourne and experimental physics at University College London. In keeping with the family's ideals, he was horrified at the extremes of poverty and wealth in London, and missed his family. He returned to Melbourne in 1882 and earned a Master of Arts degree from the University of Melbourne, as did all his brothers in the 1880s.[11]

Exhibiting the iconoclastic streak that ran through the family, William worked mostly alone, gaining respect internationally as an authority on molecular physics. He was not ambitious financially, content to support himself through private coaching, as a university examiner and through writing on scientific topics for newspapers, including Melbourne's *Age*.[12]

Uncle William enjoyed working in the garden, his special province. Margaret recollected with fondness 'a bank of flowers, balsam, nicotiana, leading up to higher cannas, delphiniums and foxgloves, and then climbing up to festooning roses—in the small secluded back garden'. Though shy, William liked children, and encouraged his nieces and nephews to accompany him on bushwalks along the Yarra River or in the Dandenong Ranges.[13] Margaret loved these excursions:

> His long years of tramping had given Willie a good knowledge of the choicest spots—and the birds, and all the wildlife that haunted the areas. A few children trailing after him seemed always welcome: he appeared to be pretty well the same age as we, and always on for an adventure. We felt no awe—only spontaneous comradeship.[14]

Like his brother George, William was a keen inventor, devising a 'strange chairlift' for his ailing sister Jane. By means of a pulley and rope, this contraption carried her upstairs to bed. To Margaret, she looked like 'a kind of queen', 'slight and dignified' on her 'squarish throne'.[15]

Margaret learned singing from Aunt Jessie, a respected teacher and accomplished lieder singer. In a gesture of devotion, Jessie, then in her mid-thirties, abandoned a promising singing career to care for Jane, fifteen years her senior.[16]

Piano lessons were more consequential. As Margaret's first 'real' piano teacher, Aunt Julia played a vital role. She had studied with Louis Pabst, a pupil of Anton Rubinstein, and was considered one of Melbourne's outstanding piano teachers. She was a gifted and expressive musician with a novel teaching approach, which was hungrily consumed by her niece. This influenced Margaret's subsequent conviction that teaching should open doors rather than indicate directions. She loved the songs of Schubert and Schumann, so Julia quickly taught her to read music by allowing her to play the vocal part above the accompaniment. This sounded very 'grown-up' to Margaret, and it 'egged her on'.[17]

The other unmarried uncle in the Stawell Street house, James, a science teacher, figured less in Margaret's life. Uncle 'Jimmie' was intensely shy, and 'rather crept into his shell'. But after George and Ada moved the family to their own home, James would visit, and developed a close relationship with Dorothy, who had a way of drawing him out. 'A new warmth came into him', wrote Margaret, in response to 'her interest and friendliness'.[18]

Shortly after arriving in Melbourne, Dorothy and Margaret stayed briefly with their Uncle Alexander, Aunt Lizzie and family at 'Dunrobin' at the University of Melbourne. Like his brothers, Alexander had an eclectic range of interests. In 1892, he retired from Carlton College with a modest income, and acquired 'Heronswood', a Gothic Revival home in Dromana that was built in 1871. In the relative seclusion of this property, he planned to devote his time to literature and scientific investigation. However, the Depression of 1892–93 thwarted this dream. He took up journalism, and wrote many articles, biographies, poems, short stories and unpublished novels over the years. Of these, *The Origin and Growth of the Moral Instinct* (1898), in which he aimed to establish that moral development conformed to evolutionary theory, won him the most acclaim, both in Australia and overseas.[19]

Alexander headed a campaign to establish a science degree at the University of Melbourne, and after his forays into journalism and some dabbling in state politics, he took on the challenging role of registrar at the university in February 1902.[20] After the death of Professor EE Morris in January, Alexander combined the role of registrar with duties as acting professor of English language and literature.

Margaret had vivid memories of her stay at Dunrobin. Apart from her debut piano performance at the dinner party (see Chapter One), there were two striking vignettes. After the first night, she woke at dawn, and pulled up the blind with 'a dramatic and confident gesture' to see a huge skeleton (of a whale) that looked like a prehistoric animal, 'possibly from outer space'. Margaret stood transfixed, her blood running cold, and looked desperately for an anchor. She snuggled with her sister Dorothy, and soon fell asleep. She awoke in daylight, her pluck returned.[21]

Later that day, the two sisters ventured out to assess their surroundings. Striding eagerly along, they passed a gardener who was 'shaping and grooming great, fantastic roots', which 'grew in and out of struggling pots of stagnant water'. Soon they noticed many pairs of bright, watchful eyes—'funny little animals, as big as half-grown kittens'. Again frightened, Margaret wondered, 'What do they do? Do they bite? Do they eat small girls? Are they friends or enemies?' They were water rats, the gardener kindly explained, and they would not bite, but were not recommended as pets.[22]

Another hurdle overcome, Margaret and Dorothy returned to the house to be greeted by their four cousins, Sheila, Lucy, Brenda and Dallas. They were older, but friendly and kind, and Margaret's shattered nerves were calmed in time for the dinner party where she performed her *Impromptu*.[23]

During this time the sisters made their first visit to Heronswood, which stirred Margaret's imagination. She clearly remembered the 'fairy palace', redolent of knights in armour, that seemed to dominate the northern slope of Arthurs Seat. After a jolting pony cart journey along unmade roads, she thought they had 'reached the end of all civilisation' at this place 'surrounded by still, blue sky and ripply blue sea'. The large house of grey-blue stone, with its erratic gables and spreading eaves, had stood rock solid through fierce gales, raging waves and the blistering heat of summer. Despite its torrid history, it was a haven of peace. When the sea was calm, it resembled a silver awning that 'caught the sparkle of faint movement when the stillness broke'.[24]

Margaret loved the rooms at the top of the house, imagining them as the fairy palace's lookouts. From the tiny balconies, there was a view over the never-ending stretch of sea, which turned into lazy, rolling breakers further out, before 'merging into the canopy of sky beyond'.[25] As might any five-year-old, she wanted to 'feel the sea air blow through wind-tangled hair'.

The orchard, filled with apple, fig and pomegranate trees that bowed low under the weight of their fruit, needed exploration. Behind the house was a hill where huge gum trees leaned over to protect the young saplings that competed for space. Awaiting discovery were gardening tools: a wheelbarrow, and a large hacksaw to cut down tree boughs damaged by winter storms. They found the first building constructed on the site, a wattle and daub cottage with a pointed shingle roof. This was 'the ancestor of them all', and Margaret wondered what sort of hermit had lived his lonely life there, using the iron kettle and hob to cook his meagre meals.[26]

George and Ada eventually bought a large two-storey house, 'Claremont', at 21 Studley Park Road, Kew. Their new home was a five-minute walk from the aunts and uncles in Stawell Street, and Margaret's father often walked her there for visits. On these occasions, she might have a piano lesson from Aunt Julia, sit as a model for Aunt Jane, or overhear one of the family's lively discussions.[27]

An established inner-city suburb, Kew had much to offer. It boasted grand houses and the picturesque, natural bushland of Studley Park that followed the twists of the Yarra River. Church steeples dotted the skyline, and horse-drawn carriages clattered along the streets. Kew's genteel residents were relatively affluent and well educated. Among them were professionals such as doctors, scientists, lawyers, politicians and educators, as well as artists, authors, literary folk and musicians. Several schools catered to the children of Kew, whose parents understood the importance of a solid education.[28]

'Claremont' was full of surprises and curiosities. At the rear were a coach house, tall gum trees, plum and apple trees, a fowl yard, and 'a man's room'—a toolshed, perhaps. There were ferns along the side of the house, and beautiful flowerbeds in the front garden. The house's verandas were edged with ironwork and lured many birds.[29]

Not yet at school, Margaret continued to benefit from mornings with her father, who chatted happily to his daughter as he worked. She was in awe of his inventing and building projects, sensing his brain ticking over. He would read to her, often children's stories he had written himself. This helped build Margaret's lifelong interest in Australian history. Occasionally they would visit Gottlieb Schuler, editor of the *Age*, whose Japanese garden was full of waterfalls and bridges that fascinated Margaret.[30]

The new family home had an upstairs studio used by Margaret's teenage sister Ruth, who had followed in Aunt Jane's footsteps and enrolled at the National Gallery Art School. Like brothers Alfred and Douglas, the teenage Dorothy was still at school, and regularly practised piano. She was studying with Aunt Julia, and dreaming of becoming a concert pianist. Ada's reservations about leaving Adelaide dissipated as she was welcomed into the stimulating Sutherland clan, who pursued similar interests to those of her own family and were, she soon decided, a positive influence on her children.[31]

Not long after the family's move to Studley Park Road, a black cloud descended when Alexander died suddenly of a heart attack in August 1902. Attributed to his stressful university roles, it was also the result of a congenital heart weakness that eventually manifested in all five brothers. His widow and children moved out of Dunrobin, and Heronswood was sold. Three watercolours of this treasured property, possibly painted by Jane or Ruth, remained in Margaret's possession throughout her life.[32]

Margaret saw John, the youngest of the Sutherland brothers, less often. He had moved with his wife Mary and two sons Keith and Leigh to St Kilda, hoping his precarious health would benefit from the sea air.[33] Mary was kind to Margaret, who in turn became very fond of her aunt.

Following university, John won a scholarship to study in London but, like his brothers, missed his family and returned to Melbourne. He published several articles and books, including *The Bonds of Society* (1914), intended for readers interested in modern thought, ethics, industry, philanthropy, art and sociology. He earned his living as an actuary, the first in Melbourne to become a fellow of the Institute of Actuaries (London) by examination.[34]

Margaret had strong memories of her stays in St Kilda. On one occasion, Uncle John revealed his amazing memory by reading a page from a book and reciting it backwards. Full of awe, Margaret held him in 'distant veneration' for the rest of her life. John loved music, but was never taught, so he purchased a pianola, a new and wonderful contraption to which he became devoted. Margaret was entranced, and the pianola received a great workout during her stays.[35]

During one visit, the American naval fleet anchored in Port Phillip Bay. This attracted 'countless tribes of men, women and children'. But a macabre incident haunted Margaret for many years. She and her cousins peeped out of the window to see a woman standing on the jetty at the foot of Marine Parade. Suddenly the woman dropped out of sight, causing a stir among the onlookers. The children set off to investigate, unnoticed by John, who was listening to Beethoven's seventh symphony. Arriving at the jetty, they witnessed people lifting a 'sad, defeated, wet figure from the waves'. The woman had committed suicide. The children were 'horrified, aghast, shocked into inaction', but managed to walk silently back to the comfort of the house. Uncle John was still engrossed, unaware that they had just witnessed a tragedy.[36]

Years later, Margaret's sister Ruth told her that she had met the manager of T&G Mutual Life Assurance Society, where John worked for the last fourteen years of his life. 'We always thought him rather strange', the manager said, 'because he would not accept the money due to him.' But John felt he earned enough to educate his sons and provide for his wife, so why take more than necessary? While this uncle had his eccentricities, Margaret did not perceive this as odd behaviour but, rather, as another example of the family's idealism.[37]

Firmly established in Melbourne life, and surrounded by this intriguing and loving family, Margaret had surmounted the 'first memorable jolt' in her existence. She was soon to experience the second: the beginning of her formal education.

CHAPTER 3

EDUCATED IN THE TRUE SENSE (1904–1913)

Nowadays we have student advisers ... They have aptitude tests, kept in tidy pigeonholes, carefully documented ... Well, callings such as music, painting, sculpting are things that dreams are made of. No power on earth can have them 'decided upon'. In fact the creative faculty is essentially a traumatic one. It cannot be tackled like the job of a stenographer.

Margaret Sutherland[1]

MARGARET'S CALLING TO music and composition was consolidated during her school years. Her family—particularly her aunts—and her school's music teacher played no small role in this. Unhappily, these years were tarnished by the serious illnesses of Margaret's Aunt Jane and her sisters Ruth and Dorothy, and by the tragic deaths of her beloved father and Uncle William. Although she wrote with emotional restraint of this time, these events left their mark, and music became a salvation.

Margaret's formal education began at age seven in 1904 at Baldur Girls Grammar, a small private school in Denmark Street, Kew. There is only one extant photo from her first years at school: in it, her long hair is loose, though pulled back off her face with a large bow. The image is small and blurred, yet elements of her developing personality are revealed. She appears mature beyond her years, serious and slightly pained, even a little reproachful. It evokes the tone of later letters expressing her outrage about musical issues.

Baldur, named after the Norse god of purity and light, was founded in 1896 in the home of a Danish woman, Andrea Magritte Tuxen. She was forced to support her family after her husband, surveyor August Tuxen, was declared bankrupt during the economic depression of the 1890s.[2]

It was not unusual for private citizens to establish small schools, which appealed to middle-class families who could not afford to send their children to more expensive ones. Baldur principally catered to the genteel daughters of the well-educated professional families living in and around Kew. The school differentiated itself through its aim to 'educate in the true sense, and instruct without cramming', and to provide a thorough grounding that would allow students to meet 'without any strain' the requirements of further advanced study. Margaret's Uncle James taught there, listed as a visiting history and geography teacher in 1907–08. Other subjects included French and German, arithmetic, scripture, botany, music, elocution, drawing, physical culture and needlework. The spirit of the Empire was inculcated through singing the national anthem, saluting the flag, and 'patriotic entertainment' events held in the Kew Recreational Hall. Important parts of the school's ethos included involving students in charity work and the Plain Needlework movement. With its mission to teach 'thrift and good housewifery' while promoting 'the feminine virtues of modesty, obedience and self-discipline', this movement reflected the prevailing attitudes towards women's roles. Among its high-minded principles was the movement's potential to increase manual dexterity, known as 'muscle culture', and to prevent 'slovenly behaviour' such as 'knocking about in gutters' and reading 'trashy romantic novels'. Sewing skills could also give women an avenue for 'gentle employment' should they fall on hard times.[3]

This movement was not the principal factor that appealed to George and Ada; the main drawcard was the school's music teacher, Mona McBurney. A friend of Aunts Julia and Jessie, McBurney epitomised the school's aim to 'educate in the true sense, and instruct without cramming'. A concert pianist and teacher, she was one of only two Australian women composers of her era who achieved prominence in their lifetimes. She and violinist, teacher and composer Florence Ewart formed 'the older generation of women composers, the inheritors of the colonial piano players'.[4]

In early twentieth-century Australia, women were still considered incapable of composing. Only in the final decades of the nineteenth century did the great European conservatories reluctantly admit women into advanced theory and composition classes. Even in the 1920s, women at London's Royal College of Music were not thought to have the same ambitions as men. While women had been admitted to the University of Melbourne in 1881 their career options were largely restricted to the teaching and caring professions.[5]

Although the quality of McBurney's compositions was recognised early, she earned her living mostly as a private piano teacher. She was not offered a teaching position at the University of Melbourne Conservatorium until 1918—and then as a tutor of Italian and French, rather than as a music teacher. Despite these limited options, she was undeterred, and achieved two major 'firsts'. In 1896, she was the first woman in Victoria to graduate with a Bachelor of Music degree from the University of Melbourne. Professor George Marshall-Hall, a dominant figure in Melbourne's musical life from 1890 to 1915, supported McBurney and her music, and was thus ahead of his time with his positive attitude towards women composers.

Second, her opera *The Dalmatian* (1905) was the first by a woman staged in Australia, albeit an incomplete performance with piano accompaniment in 1910. Although McBurney avoided the limelight, others ensured her works were performed during her lifetime. Recognition continued for a while after her death, with public performances, radio broadcasts and private recitals.[6]

McBurney was a key influence on Margaret. She gave the young musician her first 'most unorthodox' lessons in harmony, counterpoint, orchestration and composition, delivered with humour and wit.[7]

As well as imparting musical knowledge, McBurney joined Margaret's three aunts as role models of women attempting to forge careers in the arts.

McBurney's compositions were melodic and harmonious; they did not embrace the modernist style that was becoming *de rigueur.* Margaret's fierce independence led to reluctance to follow any 'fashionable' musical style, school or composer, and her approach was more experimental than McBurney's. Nevertheless, she greatly respected her teacher:

> She gave me the basic grounding, but without grinding it in, and I look back with gratitude and affection to her friendship and interest which lasted till her death. She was one of the most sensitive, gentle, yet vital persons I ever knew … She was a beautiful woman, erudite, charming though shy and retiring, a wonderful linguist possessed of a driving enthusiasm that inspired her students.[8]

A visit to McBurney's house for a lesson gave Margaret a disturbing insight into her teacher's private life, which 'stirred' her in an 'extraordinary way'. McBurney and her sister lived together with their brother, a hopeless, dishevelled alcoholic. The thought of these 'two gentle sisters, so unworldly, having to control unaided the terrorised ravings of that poor desperate brother' aroused in Margaret intense sympathy for her teacher.[9]

During Margaret's second year at school, when things had been going well, life dealt her family two cruel blows, the second more brutal than the first. Her 21-year-old sister Ruth, keen to further her art studies overseas, was nearing the end of her candidature at the National Gallery Art School and competing for the travelling scholarship awarded every three years. Sadly, this had to be abandoned when she fell desperately ill with a burst appendix that led to peritonitis.[10]

While her life was in the balance, the family waiting 'with chill in their hearts' for the latest news from the hospital, the second catastrophe struck. Soon after retiring to bed for the night, Margaret's father George was 'seized with sudden illness, and expired while medical aid was being summoned'.[11] He died of an aortic valve rupture, becoming the second of the siblings to die from heart failure in middle age—he was fifty

'There is no use trying to tell anyone what we went through', said Margaret. Ruth gradually recovered, but a slow, painful readjustment was ahead for the family. It was 'a nightmare period' during which Margaret, now nine, was sent to relatives for a few days, making her feel that she was 'allowed only on to the fringe'. She was frightened and lonely, not only because of the loss of her father, but also because her grief-stricken mother was scarcely recognisable. 'I don't believe she ever did recover from my father's death.'[12]

The family's pattern of life changed enormously as they were thrown into 'genteel poverty'. When George died, no one else in the family was earning, and they needed to start doing so quickly. As Ruth's health slowly improved, she held art classes in Claremont's attic, while her brothers left college to seek employment. Seventeen-year-old Alfred found work as a clerk, while Douglas, aged nineteen, got a job with the *Ballarat Star* as a junior reporter. Aged sixteen, Dorothy began seeking piano pupils. Margaret overheard a discussion as to whether she should move to a state school to avoid fees, but it was decided she should remain at Baldur. This decision would not have been easy, but Ada and the aunts took into account Margaret's musical aptitude and their belief in the importance of a good education.[13]

Uncle William was patient, tactful and endlessly helpful, sometimes distracting the children by taking them on country hikes to draw solace from nature. Uncle John and his wife Mary were also kind, occasionally inviting Dorothy and Margaret to stay in St Kilda.[14]

Ada faced the unenviable task of dismissing the family's maid, Lizzie, as she could no longer afford to pay her. Due to war, the Depression, alternative employment opportunities for women and improved technology, the practice of hiring domestic help largely died out in Australia in the mid-twentieth century. But in the early 1900s, it was still common for middle-class households to employ servants, and George and Ada were no exception. Ada was left with little choice but to inform her friends and relatives in Adelaide that she would welcome boarders or 'paying guests'. Her sisters—the children's aunts Hettie Bullock and Millie Kyffin Thomas—and other relatives sometimes took up this offer.[15]

The bereaved household was enlivened by regular visits from Millie's daughter, Nora Kyffin Thomas, who had recently returned after several years studying violin in Leipzig. She was fifteen years older than Margaret, but the two became close, being kindred spirits with their mutual 'addiction to music'. Margaret loved listening to Nora produce a warm, rich and glowing sound from her violin. She had a 'great feeling for the works of JS Bach', so that her rendition of Bach's *Air on the G String* once reduced Ada to tears. They referred to each other as 'Matey', and Margaret delighted in Nora's visits, because she often made a 'ridiculous fuss', expressing her pleasure with the world in what were known as 'Nora's mad half-hours'.[16]

Her older cousin gave Margaret one of her first lessons about the world beyond her family. Their bond was shaken by Nora's disapproval of a friend of Margaret's, a 'rather blousey—if good-hearted—contralto' who sang with a rich and fruity voice that Margaret enjoyed accompanying. This is one of the few times Margaret referred to friends beyond the family prior to her tertiary study. Nora treated her younger cousin to 'a gentle lecture on the kind of friends one really does not make'. This was a revelation for Margaret about 'the things one does not do'. She tucked the knowledge away and pondered it for some time. Her retention of this event suggests that within her family constellation, she had not yet encountered directives about what 'one does not do'. This might explain her later surprise and dismay at the discovery that her chosen pathway was uncommon.[17]

During the conservative early years of the twentieth century, women had few outlets to exhibit their work publicly; nor was it valued. In late 1907, when Margaret was in her fourth year at school, an event occurred in Melbourne that gave an important stimulus to Victorian women. The First Australian Exhibition of Women's Work, initiated by arts patron and governor's wife Lady Alice Northcote, aimed to recognise women's contributions to society by exhibiting their work, and to complement previous exhibitions that had consistently emphasised the handiworks of men. In addition to the fields of music and art, the domestic occupations, applied arts, needlework, dressmaking, cooking and horticulture attracted many contributors.[18]

Mona McBurney participated, conducting the premiere of her composition *Northern Ballad*, performed by an all-woman orchestra she and Florence Ewart formed. Margaret's 23-year-old sister Ruth exhibited her art for the first time, which may have provided compensation for the inability to pursue studies overseas. Naturally, Aunt Jane showed work too.[19]

In the musical sphere, women broke new ground through this exhibition. The contribution of the 3000 women musicians challenged the stereotypical image of female musicians as amateurs rather than professionals, and stretched the boundaries of what were considered suitable musical activities for women. Participants took their involvement seriously, and performances were of a high standard. Music received extensive press coverage in the major Melbourne newspapers, and most of the exhibition's concerts and recitals enjoyed considerable acclaim. The exhibition may even have played a small role in women finally obtaining the vote for the state legislature in 1908.[20]

Although only eleven, Margaret was probably aware of the exhibition, given the involvement of her sister, aunt, music teacher and school. Its recognition of women's output may have encouraged her growing desire to focus on music as a vocation.

Amid the excitement of this event, Margaret's family received another setback, felt most keenly by Ada, still grieving her husband's death. Nineteen year-old Dorothy suffered a breakdown, attributed to overwork and anxiety. She had been continuing her piano studies at the Albert Street Conservatorium under George Marshall-Hall, and teaching so as to earn money. A 'lovely-looking girl, with soft nut-brown hair and large grey-blue eyes', according to Margaret, she was 'altogether very ill', and was out of action for a long time. She never fully returned to robust health, remaining delicate and vulnerable, albeit mentally vigorous. Often confined to the couch, Dorothy read widely and received good friends for visits. She spent time with her aunts, who really loved her, particularly Jane, who painted her often. Eventually, she returned to teaching, for which she appeared to have a great talent.[21]

Margaret did not love her school subjects, apart from music, and French taught by a 'mademoiselle who adored her country and its language'. Fortunately, her teachers were tolerant and easygoing, and her pleasure in McBurney's lessons made up for her lack of engagement in other areas. Despite her professed lack of interest, Margaret did well at school, often topping her class for the year. However, her high standards, coupled with distress at home, caused her to get 'terribly wrought up' about exams (which later manifested in her reluctance to subject her piano students to them). On such occasions, her mother walked her to the violet farms in North Kew. Flowers had a special meaning for Margaret from her Adelaide daisy-chain days, and walks in the Dandenong Ranges with Uncle William added to her love of nature—flora, in particular. As with the scent of the woodbine at Claremont, Margaret was enchanted by the beautiful aroma of the violets, and after each visit, she came away 'absolutely unwrought'.[22] But music was increasingly the most important distraction, enabling her to set aside sad family events, and escape into another realm.

Throughout her schooling, Margaret's devotion to composition intensified, nurtured through McBurney's excellent coaching. But in 1911, the year of Margaret's Junior Public examination, a third devastating misfortune befell the family. Uncle Willie, 'the deservedly beloved head of the family' at Stawell Street, to whom everyone turned 'in moments of strain or indecision', died aged fifty-two, just as suddenly as his older brothers Alexander and George. On 5 October, he went for a hike at Kangaroo Ground, and visited Ada, Dorothy and Margaret, who were holidaying in a small cottage in Warrandyte. At seven o'clock, he left for Kew, appearing fine and cheerful. Having safely arrived home, he died during the night. The Sutherland family pattern of heart failure and early death continued relentlessly.[23]

Despite this trauma, Margaret passed her Junior Public examination, and continued to study harmony and counterpoint with McBurney, along with 'a few senior subjects'.[24] Although these did not hold her interest in the way that music did, she maintained her record of high marks.

Margaret had been writing down music that came into her head since she was about six, but the first compositions that reveal the fruits of her early work with McBurney date from around 1913, her final year at school. They were for voice and piano, and reveal Margaret's preference for the middle registers, where the voice naturally falls. An Adelaide *Advertiser* interview in August 1926, before a concert of her works, is helpful in dating three songs to 1913. 'Some of the songs which are to be played at the Liberal Hall on Friday were composed when I was sixteen years old', she remarked. These songs are probably *I Strove with None* (text by English poet, writer and activist Walter Savage Landor); *Edelweiss* (Australian poet Frank Wilmot); and *Wind in the Woods* (English novelist and poet Anne Brontë). There are no extant recordings or scores, though the first few bars of *I Strove with None* appear in the thematic index compiled by Margaret in 1939. These texts can be interpreted as using the beauty and perils of nature as a metaphor for a striving and ambitious spirit, and this may have been part of the appeal for Margaret at this point in her young life. At the Adelaide concert, English-born baritone and composer Clive Carey performed these songs accompanied by Margaret. The critic was impressed by Margaret's composing abilities, and the audience's reception was exceptionally warm.[25]

Another song dated to this time is a setting of Alfred Tennyson's 'Silence, Beautiful Voice' from Part 1 of his *Maud* series (1855). When first published, the series provoked protest for being morbid and hysterical, but it contains lyrical passages, of which this is one. Maud's exquisite face and wild voice conjure a world of contraries, which the narrator sees as a threat. One assumes that Margaret chose this poem for its beauty, which is maintained even when it's read in isolation from the series. There is a recording, which demonstrates sophisticated writing by the young composer.[26] It is broadly in the style of late romanticism, though exhibits tonal experimentation. The poignant melody imbues the song with a sense of unease befitting the text—an early example of Margaret's lifelong enjoyment of and skill in writing for voice.

There was no discussion of future pathways until the end of Margaret's schooling, when the headmistress recommended a career as a doctor because she was bright, and it was becoming acceptable for intelligent girls to study medicine. Margaret was appalled at being 'pigeonholed', and responded indignantly that it was the last thing she wanted to do—she planned to pursue music. She did not mention her desire to compose, because 'writing music didn't mean anything to her at all—for a woman, especially', Margaret recalled. Although she had studied for the matriculation exams, and would easily have passed, she did not sit them, maintaining that doing so was unnecessary for a career in music. The headmistress was shocked, but Margaret had never thought of doing anything else and couldn't understand why she was regarded as extraordinary.[27] In 1913, aged sixteen, she left Baldur.

Margaret's chosen pathway of composition would not be easy, particularly for a woman, but her upbringing was on her side. Family background continued to impact on women's education and contribution to musical life in the twentieth century. Even nowadays, high-achieving women have reported parental and social encouragement that enabled them to 'transcend gender typing'.[28] Women who excelled in lieder composition in the late eighteenth century and first half of the nineteenth century had usually experienced youthful immersion in musico-literary circles, and this remained true of twentieth-century composers. Lili Boulanger, for example, benefited from enormous support by a musical family of women professionals (grandmother, mother and sister). This was also true of the nine women—all born in the first half of the twentieth century—surveyed by Jill Halstead for her book *The Woman Composer: Creativity and the Gendered Politics of Musical Composition*.[29]

Margaret felt the same pressure as other family members to work after George died. While her aunts were kind and understanding, and gave her advice, she was aware that they had led secluded lives, and that she must 'strike out somehow'.[30]

PART TWO

BECOMING A COMPOSER: 1914–1927

CHAPTER 4

TO STRIKE OUT SOMEHOW (1914–1923)

Finding a foothold for some kind of career in music was a hazardous affair.

Margaret Sutherland[1]

MARGARET'S AUNTS COUNSELLED her not to submit herself to an educational institution 'just to be turned out as one of the standardised products'. The University of Melbourne Conservatorium was not the place to study music seriously, they felt, because it was staffed 'by second-rate teachers from Britain who were more concerned with exams than with musical development'.[2] Margaret internalised this opinion.

George Marshall-Hall's conservatorium was a different matter. He was a mostly self-educated, idealist bohemian who believed in art for art's sake and the power of emotive discipline—unpopular ideas among prudish Victorians. He had detractors, but his exuberance, flamboyance, wit, charisma and original approach to music pedagogy appealed to others, including Margaret and her family.[3]

Marshall-Hall contributed significantly to Melbourne's musical life through the high standards established by his orchestra, founded in 1892, and his Proms concert series. As a fine conductor, he fed Melburnians' hunger for good music, and over twenty years developed a body of players that visiting musicians recognised as comparable to those in Europe. Of particular interest to Margaret, he introduced to Australia orchestral music never before heard there. Unfortunately, the orchestra was beset by union problems and disbanded in 1912.[4]

Marshall-Hall had a troubled relationship with academia. In 1891, he was appointed the first Ormond Chair of Music at the University of Melbourne, funded by a bequest from pastoralist and parliamentarian Francis Ormond. Perceiving the need for practical music study alongside academic music courses, in 1895 Marshall-Hall founded and funded the University of Melbourne Conservatorium, in a rented space in the Queen's Coffee Palace in Carlton. After six months, he sought a more suitable, permanent site, and leveraged his friendship with prominent artists to arrange an annual lease in the Victorian Artists Society building in Albert Street, East Melbourne.[5]

In 1900, his position was not renewed, after what Margaret referred to as a 'storm-in-a-teacup upheaval' over the publication of his *Hymns Ancient and Modern*, a 'very small and very silly, provocative volume of verses'. It contained what some considered scandalous, erotic or anti-clerical poems. Undeterred, Marshall-Hall renamed his university conservatorium the 'Melbourne Conservatorium of Music'. He ran it as a private institution from 1901, and it became known as the 'Albert Street Con'.[6]

Meanwhile, the second Ormond Professor of Music, Franklin Peterson, made conservative changes to Marshall-Hall's curriculum. Margaret's Aunt Julia disapproved. When Marshall-Hall's private conservatorium, with its more innovative program, offered a scholarship at the end of 1913, Aunt Julia and Mona McBurney encouraged Margaret to apply. Buoyed by their advice, she applied for the scholarship to study piano with Czech pianist Edward Goll.[7]

Margaret prepared thoroughly for her audition, which took place at the end of 1913, shortly after she turned seventeen. She likely knew she would be playing for London-born composer Fritz Hart,

Marshall-Hall's temporary replacement while he was on leave overseas. Accordingly, she daringly chose to play her own composition. This was probably her *Sonata for Piano*, for which no score remains, and she later said was 'youthful'.[8] Youthful or not, it was a sensible and strategic choice. She made such a strong impression that she was awarded two scholarships, the first to study piano with Goll, and the other for composition with Hart.

Edward Goll was Margaret's first piano teacher after Aunt Julia, with whom she had studied for many years, and she was curious and excited about this new beginning. Classes in Goll's 'Master School' commenced in February 1914 with a group of five students, and Margaret was relieved to discover 'a fortunate, happy family'. Goll favoured group teaching, and students took turns to play and be critiqued, enabling them to learn from instruction given to others as well as to themselves. It also exposed them to a wider variety of repertoire and techniques. Students performed in recitals, with Margaret playing Brahms' *Variations on a Hungarian Song* in the 1914 end of year concert at the Melbourne Town Hall.[9]

Goll was thirty years old in 1914. Short, stocky and handsome, he had studied with Antonin Dvořák and Emil von Sauer, who had been a pupil of Franz Liszt. Margaret reflected that Goll was 'a fine teacher of musicianship', but in some ways 'a strange teacher' who 'just had what he called "ideas"'. But she liked his flexible approach and found his lessons stimulating. She remembered him as 'no instructor of beginners', being better suited to advanced students.[10]

Fritz Hart, Margaret's composition teacher, also proved gifted and imaginative. His contemporaries described him as quick in his movements, with a deep, resonant voice. Like Goll, he was a skilled raconteur. Forty years old when Margaret began her studies, he had been a chorister at Westminster Abbey before studying at London's Royal College of Music (RCM). He toured as musical director with several dramatic companies, including that of the American entrepreneur JC Williamson, with whom he arrived in Australia. When his contract with Williamson concluded, he became chief study teacher in composition at the Albert Street Con.[11]

Hart placed Margaret in his second-year diploma course of about sixteen students. They were all women, music being an acceptable feminine course of study. She also attended Hart's interpretation class, where students performed works they were studying. These performances were criticised 'more from an artistic than a merely technical standpoint', and suggestions were made 'as to poetic import, manner of interpretation, phrasing' and so on.[12]

A British musical renaissance gathered momentum during World War I, and Hart was part of it. Resisting the hold European composers had on contemporary music, patriotic Britons sought inspiration in traditional English folk music, the English 'pastoral' style and the Celtic 'twilight'. Margaret appreciated Hart's introduction to the music of British composers such as John Ireland, Ralph Vaughan Williams and Gustav Holst, all of whom he had known personally at the RCM.[13]

Hart urged his students to perform their own works in conservatorium concerts. He felt that Australian compositions should ultimately aim to develop a colour of their own; however, he did not consider Australian music as distinct from the British idiom, believing that Celticism could be drawn upon to develop a unique response to the Australian landscape. Hart's mission to raise awareness in Melbourne of British music was facilitated by audiences' changing attitude towards European music during the war—they often jeered at performances of works by German and other European composers.[14]

Margaret was encouraged by the desire of some audience members to hear Australian compositions. The Musical Society of Victoria, for example, had always aimed to elevate 'the public taste in music' and to encourage original compositions by its members. From 1914, its annual concert of Australian compositions started to receive the unanimous approval of critics.[15]

The period of calm experienced by Margaret in early 1914 was disturbed by two incidents that expanded her family's tragic story. The youngest Sutherland uncle, John, died at forty-seven from the same cardiac weakness as his brothers. This was followed soon after by the shattering declaration of war, on 4 August. When Margaret heard that her two brothers, Douglas and Alfred, aged twenty-eight and twenty-six respectively, and her cousins Dallas and Keith were contemplating enlisting, she felt that 'the air was thick with anxiety and horror'.[16]

Shortly after the declaration of war, yet another 'nearer, grossly vindictive bomb exploded' when a 'complete false, unjust and ignorant enmity towards Goll' enveloped the Albert Street Con. He was considered an enemy alien, though he was Czech and the Czechs were anti-German. Aged seventeen, Margaret was shocked by this 'outrageous nonsense', which made her 'stonily defiant'. The university conservatorium was more broad-minded. Possibly thinking that Goll would bring prestige as a student of Franz Liszt's pupil, Emil von Sauer, it offered him a position, which he accepted.[17]

Margaret remembered her education at the Albert Street Conservatorium as 'fairly sketchy', but also noted that 'windows began opening the tiniest bit, and a whole new world of sights and sounds was taking shape out of the mist, for those with their eyes and ears poised for new impressions'. Nevertheless, Goll lured his favourite student to his new institution with the offer of a three-year scholarship. Margaret could not refuse.[18]

Moving to the university conservatorium meant abandoning composition studies with Hart, who had encouraged Margaret's predilection for setting poetry to music. He advised his students to pace around the room reciting the words, so they could sense the rhythm and inflections. Before her departure for the university, some of these works were performed in an 'Evening Concert of Students' Compositions' on 11 December 1914. Margaret played her *Miniatures* for solo piano, and conservatorium violin teacher Carmen Delprat tackled her *Allegretto in D Minor* for solo violin. Unfortunately, these scores are lost. Conservatorium singing teacher Mary Campbell sang four of her songs, accompanied by the composer. One was her setting of Alfred Tennyson's 'Silence, Beautiful Voice' (1913). The other three were settings of the Brontë sisters' poetry—'Love and Friendship' and 'The Night-Wind' by Emily Brontë, and Anne Brontë's 'Lines Composed in a Wood on a Windy Day', which Margaret abbreviated to *Wind in the Woods*. Here she began to demonstrate a harmonic vocabulary that reached beyond late-romantic chromaticism towards modern twentieth-century styles.[19]

Margaret's attraction to the Brontë sisters' poetry offers insight into her personality at the end of her first year of tertiary study. An avid reader, she probably read their novels, and sympathised with the plight of women in the Victorian era as portrayed in Emily Brontë's novel *Wuthering Heights* and Anne Brontë's *Agnes Grey*. Any ambitious woman of Margaret's era would have identified with the Brontë sisters' desire to write, and to be published and taken seriously. The heroines' independent characters and the theme of the importance of education probably resonated, as did the poems' sentiments and nature motifs. Their suitability for musical settings is also likely to have appealed.[20]

In 'The Night-Wind' (also known as 'In Summer's Mellow Midnight'), a woman looks through her window at night. She hears the wind and senses the darkness of the woods, a metaphor for temptation and seduction. One interpretation is that the poem expresses the feelings of a woman facing the restrictions of her time. She cannot give in to the frightening temptation to imagine a life with more possibilities, and the inevitable end is death. Margaret used only the first three verses of the poem, ending just before the sinister element: 'How dark the woods will be!' Again, she showed proficiency with late romantic harmony, using it effectively to suggest the poem's sinister element.

The poem 'Love and Friendship' employs metaphors drawn from nature to highlight the differences between the two emotions. Anne Brontë's 'Lines Composed in a Wood on a Windy Day' uses nature as an analogy for the poet's feelings. She is initially enraptured by the beauty of nature, but there is unfulfilled desire in her wish to experience the wild ocean.

Margaret entered the University of Melbourne when women were still in the minority. The conservatorium was the exception, though most women studied single subjects, as Margaret did. Female students relished recognition of their extra-domestic talents, a situation that intensified with male students away at war. The proportion of women at the university increased from 14 to 32 per cent, and they experienced political, economic and social prominence (though they were encouraged to return to the home with the repatriation of soldiers following the war). Creative women were also likely to attract more recognition at this time of masculine crisis. It is not clear whether Margaret experienced this, but it's plausible that it was easier for her to access the teaching and performing opportunities she needed to earn a living.[21]

Initially all went well for Margaret after she switched institutions. By 'a strange stroke of fortune', George Marshall-Hall returned to the university conservatorium. Nostalgia for his striking talent and enlightened approach had been growing, and following Franklin Peterson's death, he was offered the position of Ormond Professor (*ex officio* dean) of the conservatorium from which he had been banished fifteen years earlier. With Europe at war and having failed to achieve success with his operas in England, Marshall-Hall happily accepted. There were two other incentives for the council's decision—the possible amalgamation of the university and Albert Street conservatoriums, and the chance that Marshall-Hall's orchestra would be re-formed under the university's auspices, but circumstances ultimately prevented them from coming to fruition.[22]

The return of Marshall-Hall was a significant bonus for Margaret and further confirmed that her decision to move was the right one:

> [He was] a large, long, lean man with black wiry hair, beetling brows and penetrating eyes—a man who could be terrifyingly caustic in disapproval and warmly genial in encouragement. He had the loud uninhibited guffaw of the generous, spontaneous extrovert—which indeed he was—in every sense. His attraction for the very young was enormous. He was so understandable, so vivid, so down-to-earth—and yet one felt an underlying poetic quality which held one. There was never anything vague or undefined about Marshall-Hall. He could be thrillingly dramatic, caressingly simple, and often eloquent.[23]

While Margaret was not explicit about the extent to which she directly benefited from his reinstatement, she certainly appreciated the positive impact he had on the university conservatorium as a whole. She was delighted that his 'very great gifts as a lecturer, his infectious enthusiasms, his wide knowledge, his catholicity of taste, his special talent for real communication of the sort that is all too rare', not to mention his support of women, could again benefit students.[24]

One such student was violinist Lorna Stirling, with whom Margaret became acquainted during this first year at the university conservatorium. She would be a close, lifelong friend and an important colleague in activist endeavours. Marshall-Hall's return provided Lorna with 'the stimulus of a musical champagne' that set her trajectory as a musicologist. She was especially interested in introducing musical performances to young children and in promoting music in schools.[25]

Apart from her friendship with Lorna, little is known about Margaret's social life during her years of tertiary study. Lorna was one of only two special friends Margaret mentioned. The other was Kathleen Meaghan, a gifted disabled student, with whom she shared her scholarship in her first year at the Albert Street Con.[26] Margaret focused on her studies, her needs for social interaction met by fellow students and her supportive extended family.

Sadly, the halcyon days were prematurely cut short when, in July 1915, aged fifty-three, Marshall-Hall contracted an abscess of the appendix. Surgery appeared to have been successful, but he suffered a serious relapse and died four days later. The death of the most 'honest guide to musical affairs' in Victoria left Margaret with an 'aching void—an end to something so splendid and promising'.[27]

Margaret's already firm opinions about institutional learning were cemented when William Adolphus Laver was appointed Marshall-Hall's successor. For Laver, it was the consummation of a long-term dream, but for the conservatorium, it marked the beginning of a new period of conservativism. Laver had none of Marshall-Hall's desire to progress beyond what Margaret viewed as an 'out-moded curriculum, a kind of routine going-through-the-mill' of first study, second study, harmony, counterpoint, history and aesthetics, form and analysis. She hated that the conservatorium's course still included 'English Counterpoint', which European institutions had jettisoned long ago. In her opinion, this 'dreary long-drawn-out process' ensured that 'any spark of genuine creativity dried up because of rigidity and lack of spontaneity'.[28]

This unhappy turn of events hit home. Margaret realised how privileged she was to have been surrounded by music since early childhood. Her upbringing had led her naturally to seek out information, encouraging the puzzle pieces to come together 'by means of a kind of magnetic attraction', rather than laboriously. She felt the university conservatorium's conservative learning environment could not inspire those students who hadn't enjoyed her privileges. They were deprived, for example, of the 'deserved popular Interpretation class of Marshall-Hall', which had always been 'vital, instinctive and stimulating'. Laver turned these classes into Concert Practice, where he made mundane observations such as, 'That took exactly seven minutes'. This was complete anathema to Margaret.[29]

These disappointing changes led Margaret seriously to ponder her future studies. By 1915, her teaching practice was growing. She taught pupils in their own homes, and on Saturday mornings at Allans Music in the city. This increasing time commitment made a full course of study at the university conservatorium unmanageable, and she resolved to study only those subjects that would fulfil her needs. This decision was endorsed by Goll, who became her most important mentor over the next few years.[30]

Alas, the only remaining Sutherland uncle, James, died suddenly in March 1916, again of a heart complaint. Margaret's three aunts were now 'entirely alone'. With Jane's frailty in mind, they moved to a smaller house with no stairs in Highfield Grove, Kew, and hired a housekeeper and carer, appropriately named 'Ethel Nightingale'. She was 'utterly devoted' to the aunts, and they to her. This 'charming, very shy, golden-haired young woman played a vital part in the remaining course of their lives'. Ironically, Jane lived to a greater age than her younger sisters, dying at seventy-four in 1928.[31]

Developments in the musical sphere in 1916 raised Margaret's spirits, with Goll helping to further her performing career. He introduced Margaret to energetic Belgian violinist and conductor

Henri Verbrugghen, who had arrived in Sydney with his string quartet in early 1915 as the first director of the New South Wales Conservatorium. He formed a fine state orchestra with members of his quartet leading the string sections, and was pegged to conduct a proposed national orchestra. According to Margaret, Verbrugghen and his state orchestra's presence in Sydney 'brought an enormous fillip to music in that city', and 'at once, all sorts of things began to happen'. He organised festivals, concert series and national tours, giving many high-standard concerts. More and more players were forming semi-professional and amateur orchestras in several cities, but lack of intense rehearsals was apparent in performance. By contrast, Verbrugghen's orchestra was the jewel in the crown in a climate where orchestral music was becoming more attractive to audiences, reflecting the rise to supremacy of central European traditions of orchestral writing. He was frequently in Melbourne, staying with Goll and playing music with him. Margaret drank it in and availed herself of opportunities to demonstrate her talents.[32]

Meanwhile, Margaret continued teaching, and her practice expanded in 1918 with her appointment as a piano teacher at Presbyterian Ladies' College (PLC) in East Melbourne, where Goll was musical director. This experience convinced her that she did not want a teaching career. Music was important at PLC, initially encouraged by its first principal, CH Pearson, and all students were expected to take lessons. Margaret did not condone this practice, believing that music shouldn't be construed merely as a social accomplishment. The half-hour lessons were a relentless and 'horrible grind', 'teaching little people to play little tunes'—this should not be forced on children without musical talent, she believed.[33]

Fortunately, there were moments of relief when a student failed to turn up, and Margaret could use the time for her own ends. She would practise, or stretch out on the floor and relax, her feet pressed firmly against the door to avoid being disturbed by late students or other unwelcome visitors. Although her appointment provided a much-needed source of income, it was not well paid. 'It was sweated labour', she said. Occasionally, however, promising students turned up, some of whom remained Margaret's friends for years.[34]

Alongside her own teaching practice, Margaret started to act as Goll's understudy at the university conservatorium when he was touring. She didn't love it, but needed to earn an income, and teaching, albeit underpaid, was the best option. She made additional money performing chamber music and solo recitals. This provided a welcome change from the strain of teaching and constituted the beginning of her life as a professional musician.

Margaret had performed regularly since 1916, when she was still studying at the conservatorium, and this continued until the end of 1923, when she went overseas. Her concert repertoire was generally of the conservative nature preferred by audiences at the time—standard British and European repertoire from the seventeenth to the nineteenth centuries, classified for convenience as the baroque, classical and romantic periods. But occasionally she would program more contemporary works. With her increasingly busy schedule of teaching and performing, she had little time for composition, so these performances didn't include her own works. 'You've got to be by yourself and think a lot, and I couldn't do that at all', she said.[35]

An encounter with Australia's eminent diva, Dame Nellie Melba, demonstrates Margaret's increasing prominence as a distinguished performer. This occurred sometime between August 1921 and September 1922, when Melba was visiting Australia. Amid her heavy concert touring schedule, Melba spent time at Coombe Cottage, her home in Coldstream in Victoria's Yarra Valley. She often invited friends to stay, and one honoured visitor was an English baritone named Clive. This was almost certainly Clive Carey, appointed director of singing at the University of Adelaide's Elder Conservatorium from 1924 to 1948.[36]

Margaret held Melba in high esteem:

> There was no mistaking Melba's qualities as an artist. Apart from her voice (which had a rather silver, disembodied, choirboy timbre and was unique in that one always knew it was hers, quite positively, and no-one else's), her greatness lay, as indeed it does in all outstanding musicians, in her compelling vitality and the essential pulse of everything she sang.[37]

Margaret had 'an interesting and most convincing proof of this', when she spent the day at Coombe Cottage rehearsing with Carey for a Melbourne recital.[38] After lunch, Margaret and Clive practised songs by Debussy and Fauré, while Melba retired for her afternoon siesta. The rest is best told by Margaret:

> We had not been at work longer than 10 minutes when there was a skirl and a flurry, the door opened, and 'Clive', said a voice, 'you are singing my songs and I have an uncontrollable impulse to sing myself'. Whereupon she took over, and sang one after another with an impeccable style-sense and the most compelling floating, resilient rhythm that bore them aloft and right out of sight of the essentially nice, musicianly, sincere, intelligent but unexciting and uninspired singing of the dear fellow I had been accompanying. The impression was so immediate, so electrifying, that I can recall the exact sensation even now, and get pleasure in the recalling of it.[39]

Melba's speaking voice, alas, 'was quite unbeautiful', Margaret added. 'It had a noticeable "edge" and a rather nasal quality.' The same was true of many first-rate Australian singers, she noted. 'Can it be that the resonance induced by a rather unpleasant accent is of help, not a hindrance in singing?'[40] Margaret was probably not the first to ask this question, and certainly not the last.

The same afternoon, Margaret learned something of Melba's 'dual personality'. When her impromptu recital ended, a butler delivered tea 'in extremely correct, ceremonial style'. As he offered crumpets, the lid of the 'exquisitely thin porcelain-covered dish' slipped, and smashed to smithereens on the floor:

> There was a horrified silence, before the diva, no longer in silvery tones, but in hard, strident ones with quite a touch of Billingsgate about them, told the butler exactly what she thought of him, while he slunk, beaten by the lashing of the tongue, from the room. It was a horrible anti-climax to what had been one of the loveliest experiences. But it could never obliterate it.[41]

An undated letter of invitation handwritten on Coombe Cottage notepaper shows that the respect was mutual:

> Dear Lady. Thank you so much for your song. It is too difficult for me to play so won't you come up and spend a day or two with me. I have an

orgy of music which I am longing for—you play so beautifully. Bless you, Nellie Melba.[42]

Concerts regularly organised by the university conservatorium provided further opportunities for Margaret to earn money. The venue was usually Melba Hall at the conservatorium, but there were also Victorian regional tours. Between 1916 and 1923, she performed regularly in Ballarat, Bendigo and Geelong, and went to Benalla, Warragul, Traralgon, Bairnsdale, Mildura, Rutherglen, Albury, Nhill, Echuca, Warrnambool, Port Fairy and Portland.

One such tour in June 1923 proved fateful. At the Port Fairy station, Margaret was collected by music enthusiast Dr Norman Albiston, her future husband. In his role as concert organiser, he drove her to the next venue in Warrnambool. Three years her senior, Norman was an even-featured, good-looking man, who mentioned that his first wife, Rita Stang, also a doctor, had recently left him.[43] Norman was instantly drawn to Margaret, with her attractive, demure demeanour and talent for music.

But romance was not at the forefront of Margaret's mind—she was too busy. Apart from piano solos, duets and piano trios, she accompanied instrumentalists and singers, including well-known Melbourne performers Otto Sobell, Henry Thomas, Isobel Biddell and Muriel Cheek. With popular mezzo soprano Ivy Phillips, she gave many concerts, including a fundraising event in the Melbourne Town Hall in May 1920, prior to the singer's departure for London. Contralto Mary Mack was a regular collaborator, and the two participated in a Melbourne Music Club recital at the Lyceum in July 1921. Margaret's 1913 setting of Anne Brontë's 'Lines Composed in a Wood on a Windy Day' was programmed, in what appears to be the only performance of her music during this period.

Charity and private concerts also featured in Margaret's performance schedule, with reviews suggesting that musical talent was not always the most important criterion on which women performers were judged. At an event in December 1920, Margaret played solos at a Christmas party organised by Lyceum Club member 'Mrs JM Gillespie' at Cliveden Mansions. 'The hostess wore a black charmeuse and georgette draped gown, brightened by a touch of jade green; her hat was of black tulle and jet', and the tables were 'ornamented with deep-shaded pink carnations'. Dress was similarly charmingly remarked upon after an 'at home' of the PLC Old Collegians' Club in August 1923, staged by Mary Sutherland (Uncle John's wife) to mark her retirement as president. The hostess was 'gowned to advantage in shot satin of that elusive shade known as "Mountain Mist", with trimmings of silver lace', *Table Talk* noted. As an afterthought, it was acknowledged that 'Miss Rosa Pinkerton sang delightfully once or twice, and Miss Margaret Sutherland, niece of the hostess, gave pianoforte solos and supplied the accompaniments'.[44]

Throughout this period, Goll remained a major influence. An inscription on a photograph of himself, possibly given as a gesture to mark the completion of her studies at the university conservatorium in 1918, read, 'To my very gifted pupil with all my wishes for the future'. Melbourne composer Helen Gifford raised the possibility of a romantic connection between these two attractive people. A photograph taken by Pegg Clarke, one of the few female professional photographers of this period, shows a shy-looking young woman with her hair tied back softly over the ears. She is looking downward and wears a slight smile. 'She used to hold a handkerchief for him to wipe his hands on when he was performing', Gifford related, 'and Goll loved her, because she was an attractive young girl', but 'nothing happened', because 'Margaret was altogether too correct'. Goll 'needed a rich wife', Gifford added, 'and he got one—a rich widow'.[45]

A major feature of the close musical relationship between Margaret and Goll was their performances of piano duets, a rarely programmed genre. In July 1918, Margaret had travelled with Goll, and his wife and daughter, to her birth city of Adelaide for a series of recitals given by him at Queen's Hall. Again, in 1920, the two pianists were in Adelaide, and Goll spotlighted his favourite pupil in the third of a series of concerts on Saturday 15 May. She was 'an Adelaide girl originally', he said in an interview for the *Critic*, and he considered it an excellent opportunity for his protegée. 'In this way, a student is inspired with confidence for later when she will give recitals herself', he said. 'I am sure the Adelaide public will be delighted with Miss Sutherland. She has exceptional ability.' In Bach's *Prelude and Fugue in C Minor* arranged for two pianos by Harold Bauer, the two players were evidently 'in perfect accord'. One critic noted that Goll's introduction of his 'very talented pupil, Miss Margaret Sutherland, a South Australian by birth and only twenty-two', was fully justified, since she played with 'surprising temperament and technique'.[46]

Expanding their musical horizons, in May 1921 Goll and Margaret were invited as soloists in Mozart's duo piano concerto in E flat major when Henri Verbrugghen brought the New South Wales State Orchestra to Melbourne for two concerts in the Melbourne Town Hall. Again, critics and audience were happy.[47]

Meanwhile, Margaret's reputation as a talented soloist had been growing. Between 1917 and 1920, the university conservatorium invited her as soloist in piano concertos by Brahms, Mozart and Chopin. Reviews were favourable, particularly of Mozart's D Minor concerto, for which she wrote her own cadenzas.[48]

Verbrugghen honoured Margaret with an invitation to play Beethoven's Concerto No. 4 in G Major with the New South Wales State Orchestra in the Sydney Town Hall in early December 1919. The *Sydney Morning Herald* critic considered that this 'Melbourne pianist from Mr Edward Goll's studio made an acceptable, though not a striking, debut', while the *Sydney Sun* admired her 'sound technical equipment, considerable temperament, and a fine appreciation of the music'.[49]

Reviews aside, the invitation to play with Verbrugghen's orchestra boosted Margaret's confidence. He had introduced new works and provided an 'enormously stimulating force' for music in Melbourne and Sydney. 'Every inch an artist', he had plans for the betterment of the conservatorium in Sydney. Unfortunately, it was politically controlled, according to Margaret, and his efforts to 'convince politicians of his need for expansion', and of 'his visions for a new era for music in Australia', came to nothing. In 1922, he admitted defeat, and departed to the United States with his family and quartet to become permanent conductor of the orchestra in Minneapolis.[50]

Margaret acknowledged the 'splendid work' Goll was doing in Melbourne, giving recitals of little-known music in a sea of otherwise 'conservative and unimaginative' programs. Having faced his departure overseas, she now had to contend with the loss of Verbrugghen, which left her inconsolable. He had been the driving force behind an 'excitingly fertile' period, and his departure caused her again to rethink her future. Although she continued to perform regularly, it was at this moment, aged twenty-five, that she became fully conscious of what had been brewing in her mind for a while—piano playing could never fully satisfy her. The constant practising was a 'nerve-strain' that worried her incessantly. She felt her ears were battered, and the effort to 'keep the music, after acquiring the necessary technical control' was beyond her.[51]

Most of Margaret's fellow students followed the traditional female musician's path of teaching, sometimes supplemented with performing. Margaret's aspirations were different. 'To pluck music from the air, and fashion it according to one's own whim, is quite another thing', she said. This was what made her 'heart beat faster', and what she 'longed passionately to have the time and opportunity to do'. Although 'the means were lacking', she was not dissuaded.[52]

Making an impact as an Australian composer was not easy, especially for women. Composers needed to arrange performances of their works with local players and promote themselves. This did not come naturally to most women, who had usually not been raised to seek the limelight. Neither were aspiring performers' paths easy, though Nellie Melba's rise to fame brought attention to promising singers. But with a population of only 5.4 million people over a vast continent, demand was limited, and touring unprofitable.

Although Fritz Hart and Edward Goll were introducing new music to Melbourne audiences, most contemporary European music was not yet reaching Australia. 'We had never even heard any Stravinsky', Margaret lamented. Australia's isolation during World War I helped foster nationalism and encouraged paranoia. The arrival of modernism in art, for example, caused reactionary forces to 'combine in an effort to eradicate what was considered a foreign disease'. Modernism in music posed a greater challenge. As Margaret asserted, 'Music has always been the last to get going', and with the economic downturn following World War I, and increasing unemployment, there was little funding for the creative arts.[53]

Margaret longed for a challenge and realised she would need to go to Europe. Family role models helped plant this seed. Her sister Ruth wanted to go overseas in 1905 to study art, but illness thwarted her ambitions. Cousin Stella Bowen travelled to England and Europe in 1914 and never returned, finding her artistic home in Paris.[54]

But how could Margaret afford to travel when she was barely earning enough to survive in Melbourne? A glimmer of hope appeared in early 1923, when the Golls decided to spend the year abroad. Goll asked Margaret to take over his teaching at the conservatorium, insisting she receive full fees. 'This made it possible for me to escape', she said. She continued her own teaching, alongside country tours organised by the conservatorium during university holidays. During this year of 'titanic effort', Margaret felt lonely and trapped, but at the same time excited about her future.[55]

It was not only hard work that had made 1923 'titanic'. Further blows befell the family, precipitated by the recurrence of a depressive illness in Margaret's 34-year-old sister Dorothy, the sibling to whom she was closest. Dorothy had suffered several health problems, but needed to earn, and struggled to continue teaching. But this time she suddenly became very unwell. By now, older sister Ruth had married engineer Charles Neylon, and the couple had a young son, Geoffrey, so it fell to Ada to look after Dorothy, and she slept downstairs to be near her. One morning, Margaret came downstairs to prepare for work and found her mother unconscious on her makeshift bed. She died later that morning, 8 September 1923. She had never disclosed to her family that she'd been diagnosed with Bright's disease (nephritis) two years earlier.[56]

Ada's death was a terrible shock. For Margaret, 'the feeling of desolation was crippling', and 'there seemed no purpose in life'. She felt 'blank' and found it difficult to continue her work. For Dorothy, it tipped the balance, and she had to be admitted to hospital.[57]

Margaret's sister Ruth and her family moved from their Jolimont home to Claremont, while Margaret boarded elsewhere. When Dorothy emerged from hospital, her slow convalescence was overseen by Ruth and Aunt Jessie, who was also caring for Jane and Julia. Margaret was ambivalent about departing Australia under these circumstances, and concerned her savings might not last, but she had booked her passage, and was encouraged by the family to cement her plans.[58]

CHAPTER 5

NO PROPS (1924–1925)

Creative music in Australia at that time had never developed beyond being a pale reflection of the merest fringe of music abroad.

Margaret Sutherland[1]

WITH A HEAVY heart, Margaret departed Australia on the SS *Osterley* on 19 February 1924.[2] Fortunately, her overseas sojourn was to prove formative and fertile for the ambitious young composer. Margaret's family background and her efforts to follow her musical heart began to bear fruit, despite her aspirations for a compositional career not conforming with society's dictates for women in the early 1920s.

England was a natural destination. Margaret's talent had developed on a foundation of English music, this British perspective stimulated by Fritz Hart. Indeed, one of her favourite composers was English baroque composer Henry Purcell. England offered the opportunity to study composition with well-known teachers, and to discover European musical developments. As Australians were still British subjects with strong umbilical ties to the mother country, there was the additional lure of travelling 'Home'.[3] This was the dream of many middle-class Australian women, as Margaret's cousin Stella Bowen attested:

> Going to England was called 'going home', even by people who had never been there and whose fathers had never been. We all talked with varying

> degrees of Australian accent, of which we were ashamed when we became aware of it. We regarded a real English accent with positive reverence.[4]

It was, however, unusual for women to travel overseas unchaperoned, as Margaret did. Many were accompanied by their mothers (as was Peggy Glanville-Hicks in 1932). Stella Bowen set an example when she travelled alone in 1914 but could not do so until after her mother's death. Unlike Bowen's mother, Ada had not discouraged her daughter from studying overseas. Margaret's guilt about leaving Australia so soon after her mother's death, and the impossibility for Stella of contemplating leaving until her mother *had* died, reflects the prevailing attitude that for women, family duty came first. As Stella wrote, 'It is probably reasonable to suppose that I should have ended by marrying some serious young man and settling down for ever in Adelaide, if it had not been for my mother's death'.[5]

The passage to London allowed 27-year-old Margaret time to reflect and re-energise after six years of hard work and family trauma. Luckily, on her arrival in the cool, grey damp of early spring in London, an Australian Quaker friend offered to sublet her flat in Beaufort Street, Chelsea, complete with piano.[6]

Chelsea was the artistic centre of London in the early twentieth century. It was the haunt of many eminent writers and painters, including Virginia Woolf, who set her novel *Night and Day* (1919) in this bohemian borough. Here Margaret found her version of Woolf's 'room of her own' as she embarked on absorbing as much British and European music as possible.[7]

The flat was comfortable but had its downsides. Australian architect and historian Mollie (Mary) Turner Shaw, a piano student of Margaret's who became a great friend, was also in London. The two had not yet met, but Mollie was taking dance classes on the floor below Margaret. Years later, Margaret described to Mollie how she struggled to compose to the sounds of 'a terrible gathering of women' who used to 'galumph about to the tunes of Gluck thumped out on an old piano'. Mollie didn't confess that she was among them.[8]

Shortly before her departure, Margaret had received a letter from her Port Fairy 'chauffeur', Norman Albiston. The two had 'struck up a friendship', but there is no evidence of the early development of the relationship. An accomplished pianist interested in composition, he wrote that he had sold his medical practice, and 'wanted to do something with music'. He intended to come to Melbourne to discuss his plans with Margaret, but her steamer left before he appeared.[9]

Now established in Chelsea, Margaret received another letter from Norman. He had obtained a position as a ship's doctor on a Commonwealth Bay boat from Antarctica, departing Melbourne for London in January 1924. Holding letters of introduction to English composers, 'he came after me', Margaret said. On arrival, he found lodgings opposite hers on Beaufort Street.[10]

Margaret pondered how best to spend her precious time overseas. Upholding her distaste for institutional learning, she would not embark on study at a conservatorium:

> I didn't go through the usual academic channels, because in composition, it's easy to become imitative, to lose your train of thought ... I don't think composition can be taught. It has to be there to begin with—someone can't suddenly decide in their mid-twenties that they have to write music unless they've written some before.[11]

Margaret remained adamant about this all her life. It was an unusual attitude, given that there was a consensus then (as now) that to reach one's full musical potential, formal study overseas was necessary. The prestigious Royal College of Music (RCM) in London was an obvious choice for aspiring Australian composers. Some of Sutherland's successors, including Esther Rofe, Peggy Glanville-Hicks, Miriam Hyde and Dulcie Holland, studied there in the early 1930s. Each had different motivations. Like Margaret, Rofe had a liberal upbringing. Her family was interested in music and encouraged her endeavours, and her mother was against institutional learning. However, prior to travelling overseas in 1932 at the age of twenty-eight, Rofe was largely self-taught, so the RCM offered an opportunity to acquire formal training. This was not so for Margaret, who wanted to 'see people for themselves, to know how they thought things'.[12]

Margaret's resolve not to study at the RCM may also have been due to condescending views about women composers. Women were composing in the UK but were still regarded with some contempt. She had the added burden of being an unknown female composer from 'the colonies'. Although access to the RCM was open to women, they were largely segregated from their male colleagues. Their motivations and aspirations were assumed to be different, and they were not considered men's direct competitors. Scottish music critic, author and composer Cecil Gray's comment in his *Survey of Contemporary Music* (1924) epitomised this attitude: 'A woman's composing is like a dog's walking on his hind legs. It is not done well, but you are surprised to find it done at all'.[13]

Margaret was unimpressed by English composers' efforts to establish an English-inspired idiom drawing on traditional folk music, considering it merely 'dressed-up folk song', and was selective in identifying the right mentors. Armed with letters of introduction from Hart to his friends John Ireland and Ralph Vaughan Williams, she also planned to approach Gustav Holst, with whose music she was familiar courtesy of Hart.[14]

Vaughan Williams (in his early fifties) was 'a dear old man' and Margaret admired Holst's humility. She also met English composer Cyril Scott. She did not pursue studies with any of these composers, though didn't provide detailed explanations for this. With Ireland, she did have a few lessons in orchestration, but concluded this 'was quite mistaken', because his approach was too mechanical. 'We don't have thirds any longer—turn them into fourths,' he told her. 'I must have been a horrid prig', she reflected, but I said, 'I didn't hear fourths just there'.[15]

Others dismissed her as 'somebody just come to learn accompaniment or something like that—that I wouldn't be writing anything', or they 'always had some prop to give you'. She eventually had orchestration lessons with 'an interesting woman composer', to whom she felt greatly indebted. This was Dorothy Howell, who taught harmony and composition at the Royal Academy of Music from 1924.[16]

By July, a few months after her arrival in London, Margaret had decided to approach composer Arnold Bax. He was an experienced and respected composer with many solo, chamber, orchestral and vocal compositions to his name, and was knighted in 1937. David Symons describes his music as 'essentially that of the British post-impressionist and pastoral variety' of romanticism, though 'more relatable to the "Celticism" of Fritz Hart's work, thus forming a link with Sutherland's own earlier musical associations'.[17]

Although not interested in most English music of this period, Margaret respected Bax's music, and 'more and more' she wanted lessons from him. Finding an opportunity to introduce herself was challenging, because 'He would sit right at the back of the hall, and when it was over, he disappeared by a back door ... Other composers came to the platform for their plaudits, not so Bax ... He was there to learn, not to be looked at, and that was encouraging', she said. She wrote to him, and he telephoned her, suggesting she visit, his curiosity aroused by this Australian visitor. Margaret was eager, timid and diffident, but seized the opportunity.[18]

A 'slim, gentle man', with eyes that 'had a twinkle of enquiry', Bax was forty-two when Margaret met him, and lived in a flat in Swiss Cottage. The first thing Margaret noticed on the ground floor of his apartment building was a stuffed cockatoo in a glass case, which she later concluded he had never noticed, for 'He was a man who looked only for what he wanted to see'. He informed her he was 'quite hopeless as a teacher'. He had never given lessons but said he would like to talk to her. She showed him some scores, and he quickly sought others from his shelves. The discussions began.[19]

Margaret appreciated that Bax 'had no particular method', and quickly grew to like him and his undoctrinaire approach. He insisted she complete a work before seeing him, because it was important to 'let the whole thing grow together'. They would discuss it, with reference to other composers' scores, including Bax's own. He made useful suggestions, leaving her free to develop her own imagery and style. Not 'one of those iconoclasts who make one feel that one should start everything all over again', his suggestions were always 'for the next time'. It was wonderful 'just to be able to talk with somebody who thought in the same way and didn't pontificate in the usual way, you know'.[20]

The period with Bax was invaluable, and her fondness for him obvious:

> Bax would not allow me to pay him anything. He was so genuine and so straightforward. It meant so much to me that I had known him. I just could not believe that I had found him, in that flat full of scores, books and the cockatoo. His straight-to-the-point comments on any things that I took him have always remained with me as the most valuable advice I ever had.[21]

During her first year abroad, Margaret took basic conducting lessons, which she occasionally put to use: 'We had to start conducting two pianos to begin with, but at least it gave me a bit of courage'. In a later session, 'It was organised that the wretched violas would fall out half a bar and you'd have to bring them in', she told James Murdoch in 1968. 'You really had a tense course. You knew by the devilish look in their eyes that something was up.'[22]

Margaret met interesting people, even attending a royal garden party at Windsor in mid-1924. She found time to reconnect with her cousin Nora Kyffin Thomas, who had travelled to Europe following a long recovery from a serious accident. Profoundly injured, she was never the same again. This was obvious to Margaret during a two-week visit to a convent in Sidmouth, Devon, where Nora was boarding. Although the relationship between the cousins had thawed following the 'blousey' contralto incident, and they were again on 'matey' terms, the changes in Nora were deeply disturbing. She had decided to become a Carmelite nun. Previously 'full of courage and fun', she was now 'tentative and untrusting of herself'. Distressingly, she had completely lost her love of music, and replaced it with a deep religiosity. Margaret could not understand Nora's unquestioning devotion, nor her 'extraordinary admiration for a very unappetising, freckly, pimply priest of about 19'. To distance herself, she made daily pilgrimages to 'savour a magically slender gum which grew, surprisingly, all by itself, a triumphant and lovely creamy stripling among the surrounding different vegetation'. Once again, nature came to Margaret's rescue.[23]

In September 1924, Margaret moved out of the Beaufort Street flat and embarked on another adventure. After a walking tour of Wales, she crossed the channel to visit Austria and Paris. True to form, she had no plans for formal study; rather, she wanted to see her 'way round and to know what was what' through hearing as wide a range of music as possible.[24]

Music by composers broadly described as 'modernist' particularly interested her, because they were devising new methods that greatly impacted the directions music took in the twentieth century. She heard new 'tremendously non-English music', including works by Debussy and Ravel, which manifested a French 'impressionist' style by reinterpreting tonality, form and sonority. She also heard works by Bartók, who turned to Hungarian folk music in search of new forms of tonality, and by Stravinsky, who aimed for a renewed emphasis on rhythm, and was attracted to neoclassical forms. Broadly speaking, so-called 'neoclassical' composers were reacting against what they perceived as the unrestrained emotionalism, romanticism and formlessness of late nineteenth- and early twentieth-century music. They sought a return to the aesthetic precepts of the so-called 'classicism' of the early eighteenth and early nineteenth centuries—order, balance, clarity, economy and emotional restraint. Aspects of neoclassicism in the music of Les Six, a group of six French composers who lived and worked in Montparnasse during and after World War I, interested her too. Although Margaret rejected the idea that her music was directly influenced by other composers, it is possible to detect traces of these composers' approaches in some of her later works.[25]

Vienna was musically stimulating. She attended the Musik und Theaterfest der Stadt Wien (Vienna Festival of Music and Theatre), where she 'lived on music' for a month. This was an ambitious festival, and a major landmark in Vienna's interwar cultural history. Margaret encountered Austrian composer Erich Korngold, then a sensation in Europe for his innovative approach to opera, of which *Die Tote Stadt* (*The Dead City*) is the best-known example. (He later became well respected for his Hollywood film scores.) Margaret found him impressive, as she did German composer Richard Strauss, who was conducting in the Opera House. The festival's highlight was Strauss's new opera *Schlagobers* (*Whipped Cream*). She thought the sumptuous late romantic orchestration was masterly, the production 'as exquisite as Vienna could make it', and the ballet 'as good as the Russians are, but the plot is silly—the nightmares of a little boy who has eaten too much cream cake. You see him in bed—you hear his groans!' Despite her favourable impression of his music, 'the perversity of Strauss cannot be hidden. It is that same perversity which runs through his operas *Salome* and *Elektra*'. She agreed with *Sunday Times* critic Ernest Newman, who opined that Strauss had a 'waltz complex'. As ever, she preferred works by composers who avoided 'showiness', citing the vocal and instrumental compositions of the Austrian Franz Schreker, who gained a reputation for his aesthetic plurality.[26]

Margaret loved Vienna, where classical music was embedded in everyday life. 'Though the First World War has affected most of the professional classes, they do not give up their interest in art', she remarked. 'Musical education was accessible to all.' One would find 'the newspaper vendor and the street sweeper whistling operatic arias', and 'Viennese students were all busy debating the merits of modern work'. To the casual observer, poverty was not obvious. 'The shops were as brilliant as the French ones, and the people on the streets were in the latest Parisian fashions. And everyone was so kindly—so friendly!'[27]

After Vienna came Paris. While many composers from English-speaking countries aspired to study with Nadia Boulanger, Margaret was not among them; she was not attracted to Boulanger's particular neoclassical style. Instead, she soaked up 'lovely Paris in its autumn dress!', appreciating the grand boulevards, which 'were wonderful with the bright red tints of the leaves'. She caught up with Australian arts patron Louise Hanson-Dyer, also visiting Paris. Margaret had met Hanson-Dyer in Melbourne through mutual connections with the Albert Street Conservatorium, PLC and the British Music Society (BMS), and as a fellow member of the Lyceum Club, which Margaret joined in

1922. Hanson-Dyer would become a champion of Margaret's music, publishing several of her works, including her *Sonata for Violin and Piano* (1925) in 1935.[28]

Asserting her independent thought, Margaret eschewed that major centre of Western musical history, Germany—she did not include it in her itinerary. She felt the musical impulse seemed dead there, which did not align with her opinion that, 'Everyone who composes, to be worthwhile, must sound a new note'.[29] She was not interested in entering the robust discourse across Europe about Second Viennese School innovations. Its three principal composers, Schoenberg, Berg and Webern, expanded tonality, and evolved towards extreme chromaticism. The movement's culmination was Schoenberg's serial 12-tone technique, later emulated by many twentieth-century composers.[30] This radical innovation did not resonate with Margaret's belief that music should be accessible and give pleasure. In her quest to be inventive, she preferred to bend Western classical musical rules rather than break them. Her attitude may also have been influenced by the long-lasting British rejection of this school.[31]

As if to validate her prejudice against much German music, she had this to say after watching British composer Ethel Smyth, who studied in Germany for several years, conduct her *Mass in D (Major)*:

> I heard Dr Ethel Smyth conduct her own Mass, which is a not wonderful, but sincere composition in the German style. Dr Smyth, however, is years behind the modern English school. That may sound a little critical of me, but tastes are changing so quickly in England and France that one cannot refuse to look facts in the face.[32]

But Margaret did concede that it was a treat to see German opera in London: 'The German Opera Company has two advantages over the English one, its wonderful production—never a hitch occurs—and [Maria] Jeritza, the golden-haired prima donna', who is 'all they have said of her—and more'.[33]

Returning to another London winter, Margaret savoured her happy memories, but found 'the so-called charming Chelsea most depressing'. 'Although the river can be very picturesque', she acknowledged, 'the odour quenched my ardour for its beauty'. She moved near Hampstead Heath, where she shared a flat with a Melbourne friend, medical student Rachel Gillespie. She could wander on the heath to absorb the restorative effects of nature, and enjoy the 'many interesting houses'. Ivy House, home of Russian ballet dancer Anna Pavlova, was a favourite due to its enchanting waterlily ponds.[34]

Fortuitously, Rachel was out all day, so Margaret worked in peace. Both were on tight budgets and lived frugally. 'Two meals a day would be quite sufficient', they decided. The flat was 'fairly commodious', but they found the small abode's fifteen mirrors 'a bit hard to take'.[35]

There is little evidence of Margaret's composition during this period abroad, and the few works that may have been written were undated. There are two exceptions, the first being a choral work dated 1924, a setting of 'Death and Birth', a poem written by British poet Algernon Charles Swinburne, who was attracted to opposing themes like growth and decay, pleasure and pain, and unity and division. This poem broods on the poles of death and birth, and implies the inevitability of death, a familiar theme for Margaret. It has not been published or performed, and would need a competent choir—the music is expressive and harmonically complex, if rhythmically quite simple.[36] From a beginning marked 'quietly flowing', it meanders through several key and tempo changes, with some daring dissonances. It would still come across as 'modern' today.

The most significant work from Margaret's sojourn in London was unquestionably her *Sonata for Violin and Piano*. Written at the end of her studies with Bax, it demonstrates the inspiration derived from him and represented a high point in Margaret's compositional life to date. She loved the violin—particularly for the dark sound of its lower register—and was knowledgeable about its capabilities.[37] Apart from music for piano, she wrote most of her solo instrumental work for violin, though this choice may also have been guided by having close violinist friends keen to perform her music.

Given we know of few works written before this sonata, it seemed 'to spring from nowhere'. It is a mature, deeply expressive work of considerable imagination and skill—particularly in its melodic writing and thematic development. Its freer approach to form and fluctuating harmonic centres meant it received a mixed reception when first performed in 1926 in Australia, where it was regarded as avant-garde. Its 'Baxian sensuousness', however, aligned it more closely with nineteenth-century romanticism and French impressionism than with the neoclassicism popular in Europe. Although Margaret wanted to distance herself from the excesses of late romanticism, the intensity and individuality of the sonata are far from the neoclassical style, whose 'parody and iconoclasm' were at that time foreign to her nature.[38]

Bax was impressed with the sonata, which prompted his oft-quoted utterance 'This is the best work I know by a woman'. This comment sounds patronising to today's ears but should be interpreted in context. He was probably comparing it with other women composers' work in England and Europe at the time. Margaret was flattered, not offended. Bax was sufficiently impressed to write letters of recommendation to prospective publishers, including J & W Chester in London, opining that the work contained 'some remarkable ideas and deserves your careful consideration'.[39] Margaret treasured these letters.

Valuable support was found at London's Society of Women Musicians. Margaret probably knew of its existence through one or both of two violinists—Leila Doubleday and Elise Steele—whom she met at the University of Melbourne Conservatorium. Both studied in London and became members of the society, as did Margaret in March 1925. There were many professional women musicians in Britain, but they were still struggling with the refusal to believe that a woman could play in a professional symphony orchestra or compose a large-scale, complex work.[40] In response to this attitude, violinist and writer Marion Scott, along with singer and social reformer Gertrude Eaton and composer Katharine Eggar, formed the society in 1911 to 'provide a space for women to meet to discuss musical matters and the business aspects of a musical career, as well as giving concerts that brought composers and performers together'.[41]

Margaret found the society's 1925 conference rewarding. Her *Sonata for Violin and Piano* was premiered on 11 July, with Margaret accompanying Leila Doubleday, who played 'with great warmth and virility' according to a Melbourne *Herald* review. The work was 'essentially modern in character and treatment, despite the fact that it abounds in melody', and it 'altogether had a fine reception'. Margaret also read a paper entitled 'Rhythmic Features of Modern Music', enjoying the preparation more than the delivery.[42]

Alongside working and socialising, Margaret performed in concerts, such as one hosted in Lady Evelyn Guinness's home.[43] This event probably eventuated through Margaret's membership of a musical club that organised private performances of new works in picturesque settings. Here she encountered a variety of new music, including works by Australian composer Arthur Benjamin. She also discovered the Play Actors Society, whose president was actress Lilian Braithwaite. The society produced plays that would otherwise never be staged, performing in theatres on Sunday nights when they would normally be dark, and featuring prominent professional actors who donated their time. They did this 'just for the love of the thing', Margaret said, with an altruistic spirit of support for their art that she endorsed. Here she encountered, among others, the renowned actress Sybil Thorndike, whose performance as a woman of the people in a work by German left-wing playwright Ernst Toller was the finest of hers Margaret had seen.[44]

Meanwhile, Norman's hopes of pursuing musical studies were dwindling. Short of money, he found work in a hospital, and began studying surgery, intending to qualify as a fellow of the Royal College of Surgeons. But he disliked it, describing it as 'glorified carpentry' or 'butchery'. Instead, he completed a diploma of psychological medicine in 1925, working at the Maudsley Hospital in South London and Horton Mental Hospital in Epsom, Surrey. This formal qualification was not available in Australia until the 1950s—the few psychiatrists in Melbourne in the 1920s had been trained overseas. Having shipped his grand piano to England, he filled his spare time with music, often joining Margaret at concerts.[45]

Always strapped for cash, Margaret bought cheaper seats in the 'gods' to enable attendance at more performances. She went to recitals by well-known musicians such as American–Austrian violinist Fritz Kreisler, English pianist Myra Hess and English violist Lionel Tertis, and went often to the Royal Opera House, Covent Garden. The series of Proms concerts at the Queen's Hall were an attraction, and at three shillings for standing room, she went regularly.[46] She appreciated Sir Henry Wood's 'cosmopolitan' choice of programs and his introduction of new works, and enjoyed the social aspect. 'You seem to meet everyone you know promenading during the intervals, and it is all very interesting', she said. She was disappointed with the 1925 series, however, proclaiming it to be 'very ordinary as to programmes, and extremely restricted as to artists, because old Mr [William] Boosey has banned the employment of any artist who has ever broadcasted'.[47]

Although women conductors were few and far between (and continue to be a minority), Margaret sought out their performances. 'Though the early conductors tended to be mere semaphores', she said, 'women are now coming into their own, and achieving by means of a new technique a much quieter and more efficient style'. She was particularly impressed by British conductor Ethel Leginska, whom she saw lead the London Symphony Orchestra.[48]

The orchestral works that Margaret encountered abroad meant a lot:

> It added to my work the colour I wanted; for all Australian compositions at the present have more rhythm than colour. Our development is on a par with free verse. It is very experimental, but I think there is great hope for it, for ours is a more virile rhythm, more vital, than one finds in some of the older countries. Our chief concern is to get away from the four-bar phrases—we must drop that conventionality.[49]

This demonstrates Margaret's desire to see Australian music develop a national idiom, and she now felt equipped to contribute. The source of intellectual and creative stimulus for her father, uncles and aunts had been Australia, and so it was for her. Her homeland had 'haunted' her while she was away, and with her savings running low, she decided to return there at the end of 1925. She had 'learned a great deal of a great many things', and composition now 'mattered above everything'.[50]

CHAPTER 6

RETURN TO AN UPHILL JOURNEY (1926–1927)

After having thought in terms of the writing of music all this time, the barrenness, the absolute vacuum at home, hit and hurt me.

Margaret Sutherland[1]

ENRICHED BY HER musical experiences in England and Europe, Margaret was optimistic about making her mark as a composer in her native Australia. She booked a passage home on the passenger liner SS *Oronsay*, to depart from the Tilbury docks in September 1925, but decided to delay her return, sailing instead on the RMS *Ormonde* in late October. Her decision to postpone was likely due to a reluctance to leave the vibrant cultural world of London. 'I went away for 12 months, but found even two years away only too short for all I wanted to do.' She may also have wanted to spend more time with Norman, since he remained in London for another year to complete his studies and gain experience. If Norman and Margaret corresponded during their year apart, the evidence has been destroyed. She arrived back in Melbourne on 25 November, having stopped en route in Perth, where she caught up with her brother Douglas, and in Adelaide, where she visited relatives.[2]

Margaret initially shared older sister Dorothy's flat in Toorak Road, South Yarra, and embarked on re-establishing herself in Melbourne. Her enthusiasm was soon dampened by the realisation of the impossibility in her homeland of living by composition alone. 'After having thought in terms of the writing of music all this time, the barrenness, the absolute vacuum at home hit and hurt me.' Composer Helen Gifford postulated that 'Margaret's privileged artistic environment and specialised musical upbringing led her to have unduly high expectations about her compositional prospects in Australia'.[3] The artistic, intellectual bubble in which she had grown up fed both her disappointment and her determination to create a better cultural scene in Australia.

The problem was not a dearth of opportunities to hear music in Melbourne. By the 1920s, Australia was less isolated from musical developments in Britain and Europe. Improved sea transportation enabled overseas artists and international opera companies to venture to the Antipodes. In Margaret's view, however, the impresarios 'who brought the itinerant musicians' were 'always told to give us the same old potboilers'. Nevertheless, music was reaching a broader audience. Records were being mass-produced, wireless technology was entrenched, and sound cinema was being commercialised. The Royal Melbourne Philharmonic Society (RMPS) and the Royal Victorian Liedertafel provided regular opportunities to hear choral music.[4]

Another significant factor in this enrichment was the return of Australian violinist Bernard Heinze in 1923, following service in World War I, and studies at the Royal College of Music in London, the Schola Cantorum in Paris, and in Berlin. He was to become a dominant figure in Australian music, with fingers in every major musical pie. His impact began as conductor of the University Symphony Orchestra (USO), and as founder of the Melbourne String Quartet. He lifted the USO's standards, broadened its repertoire and reach, and introduced celebrity concerts by outstanding overseas performers. A tall, urbane, charismatic and ambitious man with good business acumen, he cultivated wealthy supporters, had a gift for self-promotion, and was strongly committed to public music performances. He joined the university conservatorium staff in 1924, and in 1925 started lecturing and conducting free concerts in schools. He was appointed Ormond Professor in 1926 at the young age of thirty-two, having competed with Fritz Hart, among others, for the position. In 1927, he was engaged as RMPS conductor, and in 1929 as part-time director-general of music for the predecessor of the Australian Broadcasting Commission (ABC). He continued his involvement as ABC music adviser and conductor for many years, promoting music to younger audiences, introducing new music and supporting Australian composition, albeit with a greater focus on male composers. He did not enjoy conducting opera, however, preferring the greater visibility of conducting on stage.[5]

Although Melbourne was alive with music, and organisations such as the Musical Society of Victoria (MSV) and the British Music Society (BMS) were including Australian compositions in their programs, most remained centred around the well-known seventeenth- to nineteenth-century British and European composers. 'New music didn't come to Australia for a long time', Margaret lamented.[6]

The need to earn money led Margaret to rejoin the conservatorium staff in 1926 as 'Teacher of Pianoforte, Chief Study', where she retained the position as Goll's understudy. She already knew of Heinze and his family, but their paths now crossed regularly. Along with his ambition and appeal, Heinze could be volatile and intimidating, and their respective strong wills soon clashed. Margaret later reflected that she did not understand why Heinze was appointed Ormond Professor and dean. 'They imagined that he would toe the line and go on as they wanted', she said, 'but believe it or not, Bernard soon felt that he could be Top Dog, and that was not so easy'. He had no idea how to organise a curriculum, she thought. 'It was a shambles.' She criticised him for not learning works from the original version—she felt he mimicked other conductors. Particularly abhorrent was his comment 'Conducting? I thought you just took a stick and waved it!'[7]

Recognising Margaret's unhappiness at the 'very depressive state' of Australian music, and about her compositional prospects, a few 'warm friends' arranged a recital of her works in March 1926. This was the first of many concerts in 1926 and 1927, with her works sometimes featured. Performing helped re-establish her in the Melbourne music scene and provided much-needed income to add to her teaching earnings.

The March recital was noteworthy, both in raising her profile and for Margaret's reaction to its reception. A committee of Melbourne musical movers and shakers was established to organise and fund the concert. Its members demonstrated the useful connections Margaret had made, particularly through her membership of the Lyceum Club, but also through other musical networks. It included Ivy Brookes, Louise Hanson-Dyer, violinist Olga Kenny (née Zichy-Woinarski) and Amy Shackell (née Baillieu). The committee met in February 1926 at the Lyceum and set a concert date at the Assembly Hall in Collins Street of Friday 12 March.[8] This was carefully scheduled between an 'at home' event organised for Margaret at the Lyceum Club on Wednesday 10 March, and the opening night on 13 March 1926 at His Majesty's Theatre of ballet dancer Anna Pavlova's tour with her company.[9]

The major work on the program, and 'the most imposing', was Margaret's *Sonata for Violin and Piano* (1925), with Heinze playing violin and Goll on piano. Goll also played her *Prelude, Pavan and Passacaglia for Piano* and *Wood Nymph and Satyr* (both c. 1926), and 'more or less ruled' the concert, said Margaret. The scores for these two piano works are lost, but concert reviews provide clues as to their nature. The *Prelude, Pavan and Passacaglia* were described as short, 'charmingly simple', 'tuneful' and 'well-rounded', and *Wood Nymph and Satyr* as a 'moving and programmatic' tone poem 'of gracefully whimsical import', 'a phantasy of sylvan life with rippling cadences'.[10]

Singer and fellow Lyceum member Violet Somerset, a regular collaborator, sang six songs accompanied by Margaret. The concert program is missing, though the *Australian Musical News* (AMN) mentions a bracket headed 'Three Songs for Children's Concert', and links can be made with a similar recital of Margaret's works in Adelaide five months later. One of the three children's songs was *Hawthorn Blossoms* (Winifred Howard), and Howard's *I've Been Out Playing* was also performed. The third was *Not Yet* (Ethel Martyr), and another Martyr poem, *To a French*

Marigold, was probably aired.[11] *Edelweiss* (Frank Wilmot), and probably Walter Savage Landor's *I Strove with None*, both musical settings dated to 1913, completed the six. Sadly, these scores are lost, but their texts reveal Margaret's preoccupation with themes of life, death, nature and art.

The concert was well publicised, with notices appearing in the *Argus*, *Age*, *Herald* and *AMN*, among others. It generated much interest, with several Melbourne musical, artistic and philanthropic luminaries in the audience. Concert committee members and their spouses were there, along with violinist Nora Streeton (Arthur Streeton's wife); Fritz Hart; Mona McBurney; organist, chorus master, music critic and broadcaster Dr AE Floyd; Margaret's brother Alfred; fellow Lyceum members; friends, and many others. 'The evening was a triumph for Miss Margaret Sutherland', said one critic, and she 'was the recipient of many beautiful bouquets'.[12]

As American feminist musicologist Marcia Citron argued, critical reception is a significant 'marker on the professional path' to recognition as a serious composer. 'Reception reflects and establishes the criteria by which music is judged, and as such plays an obvious role in valuation.' The professional music critic has wielded considerable power, though it is difficult for critics to avoid imposing their own aesthetic values.[13]

There were several reviews of this watershed recital, which were generally positive, though critics' 'own aesthetic values' were evident in dubiousness regarding the perceived modernity of the *Sonata for Violin and Piano*. Observing that this was 'the most impressive work presented', the *Age* reviewer continued:

> Much of the melody follows lines of undeniable beauty, and harmonic and rhythmic invention is never lacking … Variation in the length of the phrase patterns results in an interesting exposition of rhythmic balancing, which is at present on its trial in musical experiment.[14]

The *Australasian* critic commented that 'Mr Goll and Professor Heinze collaborated in an impressive rendering' of an intriguing and charming sonata. 'The style is elusive and in some respects somewhat baffling, but the music is never negligible … Miss Sutherland clearly has something to say', and her manner 'is thoroughly individual'.[15]

The *Argus* critic began ominously, with 'Much modern music is obviously negligible', but Margaret was labelled an 'artist venturer'. 'Puzzling though they might be to people whose musical horizon is bounded by the works of the great classic composers', her compositions were 'never merely wilful, and never without some guiding purpose'. The reviewer added patronisingly that 'her work justifies itself by the only standard which can apply in these uncharted areas—it is clearly and indubitably sincere'. He continued floridly:

> Miss Sutherland's progress as a composer will be followed with very serious and sympathetic interest by all genuine music-lovers. Given favourable conditions, it is highly probable that she may retell, in the idiom of today, the ageless story of that quest which impels composers to strive ever to speak that which cannot be uttered, and to make audible the secrets which only music can with any semblance of hope discuss.[16]

The *AMN* reviewer noted that 'Miss Sutherland has been imbibing freely at the best modern tonal sources', though 'she does not reach out for much beyond a constant succession of wavelike modulations' and some 'abrupt changes'. The *Sonata* was 'evidence that Australian musicians are determined to quit the easiest roads'.[17]

Despite reviewers having acknowledged her original talent, Margaret was alert to the subtext of the comments about the novelty of the musical idiom. She later attributed her interpretation of the concert's reception to two issues. 'It was utterly unheard of for a woman to write music. In fact, people were still finding it hard to accept contemporary compositions. If you didn't employ all the old musical cliches, they used to be quite scandalised.'[18]

'The recital was well attended', she conceded, 'but no-one appeared to know what I was driving at. A frequent comment was "straight from the unconscious you know" and I began to feel I was some sort of Freudian freak'. There was 'practically no communication whatever', she felt. 'I knew then that it was going to be a desperately heart-breaking uphill journey, and I felt cold and dismayed.'[19]

Fragile with the shock of arriving home to a cultural environment not up to date with European developments, these observations fuelled

Margaret's pessimism about her future. This vignette represents one of the first obvious examples of the extent to which she took things to heart. Her mother and sister Dorothy had suffered from depression, and Margaret sometimes did too.

Most creative artists find critics hard to ignore. Over the years, Margaret kept an eye on her press and pasted favourable reviews in a scrapbook. She was aware of the critic's power, and deplored what she perceived as uninformed criticism, both of herself and other musicians. She later complained about the potential for ruthless, untrained critics to damage an artist's sensibilities. An artist 'can have his whole inside desecrated by the critic', she commented in the 1960s. In 1970, she vented her frustration in a short, tongue-in-cheek musing, 'Occupational Hazards'. Why were critics 'so often depressed and miserable', 'why so cynical', and 'why is he nearly always an introverted sort of chap?' she asked. 'Does it do him any good to sit in judgment? And is the judgment he sits in valid?' Perhaps all he should do is 'give a factual account of what happened', but that would make him 'a gossip columnist'. 'Tell me—someone—tell me, for heaven's sake. I'm going mad', she concluded.[20]

Critics' names were not always made public, but regular reviewers in major newspapers, such as Thorold Waters (the *Sun News-Pictorial* 1920s–40s), JE Tremearne (the *Herald* 1930s–40s), Neville Cardus (the *Sydney Morning Herald* 1930s–40s) and Felix Werder (the *Age* 1960s–70s) were mostly positive about Margaret. John Sinclair was a great advocate. *Herald* music critic from 1947–85, he was known for his direct and uncompromising critiques, but understood the need to hear a new work more than once to fully understand it and 'discriminate between what is good, bad and mediocre'.[21] He demonstrated the utmost respect for Margaret in reviews and articles, writing a glowing tribute to her in the *Australian Journal of Music Education* in 1969 and speaking at her funeral.

Fortunately, Margaret had her fans, who appreciated the music included in the March recital. In a letter of thanks to concert committee leading light Ivy Brookes two days after the concert, Margaret expressed her gratitude at Brookes' praise of the *Sonata*. 'I was enormously cheered when I learned from you afterwards that you had found some beauty in the Sonata', she wrote. 'It means more to me than I can possibly tell you to know this; and it is certainly the greatest incentive one can have, I think, to know that the idea behind one's work has "come through"—has made at least a definite impression.'[22]

Margaret composed little in the eighteen months after her return. Her disillusionment, and her teaching and performing commitments, precluded it. Nevertheless, composers and their music were always on her mind, and she found an outlet penning articles for the *Argus*. These reflect her frustration and despondency, and demonstrate her desire to create awareness among Australian audiences about genuinely valuable music.

'The Vogue of Bach: A Perfect Musical Balance', published in May 1936, was an attempt to express where the 'beauty' Brookes appreciated in her *Sonata* might be encountered in music. She observed 'a very natural swing of the pendulum' regarding the appreciation of Bach's works, particularly in England. Contributing to the age-old debate between absolute and program music,[23] she argued that Bach achieved a perfect balance between musical form and emotional expression:

> When we think of each phrase in Bach as a spoken phrase, brimful of import, undulating through sheer intensity of emotion, and in no way dependent on pattern or form, only then do we thoroughly appreciate its inherent value ... Emotion always first—form merely secondary. It is not Bach the geometrician, the fine draughtsman, who wins through the centuries, but Bach the singer, the interpreter of every shade of human and super-human emotion, who thrills us now with melody so pregnant, so vital.[24]

Margaret's piano composition *Two Chorale Preludes* (pre-1934)—'Herzliebster Jesu' and 'Jesu meine Freude'—constitute her first overt homage to Bach, whose music she initially came to love as a child, listening to her cousin Nora Kyffin Thomas playing violin. While listeners immediately recognise Bach's influence in these pieces, Margaret put her own stamp on them. The texture is thicker than Bach's might have been, and although the harmony is largely diatonic, she incorporated modal inflexions and occasional bitonality.[25]

Margaret made at least two trips in 1926 to Adelaide, the city of her birth, performing concerts facilitated by her cousin Kathleen Kyffin Thomas and other relatives. Foreshadowing the first visit in May, the Adelaide *Observer* published a feature article in which her 'gifted forebears' were highlighted. 'Adelaide might have permanently claimed Margaret Sutherland had not family ties taken her father to Victoria.' The article referred to her 'brilliant concert' in March in Melbourne, and to the 'excellent criticisms', which generated a wish 'that Miss Sutherland would repeat the Melbourne program in Adelaide'. During the second visit, in August 1926, this was realised.[26]

The August concerts were well promoted in Adelaide's press. The Adelaide *Mail* forewarned readers that 'Some of Miss Sutherland's works are modern in the extreme and are in somewhat unfamiliar idiom. They should be heard with interest, especially by those who wish to keep abreast of modern ideas in music'.[27]

While in Adelaide, Margaret was interviewed by a *Register* journalist, who asked about her 'modern outlook' to composition. Her response gives the first clear sense of her compositional process and confirms her frustration at having to devote time to teaching rather than composing. It also foreshadows her further development of these ideas. Margaret named Bach and Brahms as two of her favourite composers, though Purcell was another, along with contemporary composers Frank Martin, Milhaud, Hindemith, Shostakovich, Debussy and Stravinsky. But she voiced her conviction that music should develop in new ways, and should be beautiful and sincere:

> Beauty comes too, as though by accident, but the essential 'striving for' is something more actually definite. Sometimes when I am walking along, the very swing and rhythm of that movement sets something stirring in my mind … The tragedy then lies in trying to adapt oneself to the regulated life of the teacher.[28]

Margaret's answer to a question about which works she considered her most important illustrates her take on the 'modern outlook'. 'The *Sonata for Violin and Piano* … contains three movements, which are more or less continuous, and into these I have striven to weave a combination of virility and melodiousness, presented with direct simplicity of expression.'[29]

The first of Margaret's Adelaide concerts was on 10 August with the Elder Conservatorium String Quartet, led by Charles Schilsky, at the Public Library Lecture Hall in the presence of His Excellence the Governor and Lady Bridges. The group performed quartets by Mozart and Beethoven, and Brahms' *Piano Quartet in A Major*. The *Mail* was complimentary, with a further display of South Australian pride at the 'homegrown genius' of the 'South Australian-born pianist, transplanted to Victoria in early youth'.[30]

Two days after the concert, Margaret was guest at a morning tea at the Lyceum Club (Adelaide), allowing her enough time to rehearse for the important concert of her works the next evening at Adelaide's Liberal Hall. This was a repeat of the program performed in Melbourne on 12 March. Reception was hesitant: She 'brought an ultra-modern' atmosphere to the recital. 'It is unfamiliar in the extreme as to rhythmic and melodic structure, and the sonata which she played with Mr Charles Schilsky bristles with difficulties and (to the orthodox ear) harmonic irregularities.' Margaret was joined by soprano Linda Wald and baritone Clive Carey, who 'were successful in some of Miss Sutherland's own songs', of which 'two of the lyrics were written by another South Australian, Miss Winifred Howard'. Also noted was Margaret's appearance with Edward Goll on a former visit to Adelaide. Further affirming the close musical relationship between Goll and Margaret, the reviewer wrote that 'the impression then gained was that the teacher owed much to the student, whose work in conjunction with the master, rounded and completed his own'.[31]

The observation of the novelty of Margaret's music stands out in these reviews and substantiates her opinion regarding the lingering conservatism of Australian audiences. These qualms were underscored a month later in a review of an MSV concert at the Australian Church in Russell Street. The program featured music by twelve Australian composers, at least three of them women, and included Margaret's *Sonata for Violin and Piano*. The *Age* reviewer bemoaned the fact that

'Apart from the notable *Bush Symphony* [*Miniatures*] by the late Henry Tate (1873–1926), nothing immediately representative of an Australian atmosphere has appeared from local musicians'. The 'nucleus of a school of composition is not in sight', he added.

This is the sort of comment that infuriated Margaret. Tate, an important figure in Australian music, maintained that its essential character could best be gleaned through incorporating and imitating Aboriginal music and native Australian bird calls, particularly the latter, of which *Bush Symphony* is an example. Margaret was less drawn to realism. 'Australian composers should absorb the country and all its constituents including the natives, then forget it.' The influence, she felt, was the result of permeation rather than imitation.[32]

Of Margaret's *Sonata for Violin and Piano*, performed by Heinze, again accompanied by the composer, the *Age* reviewer commented that the style was exotic, and that impulse appeared to 'out-run restraint, keeping the work with its many fine moments in an undesirable state of agitation'.[33]

Before and after her trip to Adelaide, Margaret played in a series of six regional concerts organised by the University of Melbourne Conservatorium. She, Helen Hamerton (violin) and Myrtle Wise (soprano) performed a wide range of music, with Margaret judiciously programming contemporary works among those more familiar to audiences. Reviews did not offer in-depth critiques, but commented on the small audiences, and wondered whether programs presenting so-called 'high-art' classical music were a disincentive. (This problem is not new!) More so-called 'popular' music might attract a wider audience, they thought.[34]

Although the concerts were appreciated, with many encores requested, the small audiences may have reinforced Margaret's 'culture shock'. She would not have agreed that the programs should include more 'popular' items. Such comments were likely to have further confirmed her distaste for composers who wrote music for commercial gain: 'I don't know how they can do it', she said. She maintained this view all her life, though other creative artists were resigned to this fate.

Australian author Joan Lindsay, for example, stressed in her autobiography *Time without Clocks* that the main source of 'bread and butter' for her and artist husband Daryl Lindsay 'was so-called "commercial art"'.[35] Unfortunately, Margaret's high moral ground did not enhance her already slim chances to make a living as a composer.

In one of her few compositions during this period, Margaret made her first foray into stage music. Louise Hanson-Dyer, in her capacity as BMS president, decided to stage the Australian premiere of Holst's one-act chamber opera, *Sāvitri*, in a gala performance at the Playhouse in September 1926. It seemed an ideal way to secure the BMS's financial future by increasing its endowment fund. She invited Margaret to join the organising committee. Knowing Holst's high opinion of baritone Clive Carey's production of this work in London, Hanson-Dyer asked him to produce the Melbourne version, for which she designed all the costumes herself. Heinze conducted an instrumental chamber group, the Cecilia Choir members comprised the wordless female chorus, and soprano Madame A Viceroy-Goosens, tenor Norman Bennett and Clive Carey sang the roles of Sāvitri, Satyavan and Death respectively.[36]

As *Sāvitri* lasts only thirty minutes, other works were programmed, including *Clorillo and His Phyllis*, a collection of songs and duets, together with dancing nymphs and shepherds.[37] Carey devised this 'pastoral idyll' using music by Henry Purcell, and Margaret orchestrated it.

The event was not without challenges, but 'fashionable Melbourne' turned out in force. Luxurious motorcars parked outside the theatre, and Hanson-Dyer managed to raise £1000 for the BMS Endowment Fund, effectively doubling it. According to Melbourne historian and Hanson-Dyer's biographer, Jim Davidson, the rendition of *Clorillo and His Phyllis* was a 'near disaster', since the orchestra was fully challenged by the *Sāvitri* score, and ignored the Purcell work until the dress rehearsal. Unfortunately, the score for *Clorillo and His Phyllis*, featuring Margaret's apparently 'neat' orchestration, has been lost.[38] Nevertheless, Margaret's role in this event demonstrated her ability to write at short notice for a specific setting, and for a medium (stage music) she would return to several times.

Margaret took to the platform again a month later for a solo recital at the Assembly Hall. She played works by Bach, Scarlatti, Mozart, Chopin, Ravel, Albéniz and Francis Poulenc. Revealing a distaste for modern music, the *Age* reviewer opined that 'Miss Sutherland has been heard as a composer of clever artistic works in the most modern form. Her individuality may be expected to conquer the idiom in which musicians now appear willing to enslave themselves'. He appreciated Margaret's playing, however, as did the *AMN* reviewer, who nevertheless hated the program. It was 'strikingly aloof from the more emotional schools, Chopin being the one romantic to intrude', he sarcastically observed.[39]

In an attempt to enlighten readers about beauty in contemporary composition, Margaret wrote another article for the *Argus* in November 1926, 'Musical Emancipation: New Works and Old Standards'. She argued that composers should free themselves of past structures built on old formulae and find different ways to express themselves:

> We must not weigh new works on the scales with accepted classics. Comparisons are, here at all events, entirely out of place ... It is useless to say, 'But that is not beautiful', for what is beauty, when we come actually to define it, but that which stirs in us an emotion resembling in some particular the musical experience of the composer at the moment of conception? Without exception, every single innovation that has ever been in music has been 'ugly' until its meaning has become clear—until, almost imperceptibly, perhaps, the realisation has come that somewhere on this planet a fellow being has had the power to express and to share his emotional experience with those of us who are capable of responding to it.

Finally, Margaret vented her frustration that 'too often ill-rehearsed, half-considered renderings serve only to mystify us more than ever'.[40]

Norman Albiston arrived back in Melbourne in early 1927, but Margaret maintained a busy performing schedule in the first few months of that year. In the first of several concerts of piano duets, she performed with her friend and fellow Lyceum member Biddy (Beatrice) Allen at the

Assembly Hall on 15 March 1927. The program included an Irish tone poem by Bax, *Moy Mell*, as well as the only piece she appears to have produced in 1927, *Burlesque for Two Pianos*, likely composed for this concert.

The *Australasian* reviewer trivialised women's performance and compositions by emphasising the performers' dress. This was not unusual:

> Many lovely flowers were presented in the intervals in the performance, and the two young artists looked very charming as they stood before their audience with their arms full of late summer blossoms. Miss Sutherland's frock of powder blue taffeta had a hoop of tiny roses seen in the silken folds of the skirt, while another rose posy was set on one shoulder. Miss Biddy Allen wore a georgette frock in the tint of dull mauve stock, and the full skirt was hemmed with silver lace and had a twisted silver cord at the flounce waistline. Acting as ushers and helping in various ways were a number of the artists' friends, who made a pretty picture in their girlish frocks of taffeta and velvet.[41]

Thorold Waters' appraisal was more profound. 'A feeling that one of the artists had found it necessary to subdue her personality to the plane of the other was created in the more classic portions of the two-piano recital', he wrote. It was Margaret—the more experienced and accomplished player—who subjugated her talent to blend with her colleague. Of Margaret's *Burlesque*, Waters observed that it contained 'some adroit cross-rhythm'. Its 'Frenchness' was observed elsewhere and is in keeping with Margaret's affinity with French composers such as Debussy and Ravel, with whose work she became acquainted during her European sojourn. Other reviewers referred to the lightness and comicality of the *Burlesque*. With no full score to be found, it is not possible to dispute these comments.[42]

A few days later, Margaret played another Bax work at Melba Hall. In the first of the year's concerts by university conservatorium Old Students' Association members, she performed his *Trio in One Movement for Piano, Violin and Viola* (1906) with Heinze on violin and William Lambie (viola). Waters enthused that 'The players gave real illustration to its startlingly beautiful progressions', while another reviewer praised it as 'a vital and characteristic work which made a powerful impression'.[43]

There was a second appearance at Melba Hall on Friday 29 April, when Margaret gave a recital with violinist Edouard Lambert of works by Bach, Handel and Brahms, as well as 'clever interpretations of two Brahms Capriccios' for solo piano. Two months later, the RMPS performed a memorial concert for the late Alberto Zelman, the society's conductor for the past fifteen years. Included was Mozart's *Piano Concerto in A Major*, played by the MSO conducted by Heinze, with Margaret as soloist. 'She caught the spirit of the work exactly, and brought out all its poetry, lightness and sparkle', declared the *Herald* critic. The *Argus* rhapsodised that 'not often does one hear musical phraseology so persuasive and so entirely convincing; in music so treated, truth and beauty seem to meet, and no question is left unanswered'.[44] Despite her desire to compose rather than play, Margaret was in fine form.

Eleven days later, Margaret attended a reception at the Lyceum Club for renowned Lithuanian–American violinist Jascha Heifetz, but the Zelman memorial concert was her final public appearance before her wedding. The fighting spirit with which she approached life was to be sorely tested in the years following this union. The 'desperately heartbreaking uphill journey' had just begun.[45]

PART THREE

MARRIAGE, MOTHERHOOD AND COMPOSITION: 1927–1947

CHAPTER 7

THE FIRST HIDEOUS YEARS OF MARRIAGE (1927–1933)

> *I remember being absurdly starry-eyed at the thought of working things up from an extremely meagre beginning. But soon a very different picture emerged.*
>
> Margaret Sutherland[1]

MARGARET'S MARRIAGE WAS the unhappy background to the next twenty-one years. It coloured every activity and compounded her feelings of loneliness as a composer. At a time when the creation of a happy family life defined women's worth, marital strife was stigmatised, and usually borne in silence. This, combined with Margaret's tendency not to 'wear her heart on her sleeve', meant she avoided sharing her despondency with friends. According to her daughter Jenifer, she also concealed bouts of severe depression.[2]

Having completed his Diploma in Psychological Medicine in London, Norman Albiston returned to Melbourne in early 1927. Norman and Margaret's relationship took up where it had left off a year earlier. She was twenty-nine, by which age society perceived a woman as being at risk of being left 'on the shelf'. Although she had models of creative women who remained single both within and outside her family, spinsterhood was not an attractive option. As Margaret's unmarried friend Mollie Turner Shaw observed, 'spinsters were objects of derision or at best compassion, the target for cheap jokes'. Unmarried women who were dependent on the support of a relative—usually the father (not an option for Margaret)—faced many of the disadvantages, but none of the advantages, of marriage. Those who supported themselves in one of the few employment options open to women worked for relatively low pay, and many had to live with their parents, nursing them in old age.[3]

Norman 'wore her down', and the couple decided to marry when his divorce from first wife Rita Stang was settled in May 1927 after the requisite three years' separation. It was not difficult to be 'worn down' by Norman. He was 'a bit of a catch'—handsome, engaging, witty, urbane and cultured. Composer Helen Gifford recalled that 'Psychiatrists were the rage. It was the glamour of Freud from World War I on—the mind was thrilling—it was a new area of discovery. And Norman was considered one of the best-looking men of his generation—a stunner'. Alongside his strong interest in music, he enjoyed chess, billiards, snooker and photography. A competent artist who had taken lessons from Melbourne painter George Bell, he produced drawings, as well as watercolours and oil paintings, often landscapes and images from the tropics. Rumour has it that he later enjoyed sketching caricatures of his patients during sessions![4]

There are other possible reasons for Margaret's attraction to Norman. Although financial security was not her primary goal for marriage, it may have been a factor, given that it was (and still is) hard to make a living as a composer. She knew what it meant to live in financially precarious circumstances, with all the men in her family having died, compelling remaining family members to earn their own incomes. When Margaret and Norman first met in 1923, Margaret's sister Dorothy had been ill, her mother had recently died, and Norman's first marriage had dissolved. It was an emotional time for both, and they possibly derived comfort from the affection provided within a new relationship. Margaret's dejection following her return from London may also have rendered her vulnerable to Norman's 'assumption of wisdom' based on his psychological knowledge.[5]

On Saturday 30 July 1927, a cold and cloudy day that was a striking portent of the future, the couple made their vows at Trinity Presbyterian Church in Melbourne's Camberwell, presided over by the Reverend Patrick John Murdoch. No trace of the event remains. Margaret appears to have done her best to extinguish the tangible memories of her courtship and marriage, though her bitterness and sadness remained long after the inevitable divorce.

Norman's father, Arthur Edward Albiston, a Wesleyan Methodist minister and professor of theology at Queen's College, the University of Melbourne, reportedly managed the wedding arrangements. Curiously, he suggested that the couple marry in a Presbyterian church but did not attend the wedding. He did, however, lend Norman the money to buy a small house with attached medical rooms at 32 Darling Road, East Malvern. Influenced by colleagues sceptical about the likely success of a specialised psychiatric practice, Norman established a general practice. Margaret purchased the furniture, along with a small Singer car.[6]

It is impossible to know the extent to which Margaret aspired to motherhood. It was expected in the late 1920s that a woman wanted children, and the only acceptable way was through marriage. Margaret thought the mother instinct was the 'life blood of any nation, and the world *must* go on going round, mustn't it?' Contrary to the prevailing view, she may have felt, like Melbourne artist Mirka Mora, that a mother was 'first an interesting person, a mother second'. She was also aware that marriage and motherhood would necessitate career sacrifices and acknowledged her uncle John's influence in this regard. 'It is the lot of woman that her occupations in life remain less fundamentally subject to variation than those of man', he wrote in his book *The Bonds of Society* (completed 1914). 'What justification shall there be for those that find more virtue and more honour for woman in discovering scientific truths or in artistic studies than in rearing children?'[7]

These sentiments were prevalent in the first half of the twentieth century when Margaret was raising children. Women were often blamed for the dwindling birth rate and reproached for their selfishness.

A woman was expected to put her husband and children first, nurturing them and providing food and a clean house.[8]

Margaret conformed—in part—to these expectations. She took pride in maintaining a pleasant home environment, though she felt the burden of household tasks, especially when her children were young. According to her friend Mollie Turner Shaw and former Melbourne Kindergarten Training College principal Madeline Crump, she possessed strong domestic skills. She sewed well, said Crump, and created 'lovely indoor living spaces'. 'She was a good cook and a well-organised housewife, who first thing in the morning had prepared the vegetables and the puddings for the evening meal', the vegetables probably 'grown in her own garden', Turner Shaw remembered.[9]

Nonetheless, Margaret lived and breathed music, and much of her energy was devoted to it. 'She had this terrible tugging of wanting to create ... I have a picture of her almost relentlessly pursuing her music', said friend and neighbour Maureen White, daughter of Margaret's colleague, the clarinet player Thomas White.[10] Every activity revolved around music, whether it be teaching, performing, lobbying for Australian music and musicians or, above all, composition.

A talk entitled 'Chant Intérieur' (Inner Song), delivered to the Catalysts in May 1956, sheds further light on this drive to compose. Here Margaret consolidated her long-held philosophies on the nature of composers and composition, echoing views expressed earlier in her life, including those in an August 1926 Adelaide *Register* interview (see Chapter Six). Without referring to specific works, she outlined her thoughts on what constituted a 'gift for music', and what it meant to be a composer, highlighting the distinctive styles of various renowned composers. She talked about the emotional fickleness of the artistic temperament, the difference between the composer and the performer, and her views on contemporary music. But most relevant is the experience she described of composers having 'running in their heads, an almost ceaseless flow of a kind of sound-picture':

> These may be their own, or other's peoples' music. They may be even varieties of rhythms—or perhaps a kind of looser, rhapsodic music,

> formless and rather cloudy ... Many composers indeed are almost at the mercy of this insistent 'chant intérieur' which in extreme cases keeps them in a state of perpetual unrest ... The composer's mind then is full of sound—stuff—motifs, rhythmical patterns, melodies—what you will ... They are with him constantly, jogging his elbow, prodding him in the ribs, until he has time, energy and inclination to attend and give his whole mind and being to the job.[11]

In addition to experiencing this persistent 'chant intérieur', Margaret insisted, composers were given certain gifts, and it was their duty to place them at everyone's disposal rather than living in an ivory tower.[12]

The model Margaret had internalised from her extended family was of people who followed their own intellectual and artistic paths while remaining close and supportive of each other. The 'marriage plot', with its focus on the domestic realm, was never going to fully satisfy her. She yearned for a broader, more adventurous experience, and hoped to find a way to blend marriage and motherhood with a rich creative life. She was 'absurdly starry-eyed at the thought of working things up from an extremely meagre beginning'. This hope persisted as the couple went on to raise two children, Mark (born 28 December 1928) and Jenifer (7 May 1931). Nearly twenty years later, in 1946, she still maintained that music was the ideal career to combine with marriage and motherhood, 'in spite of times of stress and strain that necessarily come when such a full "double" life is attempted'. It is important to interpret this comment in context. As a mother in an era when motherhood was seen as women's primary goal and greatest fulfilment, she could hardly have given the public impression that she was prioritising her musical career.[13]

The marriage was fragile early, and the stars before Margaret's eyes began to fade. The challenges she faced in juggling her commitments were evident from early 1928. In a letter to Ivy Brookes, foundation vice-president of the Ladies Committee of the USO, of which Margaret had been elected a member in April 1927, she was 'utterly ashamed' about missing several committee meetings, which clashed with her teaching commitments.[14]

Everything hindered the success of Margaret's attempt at this 'double life'. Norman was a doctor and, as Maureen White reflected, 'Medicos were like the great almighty'.[15] He was a man of his time, who felt entitled, as head of the household, to be respected by a wife who would be a happy homemaker and mother. It was fine for a woman to be musically accomplished, so long as it remained a hobby.

Early on, Margaret tried hard to help Norman establish his career. Apart from six months' leave of absence from the university conservatorium 'on account of ill health' when she was pregnant with Mark, she continued teaching—albeit part time—while Norman built his practice. 'For the first nine years', she wrote, 'I had paid all the household expenses, dressed the children and myself, and paid for their schooling. This because I thought it would give him more of a chance to establish himself. (It did, of course, not work out that way.)'[16]

In contributing financially within her marriage, Margaret was unusual. Paid work was considered a frustration of a woman's natural destiny, and reflected negatively on her husband's ability to support her and a family. Following marriage, women usually only worked through economic necessity.[17]

Margaret still disliked teaching, but she needed the income. She was willing to focus on those students who displayed natural talent but abhored wasting time on those who did not. Two friends, fellow Lyceum members and former students, later reflected on this. 'Few of us were ever allowed to guess just how much she hated teaching', declared Mollie Turner Shaw. Elizabeth Von Rompaey noted that Margaret would much rather have spent the time composing. 'Teaching held her up in that direction.' Nevertheless, she was an inspiring teacher who developed her own methods. She disapproved of training students for Australian Music Examinations Board (AMEB) exams. 'That is for lazy teachers', she said, and she herself had always hated sitting exams.[18] 'Being in touch with a person like Margaret, if you were receptive to what she said, it really did set your mind tingling. You'd go out of that lesson pleased and happy and feeling that you knew something a little bit more than you did an hour before', said von Rompaey. Turner Shaw echoed these sentiments.

'I learned from Margaret a great deal more than playing the piano. She broadened my whole outlook on music, right from the day I met her.' Another friend and Lyceum member, Aimée Wilkins, agreed that they were 'vital and marvellous lessons ... Margaret was a wonderful teacher'.[19]

Melbourne pianist, organist and choir master Leonard Fullard also acknowledged Margaret's teaching gift. He was her student at the University of Melbourne Conservatorium from 1927 until 1934, when he departed for England. She was a tough taskmistress. When she thought his playing was not up to scratch, she could be acerbic. 'That was vile', she told him one day after he had played a Bach piece. Despite having been on the receiving end of Margaret's 'directness', he looked back with admiration:

> [She was] a beautiful player and a great teacher. She could make you play a thing in the right way just by the expression in her face ... She played so beautifully and her technique was so perfect that she could teach a lot by demonstrating. She firmly believed the technique and interpretation went hand in hand. There was none of that mechanical playing of exercises. Every piece became an exercise and she demonstrated what special technique each piece demanded.[20]

The situation at home was increasingly unconducive to blending a happy family life with an artistic career. The East Malvern surgery's waiting room, inside the house, disrupted Margaret's housekeeping and brought in infection. Although Margaret had no official role in the practice, she had little choice but to manage patients, which often necessitated embarrassed apologies on Norman's behalf. Every morning, several women and children were waiting, even before Norman arose, and he lingered over breakfast before starting to consult. He also kept patients waiting at the evening session. Eventually, at her own expense, Margaret had part of the veranda converted into a waiting room. Probably an even greater contributor to marital discord was the fact that Norman did not enjoy general practice, leaving him disgruntled about being partially dependent on Margaret's earnings.[21]

Music, which had initially drawn them together, increasingly became a source of resentment. Even before the marriage, Norman displayed ambivalence about Margaret's brilliance and self-assurance, wanting to 'cut her down' because of her airs and graces. However, he found accomplished women tantalising and had pursued Margaret tenaciously, intrigued by her musical aptitude and beguiled by her beauty.[22] Indeed, photographs of Margaret from the early to mid 1930s show an attractive woman with even features and expressive eyes, her thick, wavy hair cut in a fashionable bob.

According to Pamela Bloom, a friend of Norman's who observed his intense interest in musicians, his first wife was sometimes annoyed by his avid musical interest. She also noted a tendency on Norman's part to infiltrate Margaret's friendships with other musicians. Occasionally he would join Margaret in duets at musical gatherings at home, but she too grew increasingly irritated with his approach to music. She felt that he did not play for enjoyment, but to impress an audience, and his mechanical playing was infuriating. His inability to match Margaret's talent appears to have led to jealousy and a desire for ownership of her musical activities. His own stymied musical ambitions likely contributed to this resentment; he claimed that his father had given him only three career alternatives—the Church, the law or medicine.[23]

Norman became increasingly aggrieved by Margaret's preoccupation with music, to the extent that it seems to have affected the couple's sex life. He later argued that his wife's libido was misdirected towards music, and proposed hypnosis to rectify this 'problem'. He even suggested to a leading music critic that Margaret's drive to compose was a symptom of mental illness. Norman turned to other women early in the marriage. After he confessed to indiscretions with two of his patients, 'E. Malvern was an unhappy place', Margaret wrote.[24]

Notwithstanding Norman's attitude, Margaret persisted in trying to remain connected to the music world. As well as teaching, she wrote letters to the editor and published articles on musical topics.[25] Apart from a year's break after Mark was born, and another for about nine months after Jenifer's birth, she remained an active performer, despite there being fewer opportunities during the Depression. She took to the stage on at least a hundred occasions in the 1930s and early 1940s.

Early in her marriage, Margaret performed her *Sonata for Violin and Piano* with Bernard Heinze, an occasion that demonstrated the discord that would continue to afflict their relationship. He asked whether she would play the *Sonata* with him for a broadcast. She agreed and enquired as to when they might rehearse. He replied that as she had written it and he had played it, they could simply perform it after dinner at a soirée at the home of her student Bob Baillieu on the evening before the broadcast. 'I was astonished!' she said. 'No rehearsal?' 'You must be more professional', Heinze argued. But an average performance was not good enough for her:

> Lots of drinks: lots to eat: a great deal of talk. I was getting rattled. When to begin? Bernard was very leisurely: a very little tune-up, then a few plucked notes, and off we went. To me, it appeared to be worse and worse. Then I stood up. 'I cannot play anymore. Will you call a taxi please?' It was ghastly … I somehow had to stop it, here and now.

Margaret did not play for the broadcast. Pressured to produce a compelling reason, Heinze said that she was pregnant and not feeling well enough to play. But this was not so.[26]

Apart from occasional airings of her own music, Margaret performed works by a wide variety of composers as soloist, chamber musician and accompanist, making appearances at the British Music Society and the Assembly Hall. She played regularly at the Lyceum Club, participating in a program of her own works for a club evening in May 1938 for the Music Circle.[27] She liked the Lyceum's intimate atmosphere and sometimes used the club as a venue for other concerts. In 1932, for example, violinist Elise Steele and Margaret rented the clubroom for a subscription series of chamber music concerts.

Among her collaborating friends—many of whom were fellow Lyceum members—was Mollie Turner Shaw, who later attested that, in addition to Margaret's skills as a teacher, performer and composer, she was a more-than-capable concert impresario:

> In the early 1930s begin my many recollections of Margaret in the setting of the Assembly Hall, sometimes in recitals with colleagues such as the violinist Elise Steele, sometimes in recitals of her pupils and once of

> her own works. She always had an excellent grasp of practical matters, and soon, leaving aside my meagre musical skills, she had trained me as a kind of management assistant to look after such routines as renting the hall, making arrangements with Allans for bookings, box office, doorkeeper and ushers, coping with the printing of programmes, entertainment tax, advertising and so on; she had it all at her fingertips.[28]

Margaret and Elise Steele formed a busy duo, performing most often between 1930 and 1935, but throughout the decade. They usually appeared in Melbourne, but also in Adelaide, Sydney and regional Victoria. Steele lived with Margaret's family for about two years in the early 1930s. The motivation for this is unclear, but the two were good friends and musically compatible, and the arrangement facilitated opportunities to rehearse together. With the Depression underway, it is likely they came to a mutually beneficial financial arrangement. Steele may also have assisted with housekeeping and childminding. Middle-class families still sometimes hired domestic help, which was necessary if women were to find time for any other activities. At one stage, Margaret employed a young woman for a few hours a week while she was teaching, either at the conservatorium or privately. But any working mother would welcome on-the-spot assistance from a live-in friend.[29]

Although there is no evidence that the Albiston household suffered unduly during the Depression, the extra income from boarders was welcome. Margaret's sister Ruth and husband Charles Neylon could no longer maintain payments on their house after Charles lost his job early in the decade—he worked in construction, one of the first industries to be hit by the Depression. He moved to the country to live with his widowed mother, and Ruth and son Geoffrey were taken in by Margaret. During this stay, 50-year-old Ruth rekindled her desire to paint, setting up her easel on the back veranda. It is not clear how long she and Geoffrey remained, but the two sisters probably cooperated in looking after the three children.[30]

Dr AE Floyd collaborated with Margaret in several series at St Paul's Cathedral in Melbourne in 1927 and 1930. Other regular colleagues included Biddy Allen (piano), Margaret's piano students Mary Baillieu and Mollie Turner Shaw, Isobel Carter and Thomas White (clarinet), Violet Palmer (violin), Marston Bate (cello), harpsichord player Mancell Kirby (for whom Margaret wrote or arranged several pieces), Carrie Cairnduff and Kathleen Castles (sopranos), Howard Andrews and Clive Carey (baritones) and contralto Ivy Phillips. The latter had attracted the support of Nellie Melba, who attended an Assembly Hall recital by Ivy and Margaret on 6 June 1928. Reviews testify to continuing esteem for her playing. One was especially warm: 'Her playing is brilliant, well defined in essentials of style, and fashioned by a musical intelligence of an original and discerning order. Miss Sutherland's accompaniments were musically suggestive, faultless in taste'.[31]

With her responsibilities of caring for young children, managing a household, performing, teaching, and coping with a husband increasingly unsupportive of her composition, finding opportunities to compose presented the greatest challenge. Historically, male composers (and those men engaged in any creative pursuit) could demand the time and peace they needed. Stravinsky expected his family to eat lunch in silence, and 'sacrificed his children to his art'. And as Margaret highlighted in 'Chant Intérieur', Sibelius's 'devoted—if intimidated—wife', in a 'hang over from the 19th century', had written that 'Our home centres about my husband. For the rest of us, his life work has been all in all'.[32]

No such luxury for Margaret. But against the odds, her dedication to her art ensured that, apart from a break when her children were infants, she continued to seize opportunities to compose. Margaret did not say so herself, but these precious occasions when she could be immersed in her music likely acted as welcome moments of refuge from her tense domestic situation, just as she had found sanctuary in music as a young girl surrounded by illness and death in her family.

For obvious reasons, Margaret was less productive in the late 1920s and early 1930s. There is only one composition dated to 1928, *Movement for Two Pianos,* for which no score remains, as is the case for *Air and Bagatelle for Piano* (pre-1930), possibly also written prior to Mark's birth. When Mark and Jenifer were very young, she composed for children—*Songs for Children* for voice and piano (1929), settings for nine children's poems written by Australian poet Ethel Martyr. Published in 1929 by Allans Music, which dominated music publishing in Australia after World War I and produced *Australian Musical News* (1911–63), these were appropriately simple settings, though there is subtlety in harmony and tonality, and appropriate use of word painting.[33]

Another children's song was *Nod* for voice and piano (pre-1930). Again, no score is available, though the opening bars are in Margaret's 1939 thematic index. It is a setting of a text by English poet and author Walter de la Mare, best known for his children's works. *Cradle Song* (pre-1930) for voice and clarinet, from a poem by the Australian Louis Esson, was set specifically for Margaret's children and is one of several works incorporating the clarinet. In both text and melody, the song expresses the melancholy and unease of a lonely mother singing her child to sleep, while the father has 'gone a-shearing down the Castlereagh'. These were sentiments to which any young mother could relate. Her setting contains dissonance appropriate to the text and fails to meet the expectation of resolution to the tonic chord at the end. But conformity was never a high priority for Margaret, and she used this technique on several occasions to great effect.[34]

Some of these children's works may have been written for performance at musical plays organised for local families by Yseult Bailey, friend, neighbour and later leading figure in the kindergarten movement. Margaret wrote and arranged the music, while another friend, Dorothy Miller, acted as prompt and joined the children together in song.[35] Dorothy's singing credentials were well honed through her membership of the Tudor Singers, an ensemble formed by young people associated with the University of Melbourne, including Lorna Stirling.

As the children grew older, Margaret's and Norman's approaches to parenting grew apart, impacting on the mother–child relationship. This was particularly so with Mark, who tended to side with his father in criticising Margaret's attempts to make a career for herself.[36]

As a psychiatrist, Norman was informed by contemporary parenting theories and advice, some of which he expressed in a lecture, 'The Importance of Habit'. No doubt he attempted to impose this knowledge on his family. Margaret considered his parenting ideas unnatural and sterile. Norman had warned her of 'the crime of establishing an Oedipus complex', and she felt his insistence on this contributed to Mark's later challenges. Bringing him into bed with her was completely forbidden (though she remembered that when he was wakeful at night, she would feel his hand reach over from his cot and clutch her hair and play with it—something she did not tell her husband).[37] According to Freud, the successful resolution of the Oedipus complex for a boy involves eventual identification with his father, in order to cope with the castration anxiety caused by his unconscious desire for his mother. But as an often-absent father who had affairs and appeared not to respect his wife, Norman was not the best model.

From Margaret's perspective, Norman believed that children should be raised with no prohibitions. If she wanted to correct their son's manners, Norman would caution her to leave him alone, since he would find out later what he'd done, when he was 'ostracised by society'. 'What could be crueller?' she asked. One of many recommendations Norman made in his lecture was that parents 'Make the act produce its own punishment' and 'keep out of the picture as much as possible'. While this may seem logical, Norman does not appear to have acknowledged the benefit of preventing the need for later ostracism through early guidance. In addition, he didn't take his own advice that, as the major early influencers of children, parents need 'first to understand ourselves', which involves 'the relations of parents with each other'. His regular counsel to Mark that he should ignore his mother didn't project a solid marital relationship and was not a model of consistent parenting. It is well established that demeaning the other parent in a child's presence can lead to emotional, social and behavioural problems, and this may have contributed to Mark's later antisocial and unbalanced conduct.[38]

Margaret's relationship with her daughter Jenifer was less fraught—the two were close. 'Jenny was my greatest love', she said after Jenifer's early death in 1971. But the tension in the household could not help but affect Jenny too, and she manifested it through shyness, and in always wanting to help her mother. She was a little fearful of her father, who had an intensity that could be interpreted as intimidating, especially by a child. As an adult, Jenny had an easier relationship with Norman, often visiting him and his third wife, Valerie Cohen, with her children.[39]

Norman sometimes instilled fear in his wife too. He treated Margaret's car as his own and controlled her use of it, claiming that he needed it for his work. He forbade her from taking it to buy groceries, but drove alongside as she walked, as if to taunt her.[40]

This behaviour might now be labelled coercive control, a form of domestic abuse. American sociologist Evan Stark describes this phenomenon as 'a patriarchy in miniature, complete with its own web of rules or codes, rituals of deference, modes of enforcement, sanctions and forbidden places'. Victims are 'frequently deprived of money, food, access to communication or transportation, and other survival resources'.[41] As with physical abuse, coercive control often takes place 'behind closed doors', and can be perpetrated by men who are otherwise useful and respected members of society.

Although Margaret is unlikely to have been aware of the term 'coercive control', she did sometimes feel Norman was cruel and sadistic. She had initially given him the benefit of the doubt, thinking that unhappiness might be causing his 'cruelty'. However, she gradually realised that 'he got satisfaction—or even more—out of inflicting pain'.[42]

There are indications that Norman's mistreatment of Margaret was sometimes physical. Early in the marriage, after a mutual friend had spoken to him in an effort to help 'restore the harmony' between the two, Norman telephoned Margaret at the conservatorium and summoned her to his rooms. When she arrived, he allegedly rushed at her, seized her by the throat, and asked why she had confided in a friend about their troubles.[43] This incident may have contributed to her decision to keep her marital misery to herself. Once he calmed down, the two were able to discuss their problems, but no improvement resulted.

In a letter to fellow Australian composer and friend Don Banks in the 1970s, Margaret opened with the sentence 'I have made up my mind to tell you a bit of this horrid tale'. She implied that Norman's abuse had led to her having a kidney removed. She did have a kidney taken out (the date is unrecorded) and suffered kidney problems periodically for the rest of her life—she had a kidney stone removed in March 1966, for example. However, the condition could have been inherited from her mother, who died of a kidney ailment. Although there is no firm evidence of physical violence, the accusation has been corroborated by friends and relatives of Margaret. According to Astrid Dahl, Mark's second wife, Mark was physically violent. It is possible he took after his father in this regard, given that violence can be (though not always) perpetuated by subsequent generations of men, especially by those from family environments experiencing other adversities, including (but not limited to) family dysfunction and impaired parental bonding.[44]

By 1932, the situation at East Malvern had become what Margaret described as 'pretty untenable'. Norman decided to establish a psychiatric practice, and shared rooms in Alcaston House in Collins Street, Melbourne. In the same year, he was appointed to the board of management of the newly established Child Guidance Clinic. Along with Roy Winn, Paul Dane, John Adey, William Beattie Smith, Albert Phillips, Guy Reynolds and Reginald Spencer Ellery—married to Margaret's friend the harpsichordist Mancell Kirby—Norman was one of the early psychiatrists in Australia to become interested in Freud's psychoanalytic theories. Although he was a director of the Melbourne Institute of Psychoanalysis, formed in 1940, Norman did not join the Royal College of Psychiatrists until 1971; nor did he take part in psychiatric gatherings or seminars, aside from a few legal–medical dinners. This implies arrogance, borne out by Margaret's comment that he thought no institution had the right to examine him.[45]

The family moved to a rented house in Berkeley Street, Hawthorn. Now working in the city, Norman spent his evenings playing the card game solo, as well as chess, billiards and snooker at the Masonic Club in Flinders Street, arriving home late and sleeping in the next morning. Although his long absences reduced the children's exposure to marital conflict, they meant that Margaret shouldered a greater burden of household duties and childcare. Norman saw his children rarely, which especially affected Mark. 'It was this disparagement of home and its essential qualities which had the most devastating effects … Disparagement of the good things in life is the undoing of children', Margaret later reflected.[46]

Spending time at his club was not Norman's only evening activity. He was asked to leave Alcaston House, based on information provided by the janitor. Although Margaret never discovered what happened, she was sure it was because he was using his rooms to conduct an affair. Norman moved his practice to Lister House on the corner of Collins and Exhibition Streets (now demolished).[47]

Alongside the deteriorating situation at home came an encouraging development for Margaret's compositional aspirations. The establishment of the Australian Broadcasting Commission (ABC) in 1932, and its subsequent formation in 1936 of radio orchestras in each state capital (though not in the territory capitals of Darwin and Canberra), helped bring Melbourne out of the Depression doldrums. A policy of bringing international conductors and soloists to Australia was implemented, and the general standard of music-making and audience discernment increased. Most importantly for Margaret, it created opportunities for Australian composers.

The ABC aimed to lay the foundation for a national music literature. In its first year of operation, it provided encouragement to composers through the implementation of Composer Competitions, offering £450 in prizes. The ABC, along with other government departments, including the Department of the Interior Film Unit, 'tended to be the best employers of women as composers'.[48] In the 1933 Composer Competitions, a third of the placings went to women. Margaret was among them, winning at least thirteen awards in various categories between 1933 and 1936. By the end of the 1930s, competitions became unnecessary, as the ABC was virtually the country's only outlet and spontaneously received over one hundred works a year.[49]

'At that time a woman needed some sort of official notice or sanction for her work to justify a regular commitment to something as singular and unremunerative as music composition', Gifford noted, 'and finally this was given by the ABC with their programme of competitions providing just the incentive that she needed'.[50]

CHAPTER 8

BREAKING OUT TO COMPOSE (1933–1939)

I really gave the whole thing up but every now and again I'd break out. I didn't write very much until the children were sixteen and eighteen. Sometimes I went to stay with somebody just to write, you know.

Margaret Sutherland[1]

MARGARET BENEFITED FROM ABC sessional performing work from the early 1930s but, most importantly, from opportunities to disseminate her music. Not all her correspondence to the ABC was complimentary, but she acknowledged its contribution. 'It is impossible to praise too highly the enterprise of the ABC in giving stimulus to Australian work', she wrote in a letter to ABC chairman William Cleary in 1935. 'I feel extremely fortunate to have received such encouragement from the recent awards. Instead of writing always for the oblivion of one's own cupboard one does at least feel now that interest in what one has to say is awakened. My sincere thanks.'[2]

A 1938 *Argus* article, 'Wife, Mother, Musician and Composer', similarly praised the ABC for bringing Margaret's work to a wider public:

> Few Australians have achieved the success in a musical career which Miss Sutherland can claim as pianist and composer. Musicians and

> music-lovers have known of the quality of her work for many years, but it has been only comparatively recently, through the medium of competitions held by the Australian Broadcasting Commission for original compositions by Australians, that the general public has become aware of it.[3]

Margaret's numerous interactions with the ABC show that she cannily availed herself of opportunities. In late 1933 to early 1934, for example, she co-presented a radio series named *Foundations of Music* with Elise Steele. These recitals were part of Margaret's quest to educate Australian audiences about classical music and introduce new music, including works by women composers.

Insights into Margaret's professional life are gained through studying her exchanges with the ABC in the 1930s and 1940s. Their tone reflected the escalating frustration and tension of her domestic situation, compounded by the deaths of her Aunt Jessie in 1934, and of her older sister Dorothy, who died in 1937 aged forty-eight. There is no record of Margaret's reaction to these additions to the endless series of family losses.

The ABC letters reveal the respect shown by the commission for Margaret and her music, and exemplify her advocacy for Australian music. They also demonstrate her ability to build important networks, and a self-belief that gave her the confidence to promote her music to achieve the recognition she felt she deserved.

Women's socialisation has contributed to their reticence in openly exhibiting professional ambition, and to their lower self-confidence in marketing themselves.[4] Interestingly, Margaret was innately aware of the importance of these skills. However, there is an important distinction to make: her attempts were never purely ego driven. It was her music she wanted to promote, since she felt it had something original to offer.

In late 1938, Margaret wrote to ABC Victorian manager Robert McCall, 'in advance if possible of the influx of overseas artists' (escaping Europe ahead of imminent war), seeking assistance in two principal areas. She wanted to stage a public recital of her works in the Assembly Hall in 1939 under the ABC's direction, with 'such artists as

Tossy Spivakovsky (violin) and Edmund Kurtz (cello)', both Russian immigrants. In addition, she asked the ABC about 'getting the best artists available to perform my works':

> I feel justified firstly by the high opinion expressed both privately and publicly by many front-rank musicians regarding my compositions; and secondly by the fact that, as recipient of a good number of the ABC prizes for original work in past years, I can perhaps claim the interest of the Commission in what I have been doing more recently.

Margaret was sure McCall would agree with her 'that the composer who is not content to be merely a re-hasher, but who sincerely tries to express contemporary thought, ploughs a lonely furrow'. ABC federal controller of music William James advised her to approach these overseas artists herself, for which they were happy to give permission.[5] As the ABC has traditionally been protective of its exclusive access to artists, this may indicate its respect for Margaret and her music.

Margaret's compositional output increased from 1934 as her two children grew older. 'I just gave it away until I had time', she said. But the decision by Louise Hanson-Dyer of Éditions de l'Oiseau-Lyre to publish her works during the 1930s Depression demonstrates growing respect for her composition. Apart from her *Songs for Children* being published in 1929 by Allans, Hanson-Dyer showed the first real sign of confidence in Margaret's music.[6]

Along with performances, publication is essential in bringing a composer's music to a larger audience and enhancing recognition. It confers tangibility and a sense of permanence on a work, and enables its analysis and discussion. As feminist musicologist Marcia Citron observed, 'this boasts a poor record with regard to women: only a small percentage of their works have appeared in print'.[7]

In 1934–35, Éditions de l'Oiseau-Lyre published six of Margaret's vocal works, four of which were settings of texts by Australian poet John Shaw Neilson, whom Hanson-Dyer also championed. These included *The Meeting of Sighs* for voice and piano, and three songs for girls' choir—*Break of Day, Quietly as Rosebuds* and *The Green Singer*. At the Christmas gathering of the British Music Society (BMS) in 1934, Hanson-Dyer presented Margaret with a copy of these four songs, which had attracted her interest when she heard them in early October that year.[8] In 1935, Hanson-Dyer published two chamber works, one of which was the *Sonata for Violin and Piano*. The other was a pedagogical publication, *How to Make Pipes*, for which Margaret composed a set of pieces for bamboo pipes and a small percussion band, simply called *Australian Melodies* (pre-1935). She also wrote several pedagogical pieces for piano that were published in the late 1930s by Allans and Paling & Co.

Of Margaret's over two hundred compositions, only around sixty have been produced by publishing companies.[9] In a later reflection on the challenges of achieving publication and performances, Margaret commented as follows:

> [Having works performed was] very difficult in the past. Now we have grants. In the past many of us had to write our own parts, even orchestral parts. It was a very expensive thing to have an orchestral work performed: £250 at least. We used to have to wait years to get a first performance, but by then you would have moved on to other areas. Then it is difficult to get back there, to be able to profit from what you hear because you have passed it by.[10]

This was one reason why Margaret prioritised writing smaller chamber works, mostly for musicians she knew, but it is not the whole story. She enjoyed writing for unusual combinations of instruments and felt more comfortable with chamber music. 'I can't think of anything I'd rather do in the whole world', she said in 1965. 'I love the intimacy of writing for a small group of musicians rather than for a big orchestra. I suppose this is reasonable—women don't seem to go in for tackling epics.'[11] Again, in 1968, she equated a feminine sensibility with chamber compositions, arguing that women's musical offerings should not be devalued because they did not conform to the dominant masculine paradigm:

> A woman can contribute in a special kind of way. I don't think that women want to write the same type of things as men, but their contribution is no less important. They [men] seem to have the same yardstick all the time, this symphonic business.[12]

This attitude is intriguing, especially as it was expressed as late as the 1960s, by which time there were fewer constraints on Margaret's time, and she had embarked on her most intense period of orchestral composition. It was partly because writing for larger forces had posed challenges for Margaret,[13] but also because women were conditioned to write 'in miniature' and many had not received the necessary training to compose larger works. British composer Ethel Smyth argued that women had been barred from the requisite theoretical study:

> Face this truth: that because of what has been our position hitherto in the world of music, there is not at this present moment [1933] one single middle-aged woman alive who has had the musical education that has fallen to men as a matter of course, without any effort on their part, ever since music was![14]

Feminist musicologists argue that it was the larger genres, particularly symphonic works and opera, that were valued highly enough to be included in the Western canon. This led to women being excluded, and, by extension, from professional careers in the public sphere. In professing her preference for chamber music, Margaret was also tacitly criticising the idea that to prove herself a serious composer, she 'should not conform to the expected "feminine" pattern of small-scale composition'.[15]

Although first-wave feminism led women to challenge the status quo regarding genre and the associated prestige, and they were experimenting with larger forms, the perception lingered that it was a male realm.[16] Music critic Thorold Waters encapsulated this attitude in 1938:

> Any voyage of discovery through musical biography becomes singularly arid if one is looking for instances of major compositions from the hands of women. There is not one proved symphonist of vital force among them yet, although some few have made the effort at either true symphony or the symphonic poem ... As Creators, they have in no single instances been originators. To a woman, they have been imitative of men.[17]

Margaret also experienced this gender bias in her marriage. She commented that Norman did not mind her composing 'as long as I wrote for children' and referred to his dismissive behaviour when her orchestral works were first performed.[18] This suggests that he, too, thought women's composition should be confined to small works performed in private, non-professional settings.

An early example of Margaret's creative flowering in the mid-1930s was the patriotic song *Land of Ours* (1934), which received several performances. Scored for two-part girls' choir with accompaniment (also arranged for four-part choirs—soprano, alto, tenor, bass), the song was co-winner of the Victorian Centenary Song Competition judged by Russian-born Jewish–Australian businessman and philanthropist Sidney Myer. There were 302 entrants, and Margaret shared the £95 prize with Lindley Evans.[19]

The song represented two novelties for Margaret. First, she took up the baton to lead the choir of 4000 voices in *Land of Ours* at a performance on 4 November 1934 at Como Park, South Yarra. The large choral concert commemorated Sidney Myer, who had died two months previously. Bernard Heinze and Fritz Hart conducted the rest of the program.[20] Second, this is the only one of Margaret's vocal compositions for which she wrote the text herself:

> Land of ours, remote from other lands withdrawn,
> We hail thee now with ecstasy,
> And with one heart rejoice
> In bonds which link us strangely firm
> To yet another land which gave us Birth and Life.
> Grant to us, who love this country now so free,
> So charged with ardent youthful pulse,
> The single blessing towards
> A future of integrity
> A lasting tribute to the fount in word and deed.
> Land of ours whom we now cherish well, endeared
> Thro' much travail of war and strife
> Towards worthier ports to steer,
> Give us thy trust and let us be
> Thy willing vassals now and evermore for Peace.

The musical setting is simple, given it was written to be sung by children's choirs, and the text necessarily reflects Australian patriotism, an attitude Margaret would not have assumed without question. But she was responding to a specific brief, and certainly wanted her beloved Australia to flourish in peace, as the words suggest.

Margaret continued to encounter Heinze periodically over many years. He often conducted her music, even including it in a 17-concert tour of Canada for the Canadian Broadcasting Corporation in early 1947. The relationship remained fraught, however. In the mid-1930s, Margaret again expressed distaste for the maestro. She was disgusted with his treatment of her good friend John Bishop, South Australian pianist, conductor, music teacher, examiner and entrepreneur. Bishop and his family moved to Melbourne after several years in New Zealand, and in early 1934 he took a teaching and examining position at the University of Melbourne Conservatorium. His boss was Heinze, who was now chief conductor of the Melbourne Symphony Orchestra (MSO), having devised a plan to amalgamate the impecunious orchestra with the University Symphony Orchestra in 1933, and introduced subscription concert seasons in 1934.[21] Bishop's new role was going well until he established a music studio in Post Office Lane in the city, having identified MSO musicians' need and desire to perform chamber music. But the relationship soured when Heinze got wind of it and warned Bishop that his job at the conservatorium would be in jeopardy if he continued.

In Margaret's opinion, Heinze was threatened by Bishop's talents, 'but this time God was good!' she exclaimed. She had attended the end-of-year concert at Mark's school, Scotch College, pronounced it to be 'abysmal' and wrote to the principal, Dr Colin Gilray. 'Better to have NO music than what we had to listen to.' She received a telephone call next day from Gilray—'Can you make a suggestion?' he asked. Without hesitation, she proposed John Bishop, whom she recommended as 'exceptionally fine' and a person who 'always had ideas'. The only qualms she had—quaint but reflective of the era—were that 'his curly hair was a bit long', and he 'wore a large ring upon his hand—and I just wondered what the boys would say'.[22]

Margaret's *Trio in C Major for Clarinet, Violin and Piano* (1935), for which no complete score has been located, was an early example of her return to instrumental writing. It was joint winner in the chamber music category of the 1935 ABC Composer Competitions, which likely rendered much-needed encouragement as Margaret resumed composing chamber music. It was premiered in October 1935 at a concert of the BMS, with which she had a mutually beneficial arrangement. She regularly offered her services as an accompanist, and was an active member for many years, sitting on the committee from 1936 to 1943. The BMS in turn supported her compositions, programming them at least six times between 1928 and 1940.[23] On this occasion, Margaret, together with clarinettist Isobel Carter and violinist Elise Steele, performed 'An Hour of Music', featuring a wide variety of composers. As well as her own *Trio*, the program included Margaret's reworkings for clarinet and piano of two pieces by French baroque composer François Couperin, *Air Tendre* and *Air de Diable*.[24] Of her *Trio*, the *Age* critic (probably AEH Nickson) wrote that 'Miss Sutherland's ideas, charged with emotion sanctioned by her artistic impulse and couched in felicitous terms, appeal to mind and ear alike. The new work, original in conception and clever in structure, was well received'. The *Trio* also earned the all-important stamp of approval from German composer–conductor Dr Gerhard von Keussler, who worked in Australia from 1932 to 1936. It was an impressive composition that revealed fine technique, he opined.[25]

In February 1939, Margaret submitted to the ABC two 15-minute programs of songs she had written in the 1930s, together with three written earlier in her career. Of the fourteen songs, six were settings by John Shaw Neilson. She approached the ABC's acting manager in Victoria, AN Finlay, who wrote to William James: 'Knowing the standard of Miss Sutherland's work, we thought you might care to consider these for National Relay'. Margaret was always 'choosey about musicians' and selected the singers whom she would accompany—Howard Andrews (baritone) and Muriel Cheek (soprano).[26] The broadcasts went to air in June and July that year.

Margaret often selected female poets to set to music, but not always. Australian poet John Shaw Neilson was a favourite, and she set several of his poems over a 20-year period beginning in the early 1930s.

Along with her songs using Australian poet Judith Wright's work, her settings of Shaw Neilson's texts are among her most striking achievements in the vocal genre. Text was of supreme importance to Margaret, and she always strived to make the words stand out in the musical texture. *The Meeting of Sighs* (pre-1934) for voice and piano is a short two-verse poem, which looks back on past happiness—a typical theme for Shaw Neilson. Margaret set it simply, with the piano mostly providing harmonic support, sometimes suggesting the vocal line to come. The five Shaw Neilson settings for voice and piano were grouped together as *Five Songs* and published by Oxford University Press in 1948. Margaret also set six poems for girls' choirs in two or three parts, and three for voice and other instruments.[27]

Margaret felt an affinity with Shaw Neilson's lyrical, introspective, bittersweet poetry. She especially admired its sincerity. His themes resonated with her own experience, as she had always loved nature, and no doubt witnessed childish delight through her own offspring. The inevitability of pain and death was a phenomenon with which she was becoming all too familiar. She esteemed Shaw Neilson for his self-made achievements and couldn't understand why he seemed to be an Australian literary underdog. It is likely she related to elements of his life, including poverty and left-wing politics.[28]

The *Five Songs*—'For a Child', 'In the Dim Counties', 'May', 'Song Be Delicate' and 'When Kisses Are as Strawberries'—use the metaphor of seasons for the various stages of life, expressing the inevitability of the end of it and of love. Quirky rhythms, modal harmonies and nuanced dissonance are features of these settings.

Margaret's setting of Shaw Neilson's poem of ten four-line verses 'The Orange Tree' (1938), eventually published in 1954 by the Lady Northcote Permanent Orchestra Trust Fund, was the most ambitious.[29] The scoring for voice, clarinet (or flute) and piano may have been influenced by Schubert's *The Shepherd on the Rock* (1828), given Margaret's admiration for this composer. *The Orange Tree*'s style is richer and more complex than the earlier songs. It has a broader harmonic vocabulary, stronger dissonances, and a sense of tension as the clarinet and piano weave in and out of the texture. The poem presents a dialogue between a young girl and the poet, in which the latter seeks a rational explanation for the girl's spiritual connection with the orange tree (represented by the clarinet). For Margaret, the poem was about the opposition between intellect and intuition. On a score made by singer and copyist Elsa Haas, she noted that the tree had an indefinable quality for the girl, which words fail to express.[30]

The Orange Tree was first heard in a recital of Margaret's chamber works at the Assembly Hall on 29 March 1938 under the auspices of the BMS.[31] Among other works, the six Shaw Neilson settings for voice and piano were also premiered. Performing with Margaret were Howard Andrews (baritone), Kathleen Castles (soprano), Thomas White (clarinet), Elise Steele (violin) and Marston Bate (cello).

Shaw Neilson was unable to attend but wrote Margaret an apologetic letter in a shaky scrawl. He was sixty-six at the time, and died four years later:

> I am delighted to know that you are having some of my songs done at your Recital. I am sorry that I will not be able to attend. I am so old and tired, and I have to go to bed early every evening so as to get up in time for work next day … PS: I am really conscious that you are doing me an honour.[32]

But Shaw Neilson listened to the live broadcast of the concert, and was moved to write another charming letter:

> Although I was listening on a very bad wireless set last night, I found much beauty in all the airs. I liked the Orange Tree and I think the two next best were In the Dim Counties and For a Child. It is a long time ago since I wrote some of these rhymes. I had forgotten the lines, and the verses seem like foreigners to me. I am afraid there is a good deal of vagueness about some of them. I know that the Critics used to complain about it. Kathleen Castles seems to have a lovely voice. I was pleased to hear the splendid reception that the people gave your work.[33]

Apart from performers 'struggling against the rasping of machinery taking out foundations for a new building close to the Assembly Hall', the concert went down well. 'Songs of a mystical light … were among

Miss Sutherland's undoubted successes', wrote Thorold Waters. Of the Shaw Neilson settings, the *AMN* was most enthusiastic about *The Orange Tree*, which was 'elusive and exalted' and showed imagination.[34]

At least four critics highlighted Margaret's significance as an Australian composer.[35] Two employed an adjective often applied to her music—'intellectual'—implying that it lacked emotion: 'The character of Miss Sutherland's music is primarily intellectual' (the *Age*); 'Her best work is built upon the sure foundations of an irresistibly fascinating inspiration clarified by a constructive intellectuality' (the *Herald*).

The use of the word 'intellectual' to describe Margaret's music is curious. Music's special ability to evoke emotion was important to her, as evidenced in her 1926 *Argus* articles 'The Vogue of Bach' and 'Musical Emancipation' (see Chapter Six). Roger Covell conceded that 'Sutherland's music has a heart' but one 'ruled by a very shrewd head'. Shrewd she was, in many ways—possibly clever enough to be aware, as Thérèse Radic argued, that restraint was 'necessary in order to endure and to evade accusations of *melodramatic* (read female) self-indulgence'. Was she providing 'a superfluity of thorns' through fear of being accused of being 'sentimental', as Virginia Woolf suggested of her fictional author Mary Carmichael in *Life's Adventure*?[36] If Margaret did not always choose to 'wear her heart on her sleeve', her rich inner life, together with an overabundance of traumatic experiences, found their expression in the deep emotional intensity of many of her works.

One such composition is Margaret's watershed 25-minute *String Quartet No. 1* (1937), premiered in August 1938 in a BMS performance with Elise Steele (violin), Franz Schieblich (violin), Gladys Jones (viola) and Marston Bate (cello). In four movements, it was initially thought to be less accessible than her previous music but came to be regarded as one of the most significant works by an Australian composer. Although it displayed Margaret's mastery of traditional structures, and of the classical string quartet genre, its tonal idiom was more dissonant and striking, evoking aspects of Bartók, Hindemith, Debussy and Ravel. By now, Margaret had clearly departed from the conventions of nineteenth-century romanticism.[37]

The BMS premiere of the work startled critics and attracted approval for its seemingly more 'masculine' qualities. The *Argus* thought admirers of the romantic composers would deplore its dissonance and absence of tunes, while another observed that it would 'upset conservatives but the music will not be regarded as "advanced" by the ultra-modernists'. However, it was written by a composer who was 'not afraid to think for herself, and if, in her disdain for the writers of "pretty-pretty" music, she strays sometimes too near the camps of the "uglicista", she commands an exhilarating thrust of rhapsodic rhythm'. The *AMN* considered it a good thing that 'she is getting on the track of more virile and substantial musical facts than she has realised hitherto'. The *Herald*'s JE Tremearne agreed it was 'a virile work which reflects the modern spirit' with 'a good deal that is beautiful—a significant addition to local creative effort'. He singled out the adagio movement for its 'melody of warmth and tenderness'. Interestingly, this was a melody Margaret had first written much earlier, in her song *Silence, Beautiful Voice* (1913).[38]

Margaret's response to comments on her 'virile' *String Quartet* is not recorded. It is possible (if she read the reviews) that she didn't object to this word, given that she used it in a description of her *Sonata for Violin and Piano* in her Adelaide *Register* interview twelve years earlier. Such an equation of modern, dissonant music with masculinity was probably not questioned in the 1930s as it would be today. But to do the quartet justice, the words 'dramatic and emotionally intense' might be more fitting than 'virile', especially considering the turmoil in Margaret's personal life at the time.

She had sent the quartet score to Robert McCall at the ABC three months before the BMS premiere, wondering whether it could be performed on air, 'which I would very much like to do. The score looks interesting, and I should like you to have a look at it', McCall told James. Nothing came of Margaret's request, so she tried again a month after the BMS premiere, pointing out that her quartet had had a 'semi-public christening a week ago', and that she was hoping the ABC 'will have an opportunity to broadcast it before it goes out of their fingers (they all belong to the studio orchestra)'. A third approach was necessary before it was finally programmed for the Australian Composers' Session on National Relay on 11 March 1940.[39]

In response to a request from James for works to show two international conductors touring for the ABC—English conductor Dr Malcolm Sargent and Czech George Szell—Margaret was finally ready to submit her first extended orchestral work, *Suite for Orchestra on a Theme by Purcell* (1935): 'You will, I know, understand my desire to feel confident about it in every respect before taking such a step', she wrote to James in May 1938.[40]

A set of variations based on a theme from Purcell's St Cecilia's Day ode *Welcome to All the Pleasures* (1683), the *Suite* reflected Margaret's love of his music. She altered the theme significantly but followed the baroque practice of retaining the same key signature for all seven movements. The twentieth-century elements of this 'neo-baroque' work come through in her choice to use the orchestral sonorities of strings, woodwinds and brass, rather than the smaller baroque orchestra or the more expansive nineteenth-century orchestral forces. They also manifested in the judicious but bold incorporation of dissonance.[41]

The score was originally submitted to Sargent, and Margaret tried in vain to make an appointment with him to discuss it. He showed interest but, for unspecified reasons, did not include it in his Australian programs. Fortunately, George Szell did. After a delay in having parts copied—a constant challenge—it was decided that the work would receive three performances in Melbourne with the MSO: at the South Melbourne Town Hall on 30 May 1939, the Hawthorn Town Hall on 3 June, and as one of the Celebrity Concert Series in the Melbourne Town Hall on Wednesday 5 June. Margaret attended rehearsals, nervously expecting that Szell would want her to make changes. He suggested she remove two bars, but otherwise was happy. 'Zere is nussing to do!' Margaret mimicked. She was surprised and delighted at this outcome.[42]

In the midst of these ABC negotiations, so consequential for Margaret's career, the owners of the Albistons' rented house in Berkeley Street decided to sell it, necessitating a move for the family. A property was acquired at 20 Studley Avenue, Kew, in May 1939, for which a deposit of £250 (about $22 400 today) was paid. With this purchase, Margaret returned to the familiar and comforting neighbourhood of her childhood, close to where her family had lived on Studley Park Road, and where her single aunts and uncles had resided on Stawell Street. Their new home, built in the early 1900s, was an imposing two-storey house designed by architects Bates Smart McCutcheon (now Bates Smart). The wisteria-covered house had a dedicated music room with two pianos (at least one of which was a grand piano), where Margaret taught and composed. The new property was placed in joint names, though Margaret claimed to have found the house and paid the deposit herself.[43] Although the couple was still together, they led increasingly separate lives.

Norman did not attend the official premiere of the Purcell Suite at the Melbourne Town Hall in June 1939, preferring instead to spend the evening with his mistress.[44] His affairs had continued beyond when the children started school—Mark at Scotch College and Jenny at Tintern Grammar. (Norman's psychiatric practice was supposedly now well enough established for the school fees to be affordable, though it is possible that his parents helped.)

Sometime in the mid to late 1930s, Norman's permanent nurse had gone to Japan for three months, and Carmen had come into his life. A patient visiting from Queensland, she offered to act as a substitute nurse and soon became his lover. Margaret noted that Norman 'affected a bowler hat and dark blue velour coat (<u>she</u> liked them), and took up golf, buying the most expensive equipment'.[45] This adoption of new hobbies was not unusual. Norman tended to become obsessed with an activity, such as carpentering, but soon lost interest—a trait reputedly emulated by his son.

It was Carmen who Norman was with when Margaret's Purcell Suite was performed at the Melbourne Town Hall. He came home from work, changed into his dinner suit, and dropped Margaret off at the town hall before joining Carmen at the Menzies Hotel to dine and spend the night. 'I scarcely heard the performance', Margaret lamented. One reviewer observed that, as a member of the official party, she had dressed for the occasion in an attractive black gown, complete with slipper orchids pinned in her squirrel cape.[46] Perhaps the choice to wear black reflected not only the auspicious occasion but her mood.

Reviews were mixed, and fortunately not all chose to focus on Margaret's dress. Of the first performance, in South Melbourne, Tremearne wrote that it 'is a worthy admission to her more important compositions, which reflect a deep intellect and individuality'. The movements were well contrasted 'and the orchestration adventurous and highly interesting'. Jenkins (*Table Talk*) considered the orchestration weak—this possibly fed Margaret's lower self-confidence regarding orchestral writing.[47]

Shortly after the debacle of Norman not attending the performance of the Purcell Suite, Carmen's mother learned of the affair and approached his father. When Carmen's husband came down from Queensland and threatened divorce, 'things took on a new complexion', said Margaret. In the 'stormy and tense' atmosphere, Norman and Carmen had to part. In her misery, and in the face of Norman's apparent dismay on the morning the lovers were to bid each other farewell, Margaret was led to want 'the satisfaction of a test'. She 'cooked an enormous breakfast for Norman of chops, sausages, bacon and tomatoes, as well as all the other trimmings' and, in spite of 'the great tragedy', as she put it, 'he ate every crumb'.[48]

It is possible that Norman's affair with Carmen was a catalyst for Margaret's abandonment of teaching at the conservatorium in mid-1939, though she continued teaching privately. Norman's father had advised her to resign, hoping this would help restore a better marital relationship and make his son more responsible. An article in the *Australian Women's Weekly* headed 'Famous conductor praises woman composer' presented a sanitised and more socially acceptable reason for her resignation: 'Miss Sutherland, who is Mrs NA Albiston ... resigned recently to devote the time she can spare from her home and two children to composing'. It was not uncommon for a married woman who used her own surname in public life to have her status as a married woman confirmed in print. Nor was it unusual—during an era when a serious woman composer was an aberration—for her to be identified as a 'woman composer'. This phenomenon was particularly apparent in the *Australian Women's Weekly*, which, with its wide readership, simultaneously reflected and shaped contemporaneous expectations of women's roles.[49]

Following her departure from the conservatorium, Margaret continued to buy her own clothing with her income as a concert pianist. Norman paid her a weekly allowance for housekeeping and clothing the children, which 'caused a lot of misery'. If she asked for it, he would say she couldn't have it because she had asked. If she didn't ask, he would say it was because she hadn't asked. 'Generally eventually it was not given to me', she complained, 'but left somewhere around the house, where I was to find it in due course'.[50]

Margaret's comment in 1972 that she 'didn't write very much until the children were sixteen and eighteen' was an exaggeration. Nonetheless, it reflected her deep frustration with the struggle to compose alongside the demands of family life in an unhappy marriage, and her teaching and performing commitments. It also demonstrated the perception that society did not yet recognise women as composers. 'It's regarded as rather suspect for a woman to write music', she said in 1965. 'I suppose this is because you must shut out everything to concentrate on it, and a woman's life is conditioned by constant interruptions.'[51]

After Australia became involved in World War II in September 1939, life continued relatively normally for Margaret for the first eighteen months. As her communications with the ABC intensified, she was sometimes viewed as a troublemaker. She was certainly an agitator who periodically perceived the ABC as conservative in its programming. These ABC dialogues demonstrate her firm commitment to arguing for the best interests of her own and other quality Australian composition. Inevitably, they also reflect the stress in her private life.

CHAPTER 9

COMPELLED TO MAKE THE STRONGEST PROTEST (1939–1942)

I feel compelled to make the very strongest protest, and shall definitely decline further association with the series of 'Australian programmes' if this kind of promiscuous selection continues.

Margaret Sutherland[1]

MARGARET WASTED NO time in responding to the ABC's call for works to include in the monthly Australian Composers' Sessions commencing in late 1939. She listed fourteen works and sent scores. Acting controller of programs Ewart Chapple confirmed that the ABC would consider them, and hold the 'major' works for the Celebrity Orchestral Concerts series to be directed by visiting international conductors in 1940.[2]

In her response, Margaret alerted the ABC to her involvement in the recent formation in Melbourne of a composers' guild, 'with the idea of encouraging and stimulating work, safeguarding composers' interests and getting in touch with any younger people who are writing'. Lobbying government was a principal strategy. She thought 'it might have worthwhile results' and hoped that other states would join. The guild held its first meeting on 19 July 1939 and operated throughout the 1940s. Margaret severed connections at some stage (for unknown reasons). 'She preserves the right to dissociate herself from groups with which she feels she has insufficient sympathy, and here I refer to the Australian Composers' Guild', claimed musicologist Joyce Garretty.[3]

Four works were programmed for the Australian Composers' Sessions. *The Passing* (1938) was set for the first session, on 29 November 1939, but withdrawn without explanation. Three chamber works were selected for the second session, on 2 January 1940: *Burlesque* for two pianos (1927), *Sonata for Cello and Piano* (pre-1937) and *Rhapsody* for violin and piano (pre-1938). When Margaret saw the program, she complained to federal controller of programs Dr Keith Barry that her works were in strong contrast to others, and that this might alienate audiences.[4] The ABC made no changes, which led to a heated exchange, in which she fervently articulated her opinions.

After the second session, Margaret wrote a stern letter:

> Dear Dr Barry, The programme which we discussed when you were in Melbourne came over 3AR last night and only served to confirm my opinion that this sort of hotch-potch is pure fiasco. Without exception the songs comprising the four groups had no redeeming feature. They could not be said to contribute one iota to Australian music. Furthermore, the words of most were beneath contempt. I feel compelled to make the very strongest protest, and shall definitely decline further association with the series of 'Australian programmes' if this kind of promiscuous selection continues. May I have a word from you regarding the matter which, as you must know, concerns me very vitally?[5]

A flurry of internal ABC exchanges ensued, but the matter was left for William James on his return from overseas. Margaret took her complaint higher up the chain. In late January, she wrote to general manager Charles Moses:

> I am writing to you regarding a matter which concerns the Australian composer deeply—the lax compilation of the present all-Australian programmes. The question resolves itself into whether or not the Commission is going to sponsor as sincere and worthwhile, merely weak

> imitations of the worst and most bogus of the Victorian period of music in England. On January 2nd, a most hopeless programme was put over. Those listeners who cared for the four groups of wretched songs could not fail to loathe my instrumental works, and vice versa. In the studio the atmosphere was sheer ridicule. The songs had had to be 'doctored' by the accompanist, in many parts re-written, to be possible at all. In nearly every case the lyrics were abominable: 'Kisses for love, kisses for pain!' reiterated page after page, and so on. And yet the authors of the songs (?) according to the announcer were 'four of the foremost Australian composers'. One could almost believe that the ABC wishes to bring ridicule on Australian work. I imagine the impression of a stranger listening to a 'fair' example of Australian music. Cannot there be a more enlightened censorship of works to be performed?[6]

Missives flew around the ABC. Music editor Willy Redstone justified his choice. He did not 'contend that the vocal items were masterpieces', yet they were 'the best of a bad lot'. Victorian deputy manager James Grant agreed with Margaret. 'The majority were weak from both the musical and literary point of view, and the session was unlikely to appeal to listeners or to encourage the best of Australian composers to submit their work.'[7]

Barry acknowledged that, 'while this is not a very nice way for one composer to write about another it is, I think, based on rather a sound case'. On his return, James explained his program choices. The most suitable submissions included orchestra and/or chorus, and the Melbourne orchestra was unavailable for the second session, deeming a 'miscellaneous' program necessary. He doubted whether the series should be continued, 'in view of the comparative paucity of the material submitted'. In late March, James apologised to Margaret, suggesting a chat when he was next in Melbourne.[8] (The sessions continued for a while, with Margaret's works featured in some.)

When James programmed Margaret's *String Quartet No. 1* for March 1940, he failed to tell her which quartet would play it. But she needed to speak to the players, 'as it is a fairly complex work, and although I have marked metronome speeds there are many other things to touch on'. On learning it would be the Sydney String Quartet, she swiftly contacted its leader, George White. Unfortunately, White did not receive the parts until nineteen days before the performance—inadequate preparation time, given that 'the work had been selected weeks before, and the score and parts available', Margaret rebuked.[9]

There were two further transgressions relating to the *String Quartet*. In high dudgeon, Margaret wrote to Barry:

> Was there a muddle over the Australian programme on Monday night, or is the ABC ashamed of Australian work? It certainly seems a crime to be 'local'. No details of the programme were given at all, until on the day itself (over the air) the three other items were announced, but my quartet omitted altogether ... The only conclusion to be drawn is that these programmes are considered so little worthwhile that no care is taken to make them known. I feel this so insulting that my only course seems to be to ask for my scores to be sent back to me.[10]

The broadcast had been signalled in several publications, Barry responded, but by some 'unfortunate accident', Margaret's item was omitted from those distributed by the Victorian office. She was not placated: 'I cannot continue to be the victim of "unfortunate accidents"'.[11]

The second misdeed was the delayed payment of Margaret's fee. The ABC's respect for her usually led to polite responses to Margaret's (mostly justified) complaints, but internally they could be patronising. Grant's memo to James that it was necessary to 'pacify the lady' is one example.[12]

In the meantime, Margaret wrote separate letters to James and to chairman William Cleary, listing the ABC's litany of misdemeanours. First, she reiterated that *The Passing* had been withdrawn from the first session at the last minute, 'with no reasons given at all', and after she had herself 'copied all parts, working night and day'. Second, she repeated misgivings expressed before the session on 2 January 1940. Last, she reminded them that her *String Quartet No. 1*, scheduled for broadcast on 11 March 1940, was missing from the program list. 'Do you wonder why I am tired of such things?' she asked. 'Heaven knows composers do not wish to strut like virtuosi, but they are still capable of resenting insult. And I think you will agree with me that I have given it a fair trial.'[13]

Margaret's scores were returned to her, and Cleary promised to 'bring her representations before the Commission'. This bureaucratic process resulted in a formal letter of apology from Cleary: 'There has unquestionably been a succession of mishaps which have given you cause for just complaint', he admitted. The general manager would pay the courtesy of meeting with her during his next Melbourne visit.[14]

Margaret appreciated 'the just consideration you have given affairs I brought before your notice'. While she had his attention, she raised another issue:

> Concerning this vexed question of composers, I should like to make a point here regarding the tendency of the ABC towards relegating the works to be performed to the background. We have to subscribe, for instance, for a series of orchestral concerts extending right through the season, in entire ignorance of the fare. Yet we know all about the artists … Listeners rail against these methods, even though their opinions are not freely voiced. Could not a more equable distribution of information be arranged for those whose interests lie primarily in the subject matter?[15]

Moses professed interest in Margaret's suggestion, but whether it was actioned is unclear.[16]

The Passing (1938), Margaret's short cantata for mezzo soprano, orchestra and chorus, was the subject of a separate exchange. An unusual work for her, it set a poem attributed to an unknown poet—L Rawnsley (possibly English poet Hardwicke Drummond Rawnsley). In a note accompanying the score, Margaret interpreted its meaning as 'Death as Fulfilment, not Discord: that ultimate reality is light'. The singer represents mortality, and forms a dialogue with unaccompanied choir, which answers 'in reassuring terms … varying from intense excitement to a tolling chant'. Symons described it as a work of 'considerable harmonic clarity and radiance, with colourful tonal transitions'.[17]

Chapple submitted *The Passing* to Malcolm Sargent, who did not perform it. Margaret was disappointed, though Sargent 'was reported last year as saying that "Too much music is being written nowadays"!' 'I am inclined to agree', she added, 'but I hope he will at least examine it in spite of his prejudice'. It was finally slotted in a year later. 'Under no circumstances must this arrangement be altered', James directed, no doubt inspired by the recent exchange with Margaret regarding the ABC's 'succession of mishaps'.[18]

Thankfully, the broadcast went ahead with the MSO and Wireless Chorus conducted by Joseph Mozart Post, who lived up to his distinguished name through music teaching and choral conducting. Margaret recommended mezzo soprano Kathleen Seabrook for the solo voice, as she 'has both the quality of voice and the musical feeling for the part'.[19] There appears to be no commentary on the broadcast and, sadly, *The Passing* has passed into obscurity.

Margaret's four-minute work *Dithyramb* (c. 1939) was her first experiment with theatre—in this case, ballet. Between 1936 and 1940, three ballet companies owned by Russian ballet impresario Colonel Wassily de Basil—which traced their lineages to Serge Diaghilev's legendary Ballets Russes—toured Australia for JC Williamson's Theatres. The third company (December 1939 to August 1940) was sailing to Australia when World War II erupted on 3 September 1939. Several dancers decided to remain in Australia, creating enduring benefits for dance in this country.[20]

This third tour led to a fruitful collaboration with choreographer–dancer Nina Verchinina. Margaret's *divertissement* was written for solo dancer and orchestra, and later adapted for piano. She attended rehearsals to study Verchinina's style, resulting in a tonal work reflecting 'momentary impressions'. The variety of rhythms, textures and mood gave Verchinina scope to display her abilities.[21]

Dithyramb premiered at Melbourne's His Majesty's Theatre on 9 May 1940 in what Australian musicologist Joel Crotty described as a 'matinee charity performance for society ladies'. The *Age* observed that 'Verchinina aroused the audience to spontaneous enthusiasm with two expressive ballets: *Dithyramb,* to clever music arranged for orchestra by Miss Margaret Sutherland of Melbourne' (and a work by Handel). The work was similarly enthusiastically received four months later, at 'a midnight presentation for Sydney insomniacs', according to Crotty. The choreography was 'uncommonly vehement, and Verchinina brought to her interpretation all the force and fire which had made her work so popular during the tour', the *Age* review noted. The *Herald*'s Basil Burdett praised Margaret's music. It was 'alternately energetic and yearning in mood', and 'showed her forceful style, based on the modern expressionist mode, perfectly'. Importantly, the dancer expressed her delight in a telegram to Margaret on 20 September: 'DITHYRAMB GREAT SUCCESS CRITICS AND PUBLIC WARM OVATION'.[22]

Margaret submitted the work to the ABC in February 1941, following another request for works for the Celebrity Orchestral Concerts. Meanwhile, it was performed by the University of Melbourne Conservatorium orchestra in the Melbourne Town Hall in August 1941. Margaret played the piano part of this 'attractive' work, 'the outstanding feature of the concert', according to reviews.[23] The ABC finally scheduled it for a broadcast of Australian works by the MSO conducted by Montague Brearley, in early October 1941.

With James's encouragement, Margaret copied and submitted a score of *Dithyramb* in February 1942 for consideration by the BBC (British Broadcasting Corporation) for a concert of Australian works in London, but it was rejected on the grounds that it was loosely strung together.[24] The piece was conceived as ballet music, for which 'loosely strung' music is appropriate, so this is unsurprising. It is easy to envisage it as effective and dramatic dance music, as Australian pianist Jeanell Carrigan demonstrates on Wirripang's CD *Nostalgia*.

The orchestral version of *Dithyramb* attracted several performances in Melbourne and Sydney during the 1940s, and was staged by Laurel Martyn, Australian ballet dancer, choreographer and director at the Ballet Guild of Victoria from 1946 to 1973. She resurrected *Dithyramb* for her first season, but it 'survived only a couple of seasons in the repertoire'.[25]

At the end of 1940, Noël Coward visited Australia, encouraged by his friend Richard Casey, then minister for supply and development in the Menzies government. Margaret was approached in a precursor to later collaborations by Casey's wife, her good friend, artist, writer and aviatrix Maie Casey, to compose incidental music for a performance based on Coward's war-themed song 'London Pride'. Showing her playful side, Margaret conducted the Tudor Singers with a palm frond, with Lorna Stirling assisting.[26] It is not known whether Coward was present, the date and venue are unclear, and the score is lost. But the performance was likely connected with the Tin Alley Players student theatre group at the University of Melbourne, with whom Margaret engaged in another theatrical venture in 1941.

The Tudor Singers included Dorothy Miller, a good friend, and Keith Macartney, recently returned from Cambridge, England, to lecture in English literature at the University of Melbourne. He loved theatre and directed plays at Queen's College and for the Tin Alley Players. A resourceful director, he often featured the Tudor Singers in his productions. In April–May 1941, the Tin Alley Players staged Shakespeare's *A Midsummer Night's Dream* at the Union Theatre, to aid the Women of the University Patriotic Fund and the Union Appeal Fund. Wartime delayed delivery of the score of Mendelssohn's incidental music, *A Midsummer Night's Dream* (1842), from London, so Miller urged Macartney to approach Margaret, who produced a series of vocal, choral and instrumental songs and dances. Lorna Stirling, who helped establish the Tudor Singers, conducted the women's chorus (offstage). Performers included another three of Margaret's friends: Carrie Cairnduff and Elsa Haas (chorus), and violinist Violet Palmer, who led the instrumental chamber group.[27]

No complete score remains, but Margaret drew on music she wrote during the 1930s.[28] Her score was later arranged as the orchestral *Suite of Five Pieces: Preambule, Country Tune, Lullaby, Bergamask* and *Song and Dance.* Theatre critics noted that the score, 'although it sounded thin and tame after the famous incidental music of Mendelssohn, adorned the salient moment of the comedy with pleasant melodies', and that it 'enhanced the general effect'. Margaret was buoyed by the audience's reception and her music's contribution to the success of the production.[29] A letter from Max Crawford, chair of history at the University of Melbourne, added to her satisfaction:

> I have just written to Keith Macartney about the play, because I enjoyed it so much; and I am writing this note to you about your music for the same reason. It wasn't only the sweet, lovely music of the overture to

> the second act that I enjoyed, but throughout the sympathetic and intelligent understanding of the play that was evident in it. I hope there will be some opportunities of hearing the music played in the future.[30]

Margaret capitalised on this with an approach to the ABC in July 1941:

> Recently at the Union Theatre we had a most successful season of 'A Midsummer Night's Dream' with my incidental music. Hundreds were turned away each night in spite of an extended season. Is there a chance of making a condensed, hour's broadcast of this a little later? … I am perfectly certain it would be successful—with Keith Macartney to arrange the condensing of scenes. Will you consider this? So many have been asking for something of the sort.[31]

The ABC showed interest, but decided it was too soon after the Union Theatre season to broadcast it again.[32]

Margaret held strong views on how Australian compositions should be positioned in ABC programming, which she did not hesitate to express in mid-1941:

> You mention 2 concerts of Australian works … I feel I cannot keep here and now expressing my deepest conviction—that the policy of putting forward Australian works all on the same programme is unwise from the composer's point of view, unwanted by the public. A sprinkling of Australian works amongst all programmes is infinitely to be preferred. Why cannot this be done?[33]

Concerned she had voiced her opinion too strongly (and intelligent enough to know she should not 'bite the hand that fed her'—at least, not *too* much), she made amends soon after:

> I feel, in retrospect, that I may have sounded churlish about the proposed Australian Programmes. Actually, I make a point of saying what I mean to the persons concerned, and not muttering my objections elsewhere. As you know, I am only too anxious to see Australian works programmed, but not lumped together as something to be got over. Also, the policy of invitation concerts seems to be mistaken and what is the use of not saying so, if one is concerned in these things?[34]

Margaret did not let up. Two months later, she reiterated her point. 'The Australian programme last night went quite well', she wrote to James. 'It would have been much better, however, to have heard the things separately, not all put on one programme? Don't you agree?'[35] There is no record of James's response.

In November 1941, Margaret was soloist in her *Concertino for Piano and Orchestra* (1939) at the Melbourne Town Hall, with Heinze conducting the MSO. The score was never published and is lost, but a note Margaret sent to the ABC before this performance gives a sense of it:

> The solo piano in this work, which is scored for full orchestra, is used as an integral part of the whole, rather than as a vessel for virtuosic display. Opening in brittle, vivacious rhythmic patterns, these are quite soon quelled by a second theme of greater warmth and freer impulse. Vivid contrasts and frequent changes of mood characterise the opening movement. This is followed by the slow movement—a lullaby—lightly scored—a sensitive, almost timid interlude connecting first and last which, in their different ways, are equally impulsive and provocative. In the finale the solo instrument emerges for a short cadenza and the work ends in characteristically strenuous style.

Heinze had conducted the Sydney Symphony Orchestra in an almost identical concert of Australian composers' works in Sydney on 14 October. Caustic *Sydney Morning Herald* critic Neville Cardus produced a devastating review. 'It was devoted entirely to compositions by Australian composers', giving the impression that 'no music has been heard in this country written later than 1904'.[36] Fortunately, Margaret was spared this treatment, since her work was not performed in Sydney. But, given her negative opinion of all-Australian concerts and her perception that Australian audiences preferred music of the past, she may have agreed with Cardus.

Reviews of the Melbourne concert were less scathing, but lukewarm. JE Tremearne noted it was 'obvious at times that sufficient time had not been permitted for adequate rehearsal'. Margaret recognised this as true to form for Heinze, and other critics had noted his 'lapses in direction'. Describing the *Concertino* as 'provocative' (perhaps adopting the word from Margaret's summary of the work) and as showing 'great ingenuity', Tremearne favoured the 'charm' of the slow movement between the 'two strenuous movements'.[37]

It was 'a brilliant work in the modern manner', wrote the *Argus* critic, though 'at times it did not seem to move logically'. The *Age* found value in the work but was unsure about the 'conflicting tonalities of her apparently improvisatory figures', which tended to 'break up concord and unity'. The sting came in the last sentence: 'Had the work as much beauty as ingenuity it would have rare excellence'.[38]

Margaret's response to these reviews is not recorded, but she was disappointed with the all-Australian program and with the small audience, attributed to Cardus's negative Sydney review. She was dispirited by the orchestra's less-than-impressive rendering of her *Concertino,* and it did not help that Heinze conducted.[39]

There was a further blot on the landscape that evening. Unlike the premiere of Margaret's Purcell Suite in 1939, Norman attended, but brought his current 'lady-friend', a journalist, and both went backstage afterwards. 'Who is that woman with your husband?' asked Heinze. Margaret didn't know. On arrival home, she was so distraught that she 'took the score and put it in the fire'.[40]

In early January 1942, Margaret approached the ABC with her *Suite of Five Pieces* derived from the *Midsummer Night's Dream* production. She explained—almost apologetically—that it was 'to a certain extent "period" music, retaining an Elizabethan flavour'. 'It was very popular here in the production in April [1941] (easy to listen to)', she reassured James. Despite music editor Redstone's condescending opinion that it was 'very light in style yet in parts quite nice', he recommended that it 'should find its place in a light programme'.[41] It was broadcast from Sydney in early April 1942 in an all-Australian session conducted by Percy Code. Though grateful, Margaret reiterated her oft-made complaint:

> I am glad to know that you intend programming it, but sad to note that the all-Australian stunt is persisting! I do wish it was not such a stunt, and that our new works could be brought forward as new works and nothing else. Cannot you feel that this is the right way?[42]

This *Suite*'s performance met with hitches. The copyist misunderstood Margaret's instructions, leading to discrepancies between the score and the orchestral parts. Margaret was unhappy with Code's solutions:

> Do you mind if I bring to your notice the desirability of having first performances in the states in which the composer resides? One is so utterly helpless over the things that matter vitally—tempi and general style—when not on the spot. This seems to me another argument in favour of putting Australian works on general programmes—it is so much easier to arrange then that each new work is performed first in its home-town.[43]

On this occasion, Lorna Stirling wrote similarly to the ABC following the broadcast of the *Suite*. At last, Margaret's persistence paid off, and the ABC decided to consider 'the matter of including new Australian Works in the composer's home state'.[44]

As earlier signalled by Margaret, the copying of parts was difficult, time-consuming and/or expensive, and she lobbied for ABC assistance. In January 1942, she wrote a careworn-sounding letter in response to James's request that she submit works to the BBC. 'Of course I am most anxious to send over something', she began—

> but my impulse to do so is always paralysed by the labour involved. To put all my cards on the table (but I don't in the least mean by my explanation to sound sorry for myself): a. I am always wanting to write new things, and can't therefore face up to copying old ones. b. I have a job of work [voluntary] in connection with the University Patriotic Fund, which takes 2 days per week. c. I have no maid, and a house of 10 rooms (plus children and husband!). I struggled through the *Concertino [for Piano and Orchestra]* parts but at great agony, sitting up till the early hours. Is there any way at all in which the ABC could help composers over this almost insuperable difficulty?[45]

Margaret cited the US experience of Australian-born composer Peggy Glanville-Hicks, who alerted her to the copying facility at Fleisher's music library in Philadelphia, 'whereby out-of-work musicians are given work copying FREE'. 'Can something of this sort be done, helping refugee musicians, through the ABC?' she asked.

James was aware of the American project, but limited resources meant the commission could do no more. Referring to World War II raging in Europe, he suggested that when times returned to normal, the ABC might consider enlarging its staff to help composers with part-writing.[46]

This was not the first time Margaret had spoken on this subject. In December 1941, she had contributed to a *Listener In* article about the plight of Australian composers. Although she thought Australian music should be considered 'on its own merits', this did not mean composers didn't need assistance:

> And one boon would be a trust fund which would subsidise the publishing of Australian music for orchestral use. At present we have to write our own scores and parts if we are having a work performed: this is a strain on the musician which may detract from his work, as well as being a real and surely unnecessary labour for the composer.[47]

The impact of World War II was becoming more obvious in Australia. Norman's involvement was minor—he was not a psychologically traumatised veteran, like many other men. 'The war got him into airforce uniform', according to Margaret, and twice a week, in his capacity as a psychiatrist, he visited the Heidelberg RAAF Hospital, on the site of the 115th Heidelberg Military Hospital, opened in 1941. A 'liaison' with a Women's Auxiliary Air Force (WAAF) member followed. The woman subsequently married and had two children, but remained emotionally attached to the charismatic Norman for some time.[48]

In contrast, Margaret played her part in the war effort in multiple ways, and her public activism intensified as the 1940s unfolded. Her performing life continued, and her drive to compose did not abate.

CHAPTER 10

SOMETHING TO DO WITH UNHAPPINESS (1942–1947)

The Combined Arts Centre Movement has come into being as a serious effort to provide a house for the Arts that will belong to the people, so that we can keep faith with the ever-growing array of those who seek from life something over and above the merely hum-drum realities.

Margaret Sutherland[1]

IN 1942, MELBOURNE'S 1.1 million people were living in the shadow of World War II. One in ten Victorians was enlisted, and those who remained were battling the effects of more than a decade of financial depression. Rationing was in place, and many were struggling to put food on the table. As the war continued and her marriage deteriorated, Margaret involved herself in a wide range of voluntary activities and crusades to support the war effort and on behalf of Australia's cultural life. Despite the 'monstrous problem' of knowing that her marriage would suffer, and with her eyesight declining, she continued to write music alongside her public life and mothering duties. These pursuits helped distract her from the unhappiness of her home situation, as did the moral support of a network of kind friends.[2]

In 1939, Margaret had become involved in the Women of the University Patriotic Fund through its chief organiser, friend and neighbour Yseult Bailey, who conscripted Margaret as secretary. 'This organisation grew apace, as the war victims increased and so many seriously wounded men needed more and more comforts', Margaret said.[3] As part of this role, she helped administer a day nursery in Kew for children whose mothers had joined the workforce. Her post with the patriotic fund lasted about two years, after which time a full-time, paid secretary was required.

Through this group, Margaret, with Lorna Stirling's assistance, organised a series of lunch-hour concerts, known as the 'Middays', to raise money for the Red Cross Prisoner of War Fund. The venture's other aim was to revitalise music in Melbourne, it having slumped following the exodus of musicians serving in the war or entertaining the troops. A Red Cross fundraising event at a grand house in Kew in late November 1940 included a concert organised by Margaret and Dorothy Miller.[4] This event prefigured the Middays, as did a concert series in munitions factories that demonstrated the appeal of well-presented classical music recitals, especially during dark times.

Margaret had a great appetite for the Middays, staged weekly on Wednesdays for over two years, beginning on 17 June 1942. She saw the opportunity to build an audience for local musicians, and was not alone in keeping musical performances alive. In response to patriotic demands, the *Australian Broadcasting Act 1942* required that 2.5 per cent of works played on national or commercial stations be Australian (raised to 5 per cent in 1956).[5] As part of this effort, Heinze was released from his duties at the University of Melbourne Conservatorium to conduct the ABC's celebrity concert seasons. Partly by necessity, these included Australian soloists. Before the war, Margaret disliked the focus on overseas artists in Heinze's celebrity series, and aired her views in a *Meanjin* article in mid-1943:

> Until recently music has been largely an imported commodity. Most of our musical life centred round the visits to this country of artists from abroad. In other words, it was imposed on, rather than growing within, our community ... Now that circumstances have changed so radically,

> it is essential that we face the situation and calmly build up that within us which has been so grievously neglected—the music which grows—flourishes because it is at home here—an expression of ourselves and an inherent part of us.[6]

These thoughts were echoed in spring 1943 in an exchange of letters to the *Age* editor between Margaret and Frank Tait, director of theatrical management company JC Williamson's, which was bringing celebrity artists to Australia. Margaret railed against the importation of Italian singers, when there were Australians who 'could be trusted to provide us with operas of the highest standard, and moreover, without the footlight exhibitionism and vulgarity which have ruined some past opera seasons for us'.[7]

The Middays quickly became so popular that Margaret and her colleagues had to 'drive a hard bargain' to use the conveniently located Upper Assembly Hall venue. Management cooperated, charging only a small rental fee, and Margaret lent her Bechstein grand piano for the duration. When the hall was occasionally unavailable, concerts moved to the Russell Street YWCA headquarters, likely facilitated by Margaret's friend Constance Duncan, who had long been involved with the association. 'They were feasts of chamber music, in those days a fresh field to many of us', said Mollie Turner Shaw, 'and it was a great cooperative undertaking by a very large number of those Melbourne musicians, professional and amateur'.[8]

Most participants were Margaret's friends and colleagues, and 'all Melbourne musicians responded at once, and without reservation', she said. Performers included Lorna Stirling, Elise Steele, Isobel Carter, Thomas and Roy White, Ernest Weiss, John Bishop, Clive Carey, Elsa Haas, Keith Macartney, Violet Palmer, Margaret Schofield and others, some of whom were MSO members keen to play chamber music. Margaret also attracted international musicians such as French violinist Jeanne Gautier, who had arrived in Australia in 1939 on an ABC concert tour and stayed until the end of the war.[9]

The Midday musicians gave their time and expertise for no payment. Fortunately, the musicians' union ban on orchestral members playing gratis had been reluctantly lifted in February 1941 in the interests of the war effort.[10] A wide variety of classical music was aired—ancient to contemporary—by both local and overseas composers. In early January 1943, Margaret and Lorna gave a tea party at the Lyceum Club, inviting Midday artists. According to Lorna, this was an opportunity to thank them, but also for stewardship:

> Margaret and I gave a tea party at the Club for all the artists ... At least we asked them all but only about 16 turned up. The ABC orchestra were mostly declining on the ground that tea parties weren't in their line but promising to take part in the 1943 recitals, which was what we chiefly wanted from them of course. We also discussed programmes, everyone very co-operative, and were able to rough out a Wednesday series taking us from March 3 to the middle of June.[11]

At the same event, it was decided to maintain for 1943 the policy of a donation by audience members of a silver coin, 'even though there was a dismal preponderance of threepences', Lorna wrote. 'We're anxious to make as much as we can for the Prisoner of War Fund, but still more we want to kindle an enthusiasm for chamber music and feel we can't afford to deter anyone.'[12]

People from all walks of life flocked to the Middays, bringing their lunch, or 'their buns', as Margaret put it:[13]

> We got to know the real addicts by sight. Lots of people in uniforms popped in—Army, Navy, Air Force, Red Cross, all sorts of different nationalities. There was an atmosphere, and a feeling (for which we felt grateful) that we could provide something that undoubtedly was needed, and sought by residents ... So many people whose faces were familiar to us used to patronise the 'Middays'. There was, for instance, Dr HC [Nugget] Coombs (even then, of cultural connection), who would unobtrusively slip in and out.[14]

Margaret graced the stage at about seven of these recitals, and her own works were programmed at least twice. On 16 September 1942, her *Trio for Clarinet, Violin (or Viola) and Piano* (1936) was performed by Paul McDermott (violin), Thomas White (clarinet) and Margaret (piano). The *Argus* critic felt that 'Margaret Sutherland's trio, with the composer at the piano, had most to commend it, being more boldly written and conceived in a more lofty spirit'.[15]

From Lorna's diary, we learn about her friendship with Margaret, which blossomed through their close collaboration over the Middays. They spent time together attending concerts, exhibitions and International Women's Day events. With similar opinions on issues affecting Australian composition, including a mutual distaste for 'celebrity-mongering', the two workshopped approaches to the ABC on behalf of good-quality Australian composition.[16] On 9 January 1943, Lorna recorded that Margaret had visited her to discuss her next move in the 'controversy' over ABC controllers:

> The Government has decreed that the ABC allot 2½% of their programme time to Australian works. This is being done unwillingly and in consequence very badly by the Commission, who are taking the path of least resistance and filling the quota with dance music or 'light' music of the cheapest type. … I helped M. draft a letter to him asking for the appointment of two disinterested musicians (not composers) to systematise the quota programmes and ensure that the three types of music—serious, light and dance band—were equitably and worthily represented.[17]

Margaret was still fighting this battle eighteen months later, when the resignation of MSO concertmaster Haydn Beck provoked another letter to the *Age*:

> The resignation of Mr Haydn Beck from the leadership of the Melbourne ABC Symphony Orchestra draws attention once more to a quite Gilbertian situation, which we Australians, alas, seem to accept with no more than a shrug. Here we have an all-powerful organisation with huge sums of money at its disposal, exerting the most far-reaching influence on music, being directed and controlled by a group of commissioners. Until there is at least one trained musician on the commission what can we expect?[18]

Lending a knowledgeable ear to Margaret's new works was another way Lorna supported her friend:

> Margaret spent the evening here, bringing a setting of Shaw Neilson's verses 'The Soldier is Home' which she has done for 3 female voices in a

> perfect imitation of Purcell, sliding a ground bass and all. It's really very lovely and I wager it would deceive even ardent Purcellians.[19]

This was *The Soldier* (1943) for wind quartet, harp, celeste, percussion and male spoken voice, or, in the version Lorna referred to, for strings and three female voices. Margaret submitted it to the ABC Composer Competitions in 1943–44, where it won no prizes, and received a less enthusiastic report than Lorna's. The work was 'musicianly', and made 'ingenious use of a ground bass', but 'never really comes to life'.[20] The ABC showed interest in 1946, but this came to nothing.

At the first anniversary Midday concert on 12 June 1943, Margaret's *Quartet in G Minor for Clarinet (or Violin), Viola, French Horn (or Cello) and Piano,* also known as the *House Quartet,* was played by the composer with Paul McDermott (viola), Thomas White (clarinet) and Roy White (horn). One account judged it to be 'a well-knit and vivacious study, in which the composer successfully explored the potentialities of the four instruments'.[21]

The work enjoyed at least two further outings by the same performers in the 1940s. It was played for the British Music Society (BMS) on 5 April 1944, and at a Musical Society of Victoria (MSV) concert at the Assembly Hall a month later, the first of two 1944 MSV programs including Margaret's music. *Trio in C Major for Clarinet, Violin (or Viola) and Piano* was also programmed, this time with viola. According to one reviewer, Margaret's pieces were the 'highlights of the evening'.[22]

Margaret toured the work to Sydney in October 1945. With the White brothers and William Krasnik (viola), she performed it on 20 October in the second of two concerts at the Sydney Conservatorium of Music, broadcast live by the ABC. The often-scathing Neville Cardus praised the *House Quartet* for comparing favourably with most chamber works he knew that were composed in the 'contemporary English school of chamber composition'. Sydney *Sun* critic AL Kelly thought the *House Quartet* 'did the composer much credit'. The adagio movement was 'of unquestionable beauty', he added, and the performance 'very fine'. The *Daily Mirror* critic noted Margaret's 'impeccable and refined playing', of a work that 'has beauty and distinction rare in modern music'.[23]

Margaret and the White brothers continued their tour, performing at the Albert Hall for the Canberra Musical Society, where the novelty of her works was remarked upon.[24] The tour constituted a fine example of Margaret's practice of combining several talents at once—concert organiser, music educator and communicator, composer and performer.

David Symons observed that the *Quartet in G Minor* may 'contain an element of Hindemithian *Gebrauchtsmusik* ("utility music")' along with Percy Grainger's concept of 'elastic scoring', in that its suggestions for alternative instrumentation made it available to a wider range of performers. Given Margaret's challenging schedule, this approach made sense. 'I didn't try to do anything on a scale I couldn't cope with', she admitted. 'You can't with interruptions, you simply can't. I wrote a quartet for Piano, Clarinet, French Horn and Viola, simply because there were the players available.'[25]

As if Margaret were not busy enough with the Middays, she helped organise a series of free concerts for young people at the Assembly Hall beginning Saturday 30 March 1943. As the member of a BMS subcommittee, she devised suitable programs, while Lorna provided simple explanations of the music at the concerts. These events meshed well with Margaret's view that music must be accessible to all:

> Music must cease to be an awe-inspiring stunt. It must develop as an interchange of ideas, for after all, what is it but a language? It must begin to live within the minds of simple people who think simply—not in big headlines ... We must allow those 'simple people' to grow up on intimate terms with music.[26]

According to Lorna, the first concert was a great success, with 500 turning up, 'and they behaved admirably being I think really interested'.[27]

Through her membership of the Guild of Australian Composers, Margaret helped establish the Council for the Encouragement of Music and the Arts (CEMA) in 1943.[28] The forerunner to the Australia Council for the Arts, the national arts funding and advisory agency founded in 1968, it was modelled on its British counterpart, and aimed to bring a wide range of cultural activities to areas throughout Australia that would otherwise not have had access to them.

All these activities were intertwined with Margaret's leading role in the Combined Arts Centre Movement (CACM), which fought to have a cultural centre built in Melbourne. By 1943, there was a glimmer of hope for Melbourne's postwar cultural future, and talk in certain circles about the need for a new art gallery.

Avid art collector Sir Keith Murdoch, then editor-in-chief of the *Herald and Weekly Times,* was a key figure. In 1939, he was elected president of the board of trustees that oversaw the activities of four institutions—the National Gallery of Victoria, the State Library of Victoria, the National Museum of Victoria and the Industrial and Technological Museum—all contained within the one Victorian-era building on Swanston Street that now houses the library.[29]

The Trustees Post-War Reconstruction Committee was established in 1942, chaired by Murdoch. Following advice from three prominent architects in 1943, it concluded that new sites needed to be found for the gallery and the museum, with the library and the technological museum remaining in place.[30] The Wirth's Park site, a small triangular piece of land south of the river near Princes Bridge, was the preferred gallery venue, because of its position at the city's gateway, where ordinary people congregated.

The Wirth's Park site had been popular with the public since the late 1900s. At different times, it housed several circuses, a boxing venue, the Olympia stadium, a rollerskating rink, a cycle track and the Hippodrome. Over time, small businesses, mostly car mechanics and panelbeaters, took short leases of older, unused circus buildings, but the structures became increasingly dilapidated.[31]

In October 1943, Murdoch and the trustees were preparing their deputation to Victorian premier Albert Dunstan to present the case for Wirth's Park as the new gallery site. Concurrently, an article appeared in the *Age* with the headline 'Wirth's Park Site to Be Big Business Centre'. The Eagle and Globe Steel Company was negotiating with the government to build its offices on the site. While most members of the City of Melbourne and South Melbourne Councils thought something should be done with the forlorn site, they believed it should remain a place for the people of Melbourne.[32] Margaret agreed.

This *Age* article was her trigger for the CACM, established in late 1943. 'We needed that bit of land terribly badly', she later said. 'It was a most derelict part of the city. There were fun parlours, bits of circus-type buildings, advertisements and temporary-looking patched-up sheds that cluttered the whole area.' Margaret had been keeping a close eye on the Wirth's Park site, 'though no Act had been passed that would ensure its ultimate destiny'.[33] She sprang into action, with the full support of Lorna Stirling.

Observing that 'the demand for Art on a high level' was increasing, Margaret thought Melbourne was 'on the brink of a Cultural Renaissance'. The public's appetite for music and drama was growing, despite wartime restrictions. This was due not only to the influx of migrants from Europe; tastes in general were changing. Wartime restrictions on touring by overseas artists made audiences appreciate Australian artists, and demands for a cultural centre increased.[34]

Margaret was inspired by the director of postwar reconstruction, who felt that reform and rebuilding should have their roots among the people. She saw this as 'a vital and stimulating lead: an invitation to give voice to projected post-war cultural needs'.[35] Deeply disturbed by the prospect of Wirth's Park falling into private hands, she wrote to the press, airing her concerns and appealing for public support. The only response came from John Lloyd, a civil servant in the titles department who was interested in the arts and community service. Margaret was canny enough to know that a man's involvement would lend credibility to the campaign.

In late 1943, Lorna and John met with Margaret in her music room at the Studley Avenue home, where the 'plan was hatched'. They decided to call an exploratory meeting of prominent arts people, to gauge interest. A letter drafted by Margaret, and signed also by Lorna and John, was distributed to arts groups, inviting them to a meeting. On 26 November 1943, representatives of thirty-one organisations encompassing music, drama, ballet and the visual arts, as well as some of a more general nature, gathered with Margaret, Lorna and John at the Upper Assembly Hall in Collins Street. Music institutions included the ABC, MSO, BMS and various amateur groups.[36] Also attending were writers and literary critics Vance and Nettie Palmer, NGV director Daryl Lindsay, singer, composer and opera producer Clive Carey, and Margaret's friend Mollie Turner Shaw.

The CACM was launched at this meeting. It was resolved that a petition be presented to parliament, asking that the erection of a suitable building for the arts form part of the immediate postwar development scheme. The main objective, according to Margaret, was 'to keep hard-headed commercial interests off the site until the war ended', because there seemed to be no chance during wartime of an Act in favour of an arts centre being passed by the government.[37]

A committee was elected, whose executive included John Lloyd (chair) and Margaret (secretary), with treasurer Peggy Priestley, and members Lorna Stirling, Vance Palmer, Mollie Turner Shaw and 'Mr Lewis'. Petition forms were printed, and the executive combed the metropolitan area—'wherever we thought we had a chance of getting a worthwhile number of signatures and addresses', said Margaret. While she was standing outside the town hall collecting signatures one evening, a drunken sailor assailed her and enquired about the petition. As she had done 'a thousand times', Margaret patiently explained it. 'By gum, I'll sign my name all right—anything for Russia', he responded. She didn't have the heart to 'dampen his enthusiasm, so he signed it for Russia!'[38]

In letters to potentially interested parties, Margaret encouraged readers to spread the word:

> The Combined Arts Centre Movement has come into being as a serious effort to provide a house for the Arts that will belong to the people, so that we can keep faith with the ever-growing array of those who seek from life something over and above the merely hum-drum realities … The amount of public backing needed to prove to the Government that a large percentage of the population is seeking such a centre, is very considerable … Now what I want most particularly to urge you to do is to take [a petition] with you … introducing it in quarters where there are

> people congregated who think for themselves and have some aspirations of a cultural nature ... This cannot be left to the isolated efforts of a few. You will be surprised at how readily people catch alight and how eager they are to sign when the ultimate aim is explained to them.[39]

The Middays provided a central platform 'to display our petitions and get signatures', and Margaret took every opportunity to speak at arts gatherings. In early April 1944, for example, she addressed the Old Players' and Playgoers' Association, outlining the desired plans. The centre's main feature would be a central hall to seat about a thousand people, adaptable for intimate drama, ballet or chamber music, with provision for contemporary art shows, and possibly clubroom facilities for the various societies. The centre would grow with the community and be a non-commercial venture under neutral control. She argued for children's theatre, since 'Plays are the native diet of the child ... To the child and to the adolescent, the theatre as an extension and a reflection of the world of reality can have a profound and far-reaching effect'.[40]

Throughout 1944, the CACM's cause received support via press coverage in major Melbourne papers—the *Herald*, the *Age* and the *Argus*. *Herald* journalist Clive Turnbull was a staunch advocate:

> If proposals now being pressed for the lease to circus proprietors, dance hall entrepreneurs and a steel company of the Princes' Bridge area loosely known as Wirth's Park are proceeded with, a unique opportunity for the making of a gracious, useful and badly-needed entrance to the city will be thrown away. Here is 5 ½ acres providentially preserved to the State in the heart of Melbourne—an area which needs only intelligent development to make it one of the show places of Australia.[41]

John Lloyd hit the press on at least two occasions. In June 1944, he argued:

> For years we have suffered through the lack of facilities whereby the cultural standard of Australians could be raised ... Unless the works of the masters of music, drama, ballet, sculpture, painting and all the other pure and applied arts can be brought to the people cheaply and efficiently, the demand for the best in these arts will never be made, and worthless imitations will be accepted in their place.[42]

The following month, he wrote that 'Already a lot of hard work has gone into forwarding this movement and a lot more has to be done. All groups and societies who approve of our plan can make contact with the secretary, Miss Margaret Sutherland'.[43]

In September 1944, an initial 'Friendly Arts Centre Plan' was drawn up by John Scarborough (the University of Melbourne's Baillieu Library architect). The building would be grouped around a courtyard planned as an open-air theatre, the object being 'to avoid any "institutional" character, and to create a friendly place for instruction and enjoyment'.[44]

On 9 November 1944, a year after the initial meeting in Margaret's music room, a deputation led by CACM chairman John Lloyd arrived at Victorian Government chief secretary George Hyland's office. Margaret, Lorna and Vance Palmer were there with other committee members. They carried a petition addressed to the premier, Albert Dunstan, containing no fewer than 40 000 signatures. The huge bound petition pointed out the 'growing enthusiasm for the arts in Melbourne', but that Melbourne compared 'unfavourably with other cities of its size in the accommodation provided for art'. It emphasised the plan's educative value, and recommended that the centre be under government control, and could be made to pay for itself.[45]

As chairman of the trustees of the public library, museum and national gallery, and new patron of CEMA, Sir Keith Murdoch supported the deputation, arguing that it represented the best-informed, most idealistic and highest opinion in musical and dramatic thought and work in the state. Acknowledging that it should not take precedence over the housing, health and education needs of Victoria, he stressed the urgency of having plans ready as soon as materials and labour were available. This could be quite early, 'considering the vast employment problem that will soon be upon us'.[46]

The petition received comprehensive press coverage, with supportive articles appearing in the *Argus*, the *Herald* (Clive Turnbull), the *Sun* and the *Age*. But Mr Hyland was equivocal. He said that the project was 'in its infancy'—difficult words to hear for a committee that had

George Sutherland Snr, 1860s

Jane Sutherland Snr, 1860s

Alexander Sutherland, 1880s

Jane Sutherland Jnr, 1880s

George Sutherland Jnr, 1880s

Ada Sutherland, 1880s

William Sutherland, 1890s

Mona McBurney, 1896

Nora Kyffin-Thomas, 1902

Margaret by Jane Sutherland, c. 1904

'Heronswood', c. 1900, attributed to Jane Sutherland
Courtesy The Diggers Foundation

Jessie Sutherland by Jane Sutherland, c. 1905
Courtesy National Gallery of Victoria

'Blue and Gold', portrait of Dorothy Sutherland by Jane Sutherland, 1908
Courtesy National Gallery of Victoria

Dorothy Sutherland, c. 1915

'To my very gifted pupil', Edward Goll, 1918

Margaret, 1920s

Margaret and Mark, c. 1930

Lorna Stirling, 1930s

Jennifer and Mark, c. 1934

Con Duncan, c. 1936

Margaret, c. 1937

Margaret and Jenifer, c. 1937

Mark and Norman, c. 1937

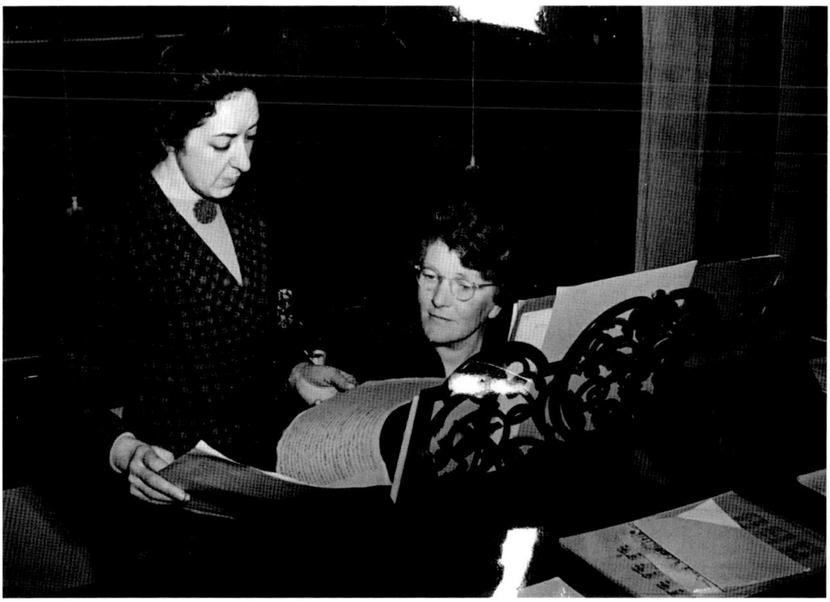

Margaret with Esther Rofe, 1941

Margaret with Harold Blair, Fitzroy Primary School, 1948

Margaret with Sophie Wyss and Dorian Le Gallienne, c. 1948

Jenifer, c. 1949

Con Duncan, c. 1950

20 Studley Avenue, Kew, today

Don Banks, Margaret and Dorian Le Gallienne, London 1952
Courtesy Jane Sinclair

Margaret, 1954

Margaret with Aaron Copland, 1960
Courtesy *The Age* and The Aaron Copland Fund for Music, Inc.

Margaret and George Loughlin, 1969

James Murdoch, 2001
Photo by Louis Seselja, courtesy
National Library of Australia

Margaret, 1974

Margaret and George Fairfax, Melbourne Concert Hall, 1982
Courtesy Australian Performing Arts Collection, Arts Centre Melbourne

Margaret, 1984
© The Estate of Athol Shmith, courtesy Kalli Rolfe Contemporary Art

been labouring for a year. The government was persuaded to reserve the Wirth's site for the arts centre, but nothing further was decided. Confirming that other needs took precedence, he acknowledged that 'the work put into this petition shows that you desire to be in the picture. I can only say that we have your petition, and that I will take it into consideration when decisions are made about the arts centre'.[47]

Meanwhile, Margaret's son Mark had entered his teenage years and their relationship was faltering. He became what she euphemistically referred to as 'an interesting person', slipping out of his upstairs window to play billiards with the boy next door. He did not take his lessons seriously, and 'drifted through school life'. In 1944, aged fifteen, he became entangled with a local girl, 'one of the over-sexed type of 15-16-year-olds', Margaret perceived. 'The two were so inaccessible, so headstrong', and this placed a great strain on an already difficult family life. It was rumoured that Mark was suspended from Scotch College for physically attacking another student, though there is no evidence in the school's records. Musically talented but otherwise average, he had to repeat Form 8 (now Year 11) in 1945 but completed Year 12 in 1946. At seventeen, he departed for Queensland with some friends, hoping to become a jazz musician.[48]

Despite the stress at home, Margaret battled on with the CACM, and her connection with CEMA offered further opportunities for publicity. In 1945, she organised the musical aspects of the CEMA Autumn Arts Festival, the Midday Series grand finale. Presented in association with the CACM, it was an excellent opportunity to demonstrate to the government the extent of Melbourne's cultural development, and thus the need for proper accommodation for the arts.[49] Running through April, the festival involved opera at the Union Theatre, drama and ballet at the National Theatre in Eastern Hill, and two free art exhibitions—the Victorian Art Exhibition and the Exhibition of Australian Aboriginal Arts and Crafts—at the Velasquez Gallery in Bourke Street. The musical events took place in the Melbourne Town Hall, where there was a series of chamber music (instrumental and vocal) and orchestral concerts.

A week of Proms concerts was the pièce de résistance, being 'one of the many activities to aid the project for an arts centre on the Wirth's site', Margaret conceded. The first was a Sidney Myer Free Concert given by the MSO conducted by Heinze in the Melbourne Town Hall on Saturday 7 April, broadcast nationally by the ABC. Included in the program were Margaret's *Dithyramb* (c. 1939) and the premiere of *Pavan for Harp and Orchestra* (pre-1938).[50] Musicians were keen to be involved. They included pianist Hephzibah Menuhin, who wrote to Margaret, saying that she was 'nearly brokenhearted about not being able to accept' the invitation to appear in the festival, because she was unable to free herself from 'the positively pernicious round of housewifely duties', which left 'no time for practising'.[51] Margaret probably sympathised.

The festival was a great success. It confirmed to the CACM that Melbourne was blessed with many excellent musicians, actors, dancers and artists, and bolstered its conviction that the city needed a proper combined arts centre.[52]

By August 1946, Mark's behaviour had exacerbated the friction at home to the extent that Norman decided he needed to get away. He joined a party of medical men who chartered a boat to visit the Barrier Reef. During this expedition, they called in at Timana Island, owned by Mrs Cohen and her two daughters Valerie (Val) and Yvonne (Von), both artists. Norman and Val were attracted to each other, 'and at the age of 53', Margaret caustically remarked, he 'found his Indian Summer'.[53]

The CACM 'kept ticking over with our more routine work', and Margaret regularly visited the Wirth's Park site, often accompanied by daughter Jenny. But there were ups and downs. An 'up' involved the arrival in Melbourne of the first Australian Aboriginal opera singer, Harold Blair. Harry Green, a trade union organiser at the Fairymead sugar mill in Bundaberg, Queensland, where Blair worked, heard him singing, and took up his cause. He approached the Queensland Government to no avail. In 1945, he arranged for Blair to appear on *Australia's Amateur Hour*, where he won a record number of votes. Green took him to audition at the Sydney Conservatorium and the University of Melbourne conservatorium. Both rejected him because, although he had a good voice, he was a beginner and not sufficiently literate.[54]

Green and Blair turned up in the CACM committee room in the Assembly Hall, where they were greeted by Margaret. She listened to Blair sing, and pronounced he had 'a good voice in essence, but utterly untrained'. Nevertheless, she wanted to help, and contacted John Lloyd, apprehensive about his response. Lloyd listened with 'great interest and attention', and when Margaret expressed her concern about housing Harold, he replied, 'Oh, that's quite simple; he can come and live with us'. It was assumed that Lloyd's wife Gwenda would agree, which she did willingly, and Blair was taken into the Lloyd household and treated like an older brother to their two children. Gwenda filled gaps in Blair's education, while Margaret, John Lloyd and Vance Palmer became trustees of a fund to enable him to continue his musical studies. He attended the Melba Conservatorium in Melbourne, then went to the US. Before Blair went overseas, Margaret assisted in at least two concerts at the Melbourne Town Hall. She accompanied him at a benefit concert on Saturday 28 February 1948, before which she was pictured with him on the front page of the *Herald*, entertaining Aboriginal children at Fitzroy Primary School.[55]

John Lloyd took an unpaid year off work in 1949, to accompany Blair and accompanist Liesel Jorg on an Australian tour sponsored by the Society for the Promotion of Australian Art, of which Lloyd was honorary secretary. At his concert in Melbourne in March 1949, Margaret accompanied Otti Veit in a cello sonata by Mendelssohn. On 24 May, she was an associate artist at Blair's concert at the Adelaide Town Hall, where he concluded his program with 'a song of the Australian bush by Margaret Sutherland' (probably one of the *Old Australian Bush Ballads* of 1948).[56]

Later in 1949, Blair arrived in New York to be mentored by African American baritone Todd Duncan. Margaret wrote to the *Age* editor, criticising those who had doubted Blair's opera-singing future. She seized the opportunity to air her long-held scepticism about institutionalised music education. After Blair had arrived in Melbourne four years before, there were 'endless problems to be faced', she wrote:

> Scores of doubting Thomases shook dubious heads, and self-styled 'friends of the aborigine' sounded sinister notes of warning. Now we read this morning that Harold Blair has been 'introduced to New York' when he attended a press conference at the house of Todd Duncan. He has also made a dignified statement on the status and need of the aborigine in this country. The ability to assess unprecedented gifts is rare. Too often unorthodox qualifications go unnoticed, or do not receive chances commensurate with the particular endowment of the individual. Therefore it is gratifying to learn that the courage and the vision for this undertaking have not been lacking, nor have they gone amiss in this instance.[57]

Margaret's championing of Harold Blair exemplified a support for Australia's Aboriginal people that had been inculcated early within her extended Kew family.[58] She was ahead of her time. By no means had Aboriginal people achieved equal rights or status by the 1940s, and it was only under the *Commonwealth Electoral Act 1949* that they were given the right to vote at federal elections. Her support manifested in several ways over the coming years.

Of the 'wide variety of vicissitudes that beset [the CACM]', said Margaret, 'one of the very serious jolts was an unexpected (not to say unimagined) takeover by Communists' in 1946. But this 'bizarre' or 'ragtime' regime 'came off rather badly in the end'. After a few months, this group was wound up, but the deposed committee, including Margaret, 'had gone on watching'.[59]

There had always been 'a sprinkling of Communists on the original committee'. Although John Lloyd deplored the actions of the takeover group, he was among their number; Margaret was not. These original committee members were more socialists than communists, she observed. They were not the 'belligerent variety' of the takeover, who were 'in it for their own sakes, not for mankind'—one of her pet hates. 'There is all the difference in the world', she said, 'between those persons who wish to disrupt the lives of others, basically for their own purpose (their own poor, unworthy egos) and those who wish desperately hard to see a better world, set for better purposes than self-glorification and aggrandisement'.[60]

By Easter 1947, Margaret's suspicions about Norman's relationship with Val Cohen were borne out. He admitted he was 'desperately in love' with Val; they were 'spiritually suited to one another'. The stress caused by Mark, intensified by a gruelling menopause, made it difficult for Margaret 'to carry on'. She asked Norman to make up his mind, but he preferred living at home, while spending time with Val. He claimed to need two women, using as a precedent the experience of a medical colleague who had successfully adopted this lifestyle. Norman was not alone in having a wife and a mistress, and in an era when divorce laws were less favourable to women, some wives chose the lesser of two evils and turned a blind eye. But Margaret was at the end of her tether and couldn't consent to a triangular relationship. 'I could not go through another six months of it', she wrote, but Norman would not budge. From then on, 'great unpleasantness existed' between them.[61]

Margaret received moral support from friends, and the Lyceum Club provided a safe haven. She remained actively involved in the club's musical life, performing a program of her works in May 1938. She organised recitals, including some of the half-hour wartime lunch concerts, and offered suggestions on matters such as the need to overhaul the piano and how to improve musical events.[62]

The Lyceum Christmas parties, complete with entertainment, were a club tradition and, with Lorna Stirling, Dorothy Miller and others, Margaret was a leading light. These 'brilliant and funny stage shows, mock operas, pageants, and straight-out farce and nonsense' allowed the light-hearted side of her character to emerge.[63] According to Mollie Turner Shaw, they were 'hilarious entertainments':

> One orchestral festival co-opted the full instrumental talent of the Club, from sedate elderly members with violins they had not played since their schooldays to others with recorders, mouth organs, and even combs and paper. Margaret conducted from the piano in the guise of Percy Grainger, with fair hair flying and huge handfuls of chords.[64]

For this event, Margaret messed up her cropped hair and entered the stage wearing shorts and an open-neck shirt. She 'literally charged to the piano and thumped out Grainger's *Country Gardens* with fantastic gusto! A storm of applause!', said club member Elspeth White.[65]

The Catalysts provided another congenial outlet. Their motto was 'Once a Catalyst, always a Catalyst', and they were mutually supportive.[66] Through monthly meetings, the group provided Margaret with friendship and intellectual stimulation. Its membership list read (and reads) like a 'Who's Who' of Melbourne's female intellectual and creative élite, which in Margaret's time included academics and historians Jessie Webb and Kathleen Fitzpatrick, and zoologist and women's rights activist Georgina Sweet. Several of Margaret's musical and Lyceum friends were members, including Lorna Stirling, Mollie Turner Shaw, Maie Casey, Constance Duncan and Dorothy (DJ) Ross, progressive principal of Melbourne Church of England Girls Grammar School.[67]

Margaret's first Catalysts talk on record took place in June 1937, on the topic of 'Aspects of Contemporary Music'. In August 1940, she organised a recital of her works involving piano, violin and voice, which she called 'Poor things but mine own'. In July 1943, she gave a talk about her beloved Purcell, accompanied by a recital of his works, assisted by Elise Steele, Lorna Stirling and mezzo soprano Winifred Gardner. And in May 1946, she talked about 'Music and Reality'.[68]

Increasingly, Margaret needed to speak more openly about her marital misery. One day at the Lyceum Club, she confided in Constance Duncan, who later became her close companion and housemate. The two probably met at the Lyceum but became more closely acquainted through their mutual involvement with the Women of the University Patriotic Fund. Con was one of the few women to be accepted into the élite inner circle of intellectuals influencing Australian foreign policy from 1922 to 1947. From 1922, she spent ten years in Japan as a 'foreign secretary' for the YWCA, then returned to Australia to a position with the Bureau of Social and International Affairs. Her familiarity with Japanese culture and society, and commitment to world peace, led to her participation in international relations at a time of heightened interest in the Asia-Pacific region, and Japan in particular. She directed the Victorian International Refugee Emergency Council, formed in 1938, and fought to dispel community prejudice against refugees.[69]

In early September 1940, Con learned through British Quaker friends that thousands of 'enemy aliens' deported from Britain were heading for Australia on the HMT *Dunera*. 'Con, being the practical and compassionate person, got immediately busy', Margaret said, finding 'clothes, cases, rugs'. In preparing for their arrival, she was accused of contravening secrecy regulations. A woman of strong principles, Con stood firm in her determination to carry out her task. The arrivals were mostly Jewish refugees fleeing Nazi persecution in Germany and Austria, and included artists, philosophers, scientists and writers. Many remained after the war, making significant contributions to Australia's economic, social and cultural life.[70]

Margaret trusted Con and felt safe divulging her despair. Con was single, with fewer fixed notions about the sanctity and permanence of marriage. Like Margaret, she had encountered discrimination as a woman. Through her role at the Federal Government's Department of Labour and Service from 1941 to 1945, she had advocated for several measures relating to children and women, including uniform divorce laws.[71] Knowledge of Con's perspective may have enhanced Margaret's willingness to disclose her story.

Con invited Margaret to her holiday retreat in Olinda in the Dandenong Ranges, where she often relaxed with friends. In this peaceful environment, Margaret revealed her problems in detail, and returned home resolved to take action. It was time to 'bust it', and the opportunity soon presented itself.[72]

In August 1947, Margaret took with her two of the many intimate letters Val sent Norman. Extremely distressed, she made a short visit to Adelaide, and on her return in early September, moved into the spare bedroom. When Norman discovered Margaret had the letters, he was furious. She knew reprisals would come. The next day, as she was washing his breakfast dishes, he approached her 'with a fearful expression on his face and said that he had collected every bit of my music, had put it in the boot of his car, and was going off to drop it in the river'. He left and took up temporary residence at the Masonic Club. Given his attitude towards Margaret's devotion to music, it is not surprising he chose her compositions as a means for revenge.[73]

Margaret consulted her solicitor (Stuart Hutchison), who referred her to Clarence Webster of Melbourne law firm Pearce & Webster (now Pearce Webster Dugdales). Webster rang Norman, ordering him to replace the music within three days. He agreed, on condition that Margaret return the letters, which she did. Just before the requisite three days were up, he went to the house and replaced the music without interacting with her. He didn't return to collect the rest of his belongings until the following year.[74]

If Margaret were alive today, she may have chosen to end the unfortunate union sooner, but she still had feelings for Norman, according to Helen Gifford. It should be borne in mind that there may be several reasons why women feel they have no choice but to remain in abusive relationships. There is also greater awareness nowadays that ending a marriage sooner rather than later can lead to better outcomes for children, given that living in a conflictual environment can cause emotional, social and behavioural problems. But although expectations were changing in the 1940s, the stigma of divorce remained and the laws were less favourable to women. Any woman—and especially a doctor's wife—would have been concerned about losing custody of her children. The views of doctors and other professionals commanded more respect than those of their wives. Reflecting her era, Margaret felt responsible for protecting her children, and didn't want to end the marriage while they were young. She finally did so when they were eighteen and sixteen, by which time she considered them 'old enough to examine things for themselves'.[75]

In an epoch when divorce was seen as a failure of morality, it is possible that the angst involved in Margaret's decision to end the marriage was eased through the model of a creative divorcee provided by her sister Ruth. Unfortunately, the veil of silence over marital strife may have prevented them from giving mutual support. Neither are the sisters likely to have shared the challenges each faced in balancing the demands of home and professional life. Ruth had been a respected artist and art critic, having written articles for the *Age* and the journal *Art in Australia*, and helped found the group 'Twenty Melbourne Painters' in 1918, which still exists today. She almost completely abandoned painting during her marriage, but successfully re-established her career after the separation. She found a teaching position in a convent, and in 1940 joined the Melbourne Society of Women Painters. She had at least one solo exhibition of her own in March 1950 at the Melbourne Book Club Gallery in Collins Street, founded by her cousin Sheila Sutherland (Alexander and Lizzie's eldest child). Margaret kept the printed list of works. Her own post-marriage experience was to resonate with Ruth's.[76]

Margaret found solace in letters received in response to news of the separation. Despite her efforts to the contrary, friends had suspected that not all was well. 'I had really feared the whole situation for you for some time, and I wondered just how much more you could take', wrote Yseult Bailey. 'I didn't know first exactly how things were, or I think I would have said much more … How on earth you've managed to put up the stand you have, I'm beyond understanding.' Keith Macartney of the University of Melbourne's Tin Alley Players admitted he had 'thought several times that life was probably not altogether easy for you'. He agreed with Margaret that 'it is much wiser for all concerned to make a break'.[77] And from Doris Carey, Clive Carey's wife:

> We are thinking about you a great deal. Of course this has come as a great shock, but my dear it may be for the best in the long run. If there is any sadism in people, well how is one to cope with it … Anyhow if the years have been a strain you may begin to live as an individual again and there is a lot in that.[78]

Margaret had not given up easily:

> Hope dies hard in me—much too hard, I fear—and I pinned a lot of it on some change in outlook over the years. For that reason I confided in no-one, for I felt if the changes were to come, all the hideous years would be forgotten … And I trusted to some extent in the Albiston stock. In this I was sadly mistaken.[79]

Despite her claims to the contrary, Margaret had not stopped composing, producing around eighty works during her marriage. But she certainly struggled to find time and the intellectual and creative space to write. She was also remarkably active as a teacher, performer and organiser during twenty-one years of married life.

After the war and leading up to the end of her marriage, Margaret made regular concert appearances. The piano she had lent for the Middays continued its life at BMS concerts, and she regularly played it as soloist or accompanist, usually for no fee. In a letter to BMS secretary Sybil Hewett about the opportunities afforded English composers during the war, Louise Hanson-Dyer commented that 'Our friend MS if she heard of it would be putting her hand in for herself saying that she was one Australian composer bar none'.[80] This seemingly spiteful comment does not align with Hanson-Dyer's support of Margaret's work, but does reflect an era when self-promotion was perceived as a distasteful attribute in a woman—even by other women. In reality, it was only occasionally that Margaret's works were performed at the BMS during this period.

As her marriage unravelled in 1947, Margaret wrote several compositions that display her versatility. The *Sonata for Clarinet (or Viola) and Piano* is further evidence of her use of elastic scoring. Although short, at around eight minutes, it is arguably Margaret's most significant chamber work of the 1940s. A lyrical, sweeping piece reflecting her earlier 'pastoral' style and her later more neoclassical style, it has overtones of Bartók and Hindemith.[81] Margaret performed it with Thomas White (clarinet) for an ABC broadcast in early 1949, and it has become one of her better-known pieces. There have been numerous performances and several recordings, as well as in-depth analyses.

While the *Sonata for Clarinet and Piano* looked stylistically both backwards and forwards, Margaret's *Six Profiles* for piano (c. 1946) abandoned romantic gestures in favour of a sparer neoclassical approach. Published by the English company Augener in 1953, these were based on six friends, whom she wisely chose not to name. 'I have always felt very vividly the link between music and the personal characteristics of human beings', she wrote. As expected, they are of varying character, ranging from whimsical to subversive to melancholic. Margaret performed them for an ABC broadcast in March 1948 after Willy Redstone described them as 'written in free style and quite unorthodox', and declared them to be 'quite suitable for broadcast'.[82]

The Selfish Giant, based on Oscar Wilde's eponymous children's story, was Margaret's second collaboration with Laurel Martyn and the Ballet Guild of Victoria. Undeterred by the tepid response to *Dithyramb* when Martyn staged it in November 1946, she commissioned a score. The dance production premiered in September 1947 at the University of Melbourne's Union Theatre, with Oscar Wilde's grandson, Vyvyan Holland, and his wife in attendance. Joel Crotty noted that 'the commission suffered from Sutherland's inability to work successfully in a collaborative venture'—she apparently refused to extend a section to allow for the character to repeat his choreographed action on the grounds that 'the score's symmetry would be broken'. It is difficult to judge whether this was because of her immoveable musical ideals, or a manifestation of the stress she was under at home, or both—or neither. As there are several documented occasions when Margaret successfully collaborated with artists both before and after composition, there were likely other factors at play apart from high-mindedness and inflexibility.[83]

Margaret suggested to the ABC that the *Selfish Giant*'s ten short dances could be linked by a spoken narrative, as in Prokofiev's *Peter and the Wolf.* Heinze was keen to include it in a 1948 school program, which was approved by William James, who thought it 'quite a fair composition, well done and orchestrated for small orchestra'.[84] It was submitted to the BBC in 1952 and rejected, and has been largely forgotten.

The evolving situation at home did not preclude Margaret's activist pursuits. She continued to further the CACM's aims, in tandem with other public endeavours relating to Melbourne's postwar cultural environment. Sir Keith Murdoch and NGV director Daryl Lindsay established the National Gallery Society of Victoria in 1947. The society's role in attracting the public's interest in viewing the gallery's treasures appealed to Margaret, and she became a member, finding her niche in organising and promoting musical recitals. Mollie Turner Shaw recalled them with affection:

> Once a year we were allowed to use the Stawell Gallery for a musical recital, and this was Margaret's special concern. On a dais in front of the great Tiepolo 'Banquet of Cleopatra' would appear the Paul McDermott [String] Quartet, Mancell Kirby at her harpsichord, Barbara Carroll with her recorder players, a quartet of rich brass from the orchestra, the oboist Jiří Tancibudek (I scurried up obscure stairs and along half-dark galleries to borrow a music stand for him from the furniture collection), Kevin McBeath reading the [Edith] Sitwell words to Walton's recorded *Façade* music—and far too many others to remember now.[85]

After the separation, Norman paid Margaret an allowance of £7 a week, except for a short period in 1949 when he was ill. Margaret filed for divorce on the grounds of desertion, and the decree nisi became absolute on 1 July 1951.[86] Norman was free to marry Val Cohen, which he did later that year, and the two remained together until Norman's death in 1979.

In 1948, artists Guelda and Polly Pyke, together with Val and her sister Von, bought an apple and peach orchard in Templestowe called Stella Park, and commissioned well-known environmental architect and builder Alistair Knox to design and build a house for Guelda and Polly, with separate houses for Val and Von. According to Margaret's grandchildren, Jenifer's children Michael and Kirsten Bunney, the two sisters were inseparable—it was uncommon to see them apart, even when Val was in Norman's company. In the mid to late 1940s, Melbourne pianist Margaret Schofield dined regularly at Melbourne's Café Latin with her friends the artist Rupert Bunny and Geoffrey and Barbara Anderson, and they often saw Norman, Val and Von at another table.[87]

Stella Park was effectively an artists' colony, and Norman moved to Val's house there following their wedding. We don't have Norman's side of the story of his marriage to Margaret, but his grandchildren, Jenifer's children Michael, Anthony and Kirsten, remember him as a fun-loving grandfather figure who delighted in making them laugh with his magic tricks. Val also painted a kinder picture of Norman. She thought him a warm and caring man who didn't need to conform to societal norms.

She claimed to want to befriend Margaret, who was not in the least interested. Val was welcoming to Norman's children Mark and Jenifer, to his grandchildren, and to Mark's second wife, Astrid Dahl, and their daughter. While Val's conviviality was paired with a strong character, she was more relaxed than Margaret, who 'was a deeply passionate, emotional person', said Helen Gifford. Val was independently wealthy and very sociable—the couple often entertained artistic friends. Margaret's son-in-law Dean Bunney's second wife, Jane, said that Val would not have put up with mistreatment from Norman, and that she was 'probably more worldly than Margaret, who came from a genteel, protected environment'.[88] Val's personality blended well with Norman's. This, together with the mellowing that comes with age, and the lack of financial constraints and any intention to have children, probably contributed to the success of Norman and Val's union.

Val was not alone in her attempts to redeem Norman's character. His great-niece, Barbara Taylor (née Albiston), remembers visiting Norman and Val in Templestowe. 'He was great fun. As a child I was a bit scared because I believed he could hypnotise, but he was very warm, and I liked him very much.'[89] Despite his being dubbed 'the bad uncle', there was family affection for Norman.

Margaret's bitterness regarding her marriage extended to the wider family. In 1942, Barbara started at Tintern Grammar, which Jenifer also attended. Younger than Jenny, she was placed in the first year of senior school, a class above her cousin. Margaret took umbrage and moved Jenny to Melbourne Girls' Grammar School's Merton Hall campus. Margaret had nothing further to do with Norman's side of the family, and Barbara's close friendship with Jenny ended. Although Margaret was not open about her unhappiness, her stress found other outlets.

The years following their separation were undeniably happier for both parties, and with 'all the hideous years' of marriage behind her, Margaret blossomed.[90]

PART FOUR

LATER LIFE: 1948–1984

CHAPTER 11

LIFE ENTHRALLS ONE (1948–1959)

I had to make a completely new life. Bit by bit it grew. And I really began being grateful for a life that mattered. Music came more and more possible. And music got written.

Margaret Sutherland[1]

APART FROM HER early childhood, the late 1940s and 1950s were the happiest years of Margaret's life. In contrast with her disastrous marriage, the stability and contentment provided by her friendship with Con Duncan enabled Margaret to flourish personally and professionally. She divided her large home, and invited Con, who was reportedly living with her family in an unsatisfactory arrangement, to share the house. Con split her time between Kew and her retreat in Olinda. At one point, Margaret rented the top floor to friends Rob and Peggy Priestley, and in the mid-1960s to Maureen White and her sister. This arrangement provided income and the company of simpatico people, akin to the Kew households of her early years.[2]

It is possible that Margaret and Con's relationship was physically intimate. There is no firm evidence, though Australian historian Renate Howe claimed that Con was open about her sexual preference for women. If Margaret and Con's relationship was more than platonic, this was unlikely to be stated publicly for two reasons. According to Maureen White, 'you'd never find from Margaret the degree of the friendship', intimating that Margaret kept her personal life private and was reticent about showing affection in public. Second, society preferred to characterise relationships between two women living together as close friendships or companionships. There remained a code of silence regarding same-sex relationships between women (and men) in 1950s Australia. Sexual intimacy was only acknowledged within circles of women with similar experiences. For Margaret, such a circle might have included friends Madeline Crump and DJ Ross. It was not until the 1970s that same-sex attraction was beginning to be accepted.[3]

Most importantly, Margaret's connection with Con was an ideal antidote to the misery of her marriage, and friends attested to their fond and affectionate relationship. A New York friend of Con's wrote to Margaret in 1955, concerned about difficulties Con was encountering at work. 'Without you to come home to each night, it would be so much more unbearable.'[4] Violinist Beryl Kimber Leske, who met Margaret in the 1950s, was 'moved by their deeply warm relationship—respect, happiness, admiration, love and humour shared. I cannot imagine Margaret without Con'. 'Connie was an absolute honey of a woman, the sort of person you'd think you could live with all right', said composer Helen Gifford. 'She was quiet, had sweet humour and tolerance—a really nice counterpart to a passionate lady.'[5]

Although Con was not a musician, she and Margaret had much in common. They fought for causes they believed in and were independent thinkers willing to go against the grain. A large, imposing woman with a big, booming voice, Con was educated at the University of Melbourne, and was often seen riding her motorcycle across campus. Margaret could understand and respect Con's achievements in the fields of international and social affairs, and her commitment to the peace movement and to helping refugees.[6]

During this period of fulfilment, Margaret organised soirées in her Studley Avenue home, launched new publishing and performance initiatives for Australian composers, and maintained her involvement in the Lyceum Club and the Catalysts, where she delivered substantial papers in 1953 ('Loose Legs in Europe'), 1956 ('Chant Intérieur') and 1959 ('One Lap Behind').

Margaret remained a committed lobbyist, activist and spokesperson for Australian music. In January 1948, she was a witness on the Parliamentary Standing Committee on Broadcasting, advocating for a £5000 fund to publish and record Australian music. Two months later, she was guest editor of the ABC *Women's Session*, where she interviewed Brian Jones from the British Council about English attitudes towards Australian composition. The next day, she was given a platform by the ABC to air her views in a program entitled *The Neglected Australian Composer*, when she gave examples of composers lost to Australia because they couldn't find an outlet for their music.[7]

Regular interactions with the ABC continued, and the gentler tone of her letters reflected her calmer life. Nevertheless, she was tenacious in pushing for recordings, broadcasts and public performances of her orchestral music, which she worked hard to bring to the notice of Sydney Symphony Orchestra (SSO) chief conductors Eugene Goossens (1947–56) and Nicolai Malko (1957–61), and Walter Susskind (1954–55) and Kurt Wöss (1956–59) in Melbourne.

Her activism was not confined to music. A program entitled *Let the Children Speak* hit a nerve. In July 1951, she wrote to ABC chairman Richard Boyer:

> Children are encouraged to lay bare a heterogeneous collection of facts—or possibly fiction—about their home life, with special reference to the relationship of their parents to each other and to the children themselves … I cannot help feeling it must have a bad effect on the children and sometimes devastating results at home. May I respectfully suggest that it should be discontinued indefinitely?[8]

Boyer agreed that the session could be 'a spur to precocity, of which heaven knows we have enough in our modern families without the aid of the ABC', but felt the program had merit. He assured her it would be kept 'on healthy lines'.[9] Margaret was dissatisfied:

> Having had first-hand experience of the disastrous effects upon children's minds of certain kinds of child propaganda, I wrote on an impulse, and possibly sounded a very school-marmy kind of female, but the harm such broadcasts could do to certain children far outweighs their value to any adults of being reminded of their own far-distant childhood.[10]

Generally, however, Margaret relaxed and enjoyed music, art, social occasions and interstate travel. In late August 1948, she opened an exhibition of Australian artist Max Ragless's work, the first held at the Book Club Gallery in Collins Street (co-directed by her cousin Sheila). Her spirits were further lifted by the news that English singer Sophie Wyss loved her songs and planned to introduce them in BBC broadcasts and concerts.[11]

The decade's end was marked by a revival of Margaret's *Suite for Orchestra on a Theme by Purcell* by the Kew Philharmonic Society on 11 May 1948, 'a splendid piece' according to *Herald* critic John Sinclair.[12] A year later, Margaret went to Sydney to hear Eugene Goossens conduct the work in an SSO Sunday matinee free concert at the Sydney Town Hall.

Although press reception was underwhelming, the trip was not wasted. Margaret was interviewed by the *Sydney Morning Herald* about the current status of Australian music and reiterated her argument for government subsidies for the publication of 'worthwhile music'. 'The composer must either go overseas to live', she argued, 'or else send his work out of this country to publishers who think twice before they risk putting money into launching the works of someone unknown to them'.[13]

Goossens had made an impact as guest conductor, and was appointed SSO chief conductor in 1947, remaining until 1956. He succeeded Heinze, who had long been pushing for permanent professional orchestras in capital cities—as Goossens continued to do—to give players employment security. (The orchestras were under the aegis of the ABC but were also funded by state governments.) This happened first in 1946, with the SSO in Sydney. Melbourne followed three years later, when the Victorian Government finally agreed to co-fund the orchestra. Sydney was advantaged by having one chief conductor for nine years; in the same period, the Victorian Symphony Orchestra (VSO) had five, the first being Heinze.[14] Nevertheless, the VSO achieved increasingly high standards, especially with fine Eastern European refugee musicians immigrating to Melbourne before, during and after World War II.

Musical evenings at Studley Avenue were a feature of Margaret's post-marriage life. These took place in her large ground-floor music room, which had two pianos and looked out onto the street through wisteria-edged windows. Some musicians were heard for the first time in Melbourne, including piano duo Max Olding and Pamela Page, for whom Margaret wrote *Pavan and Canonical Piece* (1957). Beryl Kimber Leske performed Margaret's works with her, among them her *Sonatina for Oboe (or Violin) and Piano,* and a piano and violin reduction version of *Fantasy* for orchestra (1958), both recorded by the ABC in 1958. Kimber enjoyed visiting this 'lovely house with a cultural atmosphere' and recalled Margaret's flexibility regarding the *Sonatina*'s interpretation. 'I can't remember what I wrote there', Margaret would say, 'so just play what you like—it is the overall effect that matters—no fussing!'[15] She was not averse to 'fussing' when necessary, but she trusted Kimber, and was relaxed in the context of these happy musical evenings.

Violinist Sybil Copeland and her viola-playing husband John Glickman, who arrived in Melbourne from the UK in 1955, were regulars at Studley Avenue. They felt 'fortunate to have known [Margaret] for many years, to have played with her and had some very beautiful music written for us'. Composers given opportunities to air their works were Helen Gifford, Esther Rofe and Dorian Le Gallienne.[16]

Con also hosted get-togethers, usually to raise money for welfare schemes, and invited her professional colleagues and Lyceum Club members who were mutual friends of Con and Margaret. Conversations covered a range of topics, including the challenges faced by women in pursuing careers and interests. This may have been the catalyst for Margaret joining the League of Women Voters, where she was active for a time. An atmosphere of mutual encouragement and camaraderie marked these events.[17]

In the early 1950s, Margaret was invited to join the Australian Music Advisory Committee to UNESCO, which held its meetings in Sydney. She had a good instinct for power bases and had been lobbying governments for some time. The arts fared well under John Curtin, Australia's wartime prime minister from 1941 to 1945, who wanted to establish a ministry of fine arts. As secretary of the Department of Post-War Reconstruction (1943–48), Dr HC (Nugget) Coombs proposed a federal arts funding plan. Melbourne University economics professor Lyndhurst Giblin, in his capacity as chair of the Commonwealth Financial and Economic Committee, was the government's adviser on the matter, and asked Margaret what funding was required for music.[18] Regrettably, this idea was quashed when Robert Menzies' Liberal Coalition government won power in 1949.

In her opinion, the UNESCO invitation 'was the sop to silence' her. 'I was not representing anything—everybody else represented something'.[19] Nevertheless, she remained on the committee until the late 1960s, during which time she witnessed the appointment of several national representatives, most of whom she thought were ineffectual. One was Sir Bernard Heinze (knighted in 1949), who held the role for three years in the early 1950s. His brief was to 'press for recognition by the International Society of Contemporary Music (ISCM), which worked through UNESCO for music copying, recording and distribution'.[20] Margaret's disrespect for Heinze persisted. 'We could get nowhere, because he wouldn't do his homework. He had no conception of UNESCO being a reciprocal thing.'[21]

Margaret was productive in all genres, with a noticeable surge in orchestral writing. Her compositions from this time are often referred to as her 'late works', and demonstrate her individual interpretation of English and European musical developments between the wars. The harmonic vocabulary of her earlier works remained, but she had moved beyond the more sensuous impressionism and post-impressionism. Her harmonic palate was now more strongly informed by such composers as Bartók, Hindemith, Stravinsky, Shostakovich and Prokofiev.[22]

In *Old Australian Bush Ballads* (1948), Margaret set to music thirteen Australian folk songs collected by nationalist writer Vance Palmer. He wanted to preserve contact with the simple, democratic tradition of campfire folksong, and Margaret's brief was to re-create and notate the music to which these ballads would originally have been sung. She relied on 'her instinct for appropriate melody when there was no-one who remembered the original tunes'.[23] The settings are necessarily simple, accessible, and playable by piano or guitar, evident in ABC federal music editor Willy Redstone's comment that they 'are written in the popular style (verses and refrains)'. As was often the case, Margaret used some of these settings in different contexts, drawing on melodies from 'The Banks of the Condamine' and 'The Stockman's Last Bed' as themes for two orchestral works, *Ballad Overture* (1948) and *Bush Ballad* (1954) respectively.[24]

This collection, published by Allans in 1948, was atypical of Margaret's work for three reasons. She believed that Australian identity should be incorporated in music in subtle rather than realistic ways. Second, these nationalistic poems reflect a masculine tradition. Last, the raw, uncultivated qualities of the poems contrast with the refined, lyrical and often ethereal poetry that she favoured. On this occasion, Margaret's love of nature and the Australian bush prevailed, together with her belief in the importance of recording Australia's heritage. Around this time, she also set Palmer's poems 'The Pathfinders' and 'Youth and Age', which address themes she favoured—the passing of time, and death.

The turn of the decade was notable for the first of eight settings of Australian poet Judith Wright. Between 1949 and 1951, Margaret set four poems for piano and mezzo soprano—the most natural vocal range, in her opinion: 'Bullocky' from Wright's 1946 collection *The Moving Image*, and 'Midnight', 'Woman's Song' and 'The Twins' from *Woman to Man* (1949). In 1962, she set two more poems, 'The Old Prison' from *Woman to Man* and 'Winter Kestrel' from *Birds*. These were published as *Six Songs* in 1967 by Allans. Her other two Wright settings were 'And Mr Ferritt' from *The Two Fires* (1955) in choral and string quartet versions, and 'The World and the Child' (1959) from *Woman to Man* for voice and string trio.

As with John Shaw Neilson, Margaret's relationship with Wright was artistic—they did not know each other well, but Wright's poetry suggested to her something beyond words. 'Judith's writing seemed to me to be meaningful—even musical.' They were kindred spirits on two subjects: love of the Australian landscape, and the feminine themes of procreation, motherhood and childhood, particularly evident in Wright's *Woman to Man* series. The *Six Songs* incorporate themes of birth, death and rebirth, elemental life and its attendant mysteries, and time, decay and transformation from the perspective of Australian heritage.[25]

From the early 1940s, when she was in her mid-twenties, Wright was going deaf, and did not consider herself musically educated. She was ambivalent about the transformation of her poetry into music, but admired Margaret's work:

> Of course I am delighted that you have set some of my verses to music, especially that you have found their auditory qualities good enough for the purpose. I always feel that verse ought to be close enough to music for them to meet somewhere, but have doubted whether I myself manage to keep my own rule; I seldom feel I get a really good vowel-pattern either for speech or singing. I very much hope I shall hear your settings one day.[26]

With a temporary improvement in her hearing, she listened to them, and appreciated the results, particularly 'Woman's Song'.[27]

In early May 1950, Margaret visited Adelaide with Lorna for the first Festival of Australian Contemporary Music at Adelaide University's Bonython Hall, where several of her works were performed. In anticipation, the *Advertiser* published an article about the importance of showcasing Australia's female composers. Pointing out that the festival would 'provide a long-awaited opportunity for the works of leading Australian composers, both men and women, to be presented', the author noted that 'Margaret Sutherland is recognised as one of Australia's outstanding composers. Her work has a distinctive quality rare in much contemporary music. It is never static because she is constantly experimenting'.[28]

In the opening concert of choral and chamber music on 2 May, Margaret's Shaw Neilson settings, the *Five Songs*, were performed by soprano Kathleen Glastonbury and the composer. Clarinettist Cleve Martin joined from offstage in *The Orange Tree*. In a program with some 'richly rewarding moments', wrote John Sinclair, 'good, bad, and indifferent works rubbed shoulders in a highly indigestible mixture of styles and standards'. Fortunately, he placed Margaret's songs in the first category. 'She chooses her poetry with extreme care and disciplines her setting with sensitive craftsmanship and fine taste.'[29]

In the second concert two days later, South Australian Symphony Orchestra (SASO) concertmaster Sam Bor and Margaret played her *Sonata for Violin and Piano* (1925). They 'conveyed a feeling of nostalgia' in the first movement, and 'seemed to conjure up the atmosphere of the birds and trees and great open spaces', thought *Advertiser* critic Harold Tidemann. The *House Quartet* (1942) made a reappearance, with Cleve Martin (clarinet), Robertson Collins (viola), Eldon Fox (cello) and Margaret on piano combining 'to produce an exquisite whole'.[30]

Orchestral compositions performed by the SASO under John Bishop—by then head of Adelaide's Elder Conservatorium—featured on 6 May. The *Suite for Orchestra on a Theme by Purcell* (1935) was Margaret's contribution. Tidemann pronounced it a 'brilliantly clever' work that 'contained everything one likes to hear in such a work—a delightful variation on the theme, a gambolling scherzo, a blustering gigue and an intriguing Passacaglia with fragments of the theme wandering round like disembodied spirits. A country dance and dramatic finale concluded a successful work'. In contrast, the *News*'s Nadra Penalurick considered it 'an unusual piece of writing' that 'called for some imagination on the part of the players'.[31]

Margaret was 'disappointed with the apathy of sections of the Adelaide public' about the festival but delighted with the 'tremendous amount of work and organisation' that made it a success. Presaging the biennial Adelaide Festival of the Arts that started ten years later, she asserted that the festival 'could develop on still grander lines', envisaging 'a future programme that would include drama and ballet as well as music'.[32]

With more time on her hands, Margaret tackled orchestral works. Her ambition to prove herself in music's most valued realm overruled her earlier preference for chamber music. Orchestration was challenging, partly due to her failing eyesight and the time required to copy parts, but also because she sometimes struggled to write in the most appropriate range for some instruments. A friend, composer Robert Hughes, assisted with several orchestral works from this period. *Haunted Hills* (1950), arguably her most symphonic work, was the first.[33]

'It has been the fashion over the last twenty years', Margaret wrote in 1958, 'for composers to give general, non-committal titles to their works'. While there was much to be said in favour of a 'classifying' title, there were times 'when a descriptive title seems the only appropriate one'. The title may have originated from the name given to hills near Moe in Gippsland, Victoria, but Margaret sketched *Haunted Hills* in the Dandenong Ranges east of Melbourne in the autumn of 1950. The work reflects her profound appreciation for Australia's natural environment. 'The underlying urge, or feeling, was born of the sheer physical age of these hills', she wrote. It was also 'a sound picture written in contemplation of the first people who roamed the hills—their bewilderment and their betrayal', with the seeming gaiety of its frenzied dance 'born of despair'.[34]

As suggested by Margaret's support of Aboriginal tenor Harold Blair in the 1940s, she was sensitive to the plight of Australia's Indigenous peoples through white exploitation of their culture. Although she later admitted that this was why she wrote it, she initially preferred not to emphasise the role of Aboriginal people in inspiring *Haunted Hills*; it should be 'about the future, to get away from the ghastliness' of their predicament. Her diffidence is equally attributable to her distaste for those composers who mimicked sounds or rituals to express 'Australianism'.[35]

In October 1950, Margaret showed the score to Goossens, who wanted to premier it in March 1951 in Sydney. She immediately sent it to William James. As ever, the process of parts copying was fraught, and after her request for assistance, the ABC struck a deal that it would take care of the strings if she did the woodwind and brass parts. Goossens and the SSO performed it on 22 March. One review suggests that Hughes's input occurred later: it 'showed evidence of imagination and sensibility, despite a lack of formal cohesion and a pianistic approach to orchestration'. Goossens conducted the piece again at a VSO concert at the Melbourne Town Hall on 13 October. The *Argus*'s Biddy Allen thought it achieved Margaret's aim, referring to it as a significant example of Australian 'nature-music' that 'conveys the inner mood of our alternately hostile and alluring bush'. *Herald* critic John Sinclair was tentative. Possibly responding to the work's modern, assertive dissonance, he determined that it was worthy of respect, 'but several more hearings would be necessary before I could feel confident of understanding its essence'. The ABC federal music editor, composer John Antill, wrote a disparaging report when the work was under consideration for recording in 1955. 'Little of musical consequence eventuates in this piece', he wrote. 'The emphasis is on effect rather than on melodic interest and, in this direction, it appears fairly successful and justifies its title.'[36]

Margaret attended another performance of *Haunted Hills* at the Adelaide Australian Music Commonwealth Jubilee Festival in late August 1951, with John Bishop leading the SASO. Enid Robertson of the *Advertiser* liked its atmosphere and scoring, though noted 'some queer things going on among the horns'.[37] At the opening concert on 22 August, Margaret accompanied Cleve Martin in her *Sonata for Clarinet and Piano,* and the Adelaide Singers performed her Shaw Neilson choral setting of *Quietly as Rosebuds* (1934). Her *String Quartet No. 1* was played at the third concert on 27 August.

By this time, Margaret and Con were planning an extended trip to Europe, both for leisure and to promote her music. Margaret's brother Douglas had died in Perth five years earlier and left her a small sum of money, which financed the adventure for both.[38]

They could not depart, however, until after a recital devoted to Margaret's chamber works at the Assembly Hall on 5 November. This was the second in a series of three concerts featuring Australian composers organised by the University of Melbourne Conservatorium of Music, the ABC and the *Argus* as part of the Commonwealth's Jubilee year. Included was the first performance of the three settings from

Judith Wright's *Woman to Man* collection ('Midnight', 'Woman's Song', 'The Twins).[39] Margaret accompanied Elsa Haas, and Thomas White (clarinet) joined for *The Orange Tree* (1938). Also programmed was the *Serenade for Oboe and String Quartet* (1950) in a version for clarinet and strings, and the *Trio in C Major* (1935), usually for clarinet, violin and piano, but on this occasion with VSO principal bassoonist Tom Wightman substituting for the violin. The *Canon* reviewer found the *Trio* the most interesting. It 'showed a side of the composer's character which is not often foremost in her music—urbane and accomplished, conversationally witty, content to make an effect only incidentally'. This ambiguous statement upheld the *Canon*'s disclaimer: 'The contents of a review express the subjective reaction of the author at a particular time, and there may be as many views as there are critics'.[40]

Following this farewell concert, Margaret and Con had three weeks to prepare for the long sojourn abroad. Margaret wrote to James at the ABC, asking for letters of introduction, and he quickly obliged, with letters addressed to the ABC's representative in London, Thomas Bearup, and to Leslie Boosey at music publishing house Boosey & Hawkes.[41] On 27 November, they departed Melbourne on the QSMV *Dominion Monarch* for the four-week voyage to England. In Cape Town, they visited Margaret's friend singer Ivy Smuts (née Phillips), who had married the cousin of South African prime minister Jan Christian Smuts and settled in South Africa. They stopped at Las Palmas in Spain, where Margaret remarked upon the exotic landscape, camels, donkeys and ancient buildings, but she and Con were saddened by poor and hungry cave-dwelling families.

They docked at sunny Southampton on 26 December and boarded a train to London's Waterloo Station. They stayed at Helen Graham House, a hostel with a 'grand friendly feeling' opposite the British Museum in central London. In January 1952, they moved to longer-term accommodation in Bramham Gardens, South Kensington.

The two quickly embarked on sightseeing and social engagements. Three days after their arrival, they visited Southwark Cathedral and the British Museum before dining with Clive Carey and his wife Doris at the International Music Council. Then followed several months of sightseeing, social commitments, concerts, opera, theatre, movies, art exhibitions, and horticultural and flower shows. There were walks in Hyde Park, Regent's Park, Hampstead Heath, Kew Gardens, Windsor Great Park and Epping Forest, and talks on a variety of cultural, political and scientific topics.[42]

On New Year's Day 1952, Margaret attended a concert at the Society for the Promotion of New Music, where she met composers including London-born Elisabeth Lutyens and Australian-born Arthur Benjamin, then resident in London. The next day, she deposited scores with Boosey & Hawkes. These included the three-movement, twelve-minute *Concerto for Strings* (1948–49), which has achieved almost legendary status for its rejection by this publisher. In pointing out the 'frightful prejudice' she had encountered over the years, Margaret often cited this example.[43] Initially interested in the work, they changed their minds once they discovered M Sutherland was a woman.[44] Discrimination against women's music, conscious or unconscious, was alive and well in England in the 1950s, further confirmed by the BBC's response to Margaret's music.

Stylistically the concerto could be categorised as neoclassical. Despite its overtones of English music, with some resonances with Shostakovich and Bartók, it is quintessentially Margaret. Each movement is based on a single theme that nods to baroque music, but there are modal harmonies and judicious use of dissonance, as well as variations in mood from the melancholic to the exuberant.[45]

Margaret did not give up. In early 1953, she sent the score to James at the ABC. 'It is (I think, and I am told) effective and incisive for strings and I have good parts for reproduction.' It was published in 1953, and in 1955, the ABC made a poor recording of it, which Margaret later refused to have included in a commercial recording by EMI. The work was nominated with six Australian works for inclusion in concerts at the first South-East Asia Regional Music Conference in Manila in August. It was also chosen by Susskind, Bishop and Goossens, who comprised the Australian Score-Reading Committee to select works for submission to the ISCM World Festival in Baden-Baden. It didn't get past the ISCM jury, however, and was not publicly premiered until 1956, when Heinze conducted the SASO.[46]

Concerto for Strings was well received in Australia, vindicating Margaret's persistence. When Australian pianist and composer Una Bourne heard the broadcast of the first performance, she wrote to Margaret:

> Best congratulations. We've listened to your *Concerto for Strings*. It came over the air splendidly, and <u>what</u> a warm, spontaneous reception it received. We were thrilled when you were at last 'found' in the audience and the tumultuous applause nearly broke our radio.[47]

When it first emerged, Australian composer Peter Sculthorpe was 'tremendously impressed with the work'. 'It was like no other music I had ever heard, and I felt that this was my first encounter with a truly original and Australian voice.' The work has stood the test of time. In an *Age* review of a 2012 performance at BMW Edge in Melbourne, Clive O'Connell similarly observed its originality. 'It raises no eyebrows these days', he observed, but in its time 'it stood in severe contrast to the blandness that passed for new Australian music'.[48]

Margaret visited several more London publishers, including Chester Music, Elkin and Augener, but only the latter published a work—her *Six Profiles* for piano (c. 1946) in 1953. She also approached the BBC, despite having had no luck in earlier years, except for her *Trio in C Major for Clarinet, Violin and Piano* (1935), performed in 1937. She submitted sixteen (mostly chamber) works, which she thought would be quickly evaluated, but possibly inadvertently sabotaged her chances by not submitting orchestral or vocal works. It is notable that panel members (all male) had the orthodox musical education that Margaret had spurned. Their reports were condescending and sometimes hostile. She was criticised for amateurism, domestic (Australian) content, instrumental choices, accompaniment writing, musical instructions, melodic development and harmonic progressions.[49]

By contrast, although the ABC didn't accept everything Margaret submitted, it recorded at least fifty-six of her works, several of which were released commercially. Naturally, it was more invested than the BBC in disseminating Australian compositions, and Margaret had established a level of rapport she could never have had with the ABC's UK equivalent. Her response to the rejections is not recorded, though she may have found consolation through being in good company. Many eminent contemporaries—particularly women—received the same treatment. Elisabeth Lutyens attested to experiencing discrimination, even with the obvious advantage of being English rather than 'from the colonies'.[50]

On 16 February 1952, Margaret attended the launch of the Australian Musical Association (AMA) at Australia House in London. The AMA was formed by Australian composer Don Banks in response to the perceived need to support Australian musicians in the UK and raise their profile. It existed for twenty years. Margaret contended that Australian musicians should study overseas but return to Australia, as she had done. 'We produce an astonishingly high proportion of fine musicians; they go overseas and there they stay—and few people ever realise that they originally came from Australia.'[51]

Margaret was extremely fond of Banks and revered his music. He became a close friend with whom she corresponded regularly, candidly and affectionately for twenty-five years. She offered suggestions for promoting his music in Melbourne and bemoaned the Australian musical climate, but also wrote about personal issues. Margaret's trust in and respect for him meant that, along with other Australian musicians, including Australian conductor Charles Mackerras, she was happy to help administer the AMA:

> After several meetings we decided to arrange concerts and to publicise the activities of our musicians, as well as to establish a library of musical scores and records and to submit our best work to both British and international organisations ... One of the most important functions of the association ... will be to advise students, many of whom come from Australia with all too little knowledge of what lies ahead.[52]

The AMA provided information on grants, scholarships, competitions, prizes, concerts, lectures and summer schools, and options for mentorship and accommodation. Through this work, Margaret connected with the Composers' Guild of Great Britain, which showed interest in collaborating with Australian composers. She became the guild's musical adviser for Australia for three years from 1952. She also joined the London Contemporary Music Centre, with her music included in a concert of Australian composers on 29 February.[53]

With her eyes deteriorating, in early March Margaret consulted renowned Scottish ophthalmologist Sir Stewart Duke-Elder, founder of the Institute of Ophthalmology, surgeon–oculist to royalty and long-time editorial committee chairman of the *British Journal of Ophthalmology*. He said her 'old trouble' was stable, but she had cataracts. Perhaps she had glaucoma—though there appears to have been no family history—or a form of macular degeneration. According to her grandson, Anthony Bunney, Margaret blamed her poor eyesight on an excess of the close work involved in composing.[54]

May 1952 was a busy month. Margaret played at a contemporary music recital at the Mercury Theatre on 15 May. Soprano Sophie Wyss and clarinettist George Draper performed her *September* (1930s) for voice and clarinet, and Margaret joined them for *The Orange Tree* (1938). In the audience was Don Banks, who provided much-appreciated praise. On 29 May, Margaret and Con attended the first AMA concert, an informal event presenting French, British and Australian works, which had been 'ticklish to arrange'.[55]

At the end of May, Margaret accompanied Jack Brymer in her *Sonata for Clarinet and Piano* (1947) in a private recital in Hindhead (southwest of London). He 'gave a really eloquent performance', Margaret wrote. At the same event, Sophie Wyss made up the trio for *The Orange Tree*. Brymer thanked Margaret for the opportunity of playing her sonata 'with your excellent accompaniment; I enjoyed it very much and had very much hoped to broadcast it with you before your return—but the BBC is not an easy body, as you know'. He requested a copy, 'and you can be sure lots of people will both try it and hear it', he reassured her.[56]

Margaret and Con ventured beyond London, visiting Devon and Cornwall in April, and Cambridge and Canterbury in May. These short trips provided a taste of what was to come—a six-week trip to the

Continent in 'Maggie the Magnificent'. Maggie the car was owned by the family of two young Australian women Margaret had met at an AMA event, who had casually suggested that she and Con join them for their European escapade. 'There could be no possible doubt as to the answer', wrote Margaret, and they 'turned out to be a most harmonious quartet. There were never any tempo troubles', and they 'entirely agreed on the "louds and softs"'.[57]

The day after the Hindhead concert, they were off. After a soothing night in a seafront B&B in Folkestone, where there were 'masses of doilies and crochet-ing and tatting and photographs in silver frames', they drove Maggie, with 'a load of Amazonian proportions' onto the ferry and sailed for Ostend in Belgium. Their road trip took them to Bruges, Ghent and Brussels in Belgium, then to the north of France 'through all the country made so deeply familiar to Australians during World War I'. These travels 'were really golden days', wrote Margaret. 'Lunch was an affair of cheese, tomatoes, rolls, and cherries as large as plums, followed by *vin du pays*, under a beech, or an elm, while Maggie browsed contentedly nearby.'

Paris was next, where 'Madame-on-the-boulevards was as exquisite as ever', and Margaret paid a visit to Louise Hanson-Dyer. While French villages such as Vézelay were enchanting, others were 'pock-marked and severely bombed … testimony to the recentness of their grim ordeal'. Italy was next—Rapallo, Pisa, the Carrara Mountains, 'dreamlike' Florence, Ferrara, and Venice, where Margaret experienced the lack of tooting vehicles as heaven, and they lapped their way ecstatically along the canals. St Mark's was 'just as the story books said' and 'beatific contentment spread over us', Margaret rhapsodised, 'as the quiet softness of Venice enfolded us'.[58]

Via the beautiful Grossglockner Pass, they continued to Austria. After a 'most soul-satisfying drive' they reached Salzburg, where the ISCM's annual festival was underway. This proved disappointing due to a new rule that every financial member-nation must be represented, regardless of quality, which resulted in unbalanced programs. Lack of rehearsal was another problem, and the score for the only Australian work performed—a fine work by Don Banks—was not seen by players until the afternoon of the concert. But to wander in woods near Salzburg was 'sheer delight', and the quartet lunched, browsed and 'drank beer in unblemished peace'.

After visiting Innsbruck, they departed for Switzerland—Zürich, Interlaken and Lucerne—'lingering beside the tranquil lakes as the light changed from drenching sun to the intense blue of early twilight'. Germany was next, with war-damaged Freiburg first on the list, followed by Heidelberg. In Bacharach, they were forced to halt to witness 'the most spectacular of Wagnerian storms'. In Cologne, Margaret and Con parted from their friends and boarded the overnight train to the Hague via Rotterdam, where they talked far into the night with their hosts. Amsterdam was the final stop of a wonderful few weeks that reminded Margaret that 'life as it is being lived—at this very minute—enthralls one'.[59]

Although Margaret was sad to leave the Continent, there were events to look forward to before she and Con returned to Australia. The second AMA gathering on 10 July attracted a full house of 120. Unfortunately, the musical program was marred by critic Neville Cardus, who had returned from Australia to live in London. Addressing the audience, he 'wiped off all Australian composers' to date. Margaret was horrified and tackled him afterwards in 'a ding-dong argument wherein he tried to be as rude as he knew how to me'.[60]

More pleasant experiences included a UN garden party at 10 Downing Street with Con on 13 July. On 9 August, it was off to Glyndebourne in 'lovely rolling country' near Lewes, East Sussex, which has hosted an annual opera festival since 1934. Margaret and Con heard a program of British composers Purcell and Britten given by the Glyndebourne Opera Chorus and the London Philharmonic Orchestra.

The annual Edinburgh International Festival of Music and Drama was a must. On 17 August, Margaret and Con attended the opening ceremony—full of pomp and circumstance—where the Duke of Edinburgh and the Chilean president spoke. At the opening concert, they heard British conductor Sir Thomas Beecham conduct

London's Royal Philharmonic Orchestra in Sibelius's *Symphony No. 1*, 'a thrilling performance of a work that can be so torpid and dull', Margaret declared.

The pair spent a late August day surveying the abbey and Roman ruins in St Albans, northeast of London, and then enjoyed a nine-day 'farewell idyll' in a friend's 'sweet, airy, polished-up little cottage' in Bramley, southwest of London. There were 'apples everywhere, and lovely fresh brown eggs', and they enjoyed the 'simple life', walks, drives and sightseeing. It was here that Margaret heard of Jenifer's engagement to Dean Bunney (they married in 1953), which came as a 'bombshell', possibly because Margaret had met Dean only once. While sad to leave, the break was refreshing, and Margaret felt 'reconciled to taking up the reins at home once more'.

After helping organise the AMA's future management on 11 September, Margaret and Con had a final weekend away in a friend's 'dear little white-washed thatched cottage' near Chelmsford in Essex. 'A little down, a little forbidding', Essex nevertheless had 'simple unconscious charm'.[61]

There were more plays and concerts before a melancholic farewell at St Pancras Station in London on 26 September. Margaret and Con boarded the *Orontes* the same day and found their 'commodious cabin' for the voyage back to Melbourne. They docked at Station Pier, Melbourne, on 29 October 1952.

Life in Melbourne took up where it left off. Con was appointed city organiser of the University of Melbourne's International House Appeal, which occupied her until 1955.[62] Plans for the arts centre were bubbling away. The *Melbourne South Land Act*, drawn up in 1946, had never been proclaimed, and a 1953 Melbourne Master Plan that protected the site from commercial interests was yet to become law. After Keith Murdoch's death in 1952, the National Gallery trustees, National Gallery Society and the newly formed Arts Council of Australia (formerly CEMA) made deputations to successive state governments, but it was a period of unstable government, making raising funds and securing the site difficult. Campaigners could do little more than keep the venture on the political agenda, and in the newspapers—particularly the *Sun* and the *Herald*. Margaret did her bit, lobbying to have HM Queen Elizabeth II lay the foundation stone during her visit to Australia in February 1954. She hoped this would 'force the Government's hand and bring up public opinion in a big way, but all such moves are hard-going', and the attempt was unsuccessful.[63]

Margaret again expressed her opinion about the ABC in letters to the *Age*. On 27 March 1953, she complained about the commission's failure to provide advance notice of 'important works to be heard during the season'. Six weeks later, she wrote asking whether her recommendation had been made to the ABC.[64]

Spurred on by her musical experiences in Europe, Margaret founded the Camerata Society in 1953. The aim was to present concerts of twentieth-century music, with a focus on local composers, and her own 1950s works were often premiered.[65] Lack of funding meant it did not last beyond the late 1950s, but it was the precursor to the Melbourne branch of the ISCM established in the 1960s by James Murdoch. Margaret also reactivated her connection with the British Music Society, where the three songs from Judith Wright's *Woman to Man* collection were performed by Elsa Haas and the composer on 20 November 1952.

Keen to return to composing, Margaret wrote at least four works in 1953, including her second string quartet, *Discussion*, so-called because she wanted to emphasise the conversational nature of the medium, and share thematic material democratically among the four instruments. One of her major chamber works of the 1950s, this eight-minute, one-movement piece was first performed by the Paul McDermott String Quartet on 9 August 1954, when it made 'an excellent impression'. It was heard again on 16 July 1956—the 'animated and concise' piece 'was doubly welcome at its second hearing'. It has the free rondo-like structure adopted by the composer in several chamber works, though more dissonant. However, its chromaticism suggests an affinity with

Bartók and Hindemith, rather than with the Second Viennese School of Schoenberg, Webern and Berg, about which Margaret was dubious at best. The *Herald*'s John Sinclair considered it 'a vigorous, cleanly-written and tersely constructed work, packed with invention and wit'. The *Age* critic tried his own brand of wit in a patronising review: 'All four instruments aired their own views, none of which appeared to be compatible, and the argument became rather heated towards the finish. It could have been a discussion between four women about a hat or a piece of bric-a-brac'. Clearly Bishop, Goossens and Susskind had a higher opinion, since they selected it (with *Concerto for Strings*) for the ISCM World Festival in Baden-Baden in 1955. Adelaide's Gerhardt String Quartet also liked the piece and recorded it for the ABC in 1958.[66]

Margaret produced two orchestral works in 1953—*Homage to JS Bach*, a relatively simple work, which combined with two other pieces, *Pastorale* and *Walking Tune*, to become *Threesome*. The second was *Open Air Piece*, an overture intended for youth orchestras and audiences. It was premiered and recorded by the SSO under Goossens in April 1955 and won the £150 prize in its section of the Queensland Centenary Competition in 1959. Although this work 'captures the sounds of the wind and galloping horses', 'these are merely suggestions of mood, and have no hint of "programme"', Margaret claimed.[67]

Back in the mid-1940s, Margaret had composed *Four Symphonic Concepts*, which she referred to variously as studies, a suite and a symphony. She entered it in an Australian Jubilee symphony competition in 1951, where it was judged among the top ten of eighty-seven entries. It won no awards, as it possibly failed to satisfy traditional criteria for a symphony. It appears never to have been performed in its entirety, but the VSO, conducted by Goossens, played it on 31 July and 2 August 1954 without the fourth movement, and renamed *Triptych*. According to Margaret, she hadn't completed the fourth movement, but Goossens 'wanted something quickly'.[68]

It may have been this occasion that prompted Margaret's negative view of Goossens. She was dismayed when he shortened the work to fit into a preordained timeslot. Wearing his hat as a composer—not a good one, according to Margaret—'he proceeded to cut bars here and bars there, till the work was completely changed and disconnected'. When she complained, he responded that he knew what he was doing, 'so he just took over'. She vowed never to allow something so 'frightful' to happen again.[69] The fourth movement, 'Vistas', was not heard until it appeared in a free ABC MSO concert in late August 1968.

The *Age* critic (possibly Dorian Le Gallienne) commented that 'the strength of this work was its pervading femininity'. This term was not usually applied to Margaret's music, which on several previous occasions had been referred to as 'virile'. It might be interpreted as sexist nowadays but was clearly intended as a compliment in 1954. The *Herald*'s John Sinclair's assessment demonstrates a more nuanced understanding of Margaret's intentions. 'It is the music of a sensitive writer searching for a personal language. Its essence is rather elusive, perhaps because Miss Sutherland tends to avoid the obvious and to approach her central thought by a series of oblique references.'[70]

In 1955, Margaret wrote the *Trio for Oboe and Two Violins*, notable for several reasons. It was written for three musicians who had recently arrived in Melbourne, and who were to become regular collaborators. They were married couple Sybil Copeland (violin) and John Glickman (violin/viola) and oboist Jiří Tancibudek. The latter had arrived in Sydney in 1950 after escaping the communist regime in Czechoslovakia and was appointed principal oboe in the VSO in 1953. Margaret admired Tancibudek's playing and wrote several works with him in mind—*Serenade for Oboe and String Quartet* (1950s), *Sonatina for Oboe (or Violin) and Piano* (1954) and *Concertante for Oboe and Strings* (1961). Tancibudek considered Margaret one of Australia's most original composers, whose extraordinary qualities were reflected in her music. She was an interesting person who knew what she wanted, he thought, though there was something negative that he couldn't describe. Perhaps he detected in her demeanour the collective impact of her life's trials and traumas, both personal and professional. The *Trio* was first performed in October 1955 at a concert of the Soirées Musicales Chamber Music Society, formed by Ukrainian immigrant violist Mischa Kogan in 1950.[71] The same musicians performed it during Musica Viva's Olympic Festival in Melba Hall in December 1956.

Second, it is another example of Margaret's penchant for unusual instrumental blends. Third, it attracted the interest of two world-renowned Ukrainian violinists, father and son David and Igor Oistrakh, who asked her for a work for two violins in late 1958.[72] In a letter dated 6 July 1959, David Oistrakh wrote to Margaret:

> Now I and Igor are studying your Sonata with growing interest, and are looking forward that it will be possible to perform it, so as trio for two violins and oboe, during the winter season in Moscow to make us musically acquainted with your art. We are very thankful for your intention to dedicate it to us.[73]

Fourth, it was recorded by Brolga (named after an Australian native crane bird), a recording company Margaret helped found, and was one of only a handful of her compositions commercially recorded before 1960. Finally, it was published in the late 1950s by Kurrajong Press (named after the Australian tree), established by Margaret in 1957 with funding assistance from businessman and philanthropist Kenneth Myer. The press's express purpose was to publish Australian compositions, since, according to Margaret, other music publishers were not committed to doing so. But works should not be 'complex or lengthy', she counselled Sculthorpe in her invitation to submit works.[74] Unfortunately, neither Brolga nor Kurrajong Press was a commercial success, and existed only briefly. They were, nevertheless, further testimony to Margaret's persistent efforts on behalf of Australian music.

This letter to Sculthorpe was the first in an exchange that lasted until 1963, when Margaret lost respect for his music. Of *Sun Music* (1965) she commented in 1968, 'Even the opening phrase cloys with me now. Turgid portly music'. Her opinion had not changed by 1972, when she decided that he 'was just out for commercial gain', and 'had only really written one thing because it's over and over and over and over'.[75]

Meanwhile, there were developments with the arts centre. In 1954, Radio Corporation, whose parent company director, Arthur Warner, was Liberal MP for the state seat of Higginbotham, was given permission by the government to build a factory on the Wirth's Park site to manufacture vinyl records. Warner's action aroused such public indignation that support for the art gallery and arts centre strengthened. In his campaign in 1955, Henry Bolte stated that if elected, his Liberal government would appoint trustees to control the Wirth's Park area. True to his word, among the rush of new legislation introduced in his first few months of office, the *Melbourne South Land Act* was finally proclaimed in 1956, setting up a trust fund to receive the revenue from Wirth's Park leases and public contributions. The Act led to the appointment of a National Gallery and Cultural Centre Building Committee, which officially took control of the Wirth's Park site and assumed responsibility for the creation of the new gallery and arts centre.[76]

Margaret persisted with her arts centre lobbying as her dear friend Lorna Stirling was dying prematurely, of cancer, finally losing the battle on 9 February 1956. Margaret's response to this is not documented, but one can only imagine that Con and other friends supported her through what was yet another period of grief—the one sad event in an otherwise happy and productive decade.

To Margaret's surprise, Heinze supported her music in two ways in mid-1956. His biographer, Thérèse Radic, affirmed that audiences loved him, but his players 'generally considered him dictatorial, anti-female, and someone to be feared. His extensive influence ensured that a word in the right quarter could make or break a career'. There were, indeed, occasions when Heinze exercised his influence in ways unhelpful to Margaret's career. For example, according to John Hopkins, whenever he brought up Margaret's name at Commonwealth Assistance to Australian Composers (CAAC) board meetings, Heinze 'would go "B-b-b-boo-boo! Not an important composer"'.[77] Heinze was not always so dismissive, however. In early July, he wrote to Louise Hanson-Dyer to canvas her interest in publishing LP records of Australian chamber music. To this end, he asked the ABC whether it might send tapes of Margaret's chamber music to Éditions de l'Oiseau-Lyre.[78] And in August, Margaret received a letter reporting on a successful performance of her music. Three years earlier, she had composed *Adagio and Allegro Giocoso for Two*

Violins and Piano (1953), and the orchestrated version of the *Adagio* was programmed by Heinze for a tour of New Zealand with its national orchestra in August 1956:

> I feel sure that had you been present, you would have been delighted with the warm reception it received from the public. And I was so delighted and proud to have had the opportunity of presenting it here in New Zealand. I am looking forward to seeing you when I return.[79]

Margaret never trusted Heinze, but her vitriol was possibly as much directed at his public persona as at his treatment of her personally. They even agreed on some matters—for example, they both disputed that the development of original Australian music meant adopting Aboriginal rhythms or Australian bird song.[80]

The *Adagio and Allegro* were simpler harmonically than other works composed for two unaccompanied violins in the 1950s—*Contrasts* (1953) and *Six Bagatelles* (1956), which are models of conciseness. The *Bagatelles* originated from Margaret's work *Two Occasional Pieces*, with the four remaining movements added to provide a more substantial piece for Sybil Copeland and John Glickman, who performed it on several occasions. The first was at a recital of Margaret's music at the National Gallery of Victoria, to mark the opening of the watershed UNESCO Seminar on the Role of Music in Education in May–June 1956. Education was a cause dear to Margaret's heart, and as a member of the organising party, she played a major role in the ten-day seminar of lectures, discussions and music.[81]

The year 1956 brought a further example of Margaret's love of unusual instrumental blends: her *Quartet for Cor Anglais, Violin, Viola and Cello*. It was composed for Copeland and Glickman, who recorded it for the ABC in 1958 with David Woolley (cor anglais) and Otti Veit (cello). Margaret wanted to avoid treating the cor anglais as soloist and to give the instruments equal footing, and aimed to balance modal, tonal and chromatic harmonies. It was first performed at a memorial concert for Lorna Stirling in a program of works by Australian composers in the Assembly Hall on 1 April 1957, and again for the Camerata in June 1960.[82]

A year later, Margaret wrote her third major song cycle, *Four Blake Songs*—'Memory Hither Come', 'Piping Down the Valley Wild', 'How Sweet I Roamed' and 'The Jocund Dance'. Again, she was attracted by a mystical poet who celebrated the natural world. The songs having been written to mark the poet's bicentenary, Margaret 'tried to get the feeling for Blake as an Englishman'—probably an eighteenth-century gentleman, since they evoke English dances of that period. The songs are through-composed in Margaret's late neoclassical manner, and gracefully evoke melancholy and irony. John Antill recommended that the ABC record them separately, since they were 'quite interesting and acceptable as separate identities', but 'together the idiom becomes tedious'.[83] The recording went ahead in mid-1958, with mezzo soprano Muriel Luyk and Margaret at the piano.

On 1 June 1958, Margaret was honoured to meet David Oistrakh, who was touring Australia and had given his Melbourne recital on 29 May. Oistrakh wanted to hear some Australian compositions and was given a recital at Melba Hall. Margaret accompanied three of her *Blake Songs* (1957), sung by Muriel Luyk, and *Sonatina for Oboe (or Violin) and Piano* (1954) played by Beryl Kimber Leske. Other featured composers were Dorian Le Gallienne, Felix Werder and Harold Badger. Oistrakh 'responded with a superb performance of the Prokofiev D Major and some [Polish composer Karol] Szymanowski', Margaret enthused. It was possibly through Margaret's friendship with Kimber Leske that the recital came about. She had achieved first distinction (violin) at the first International Tchaikovsky Competition in Moscow in March that year and had studied with Oistrakh while there.[84]

The year 1958 was productive for orchestral compositions. Margaret entered her *Outdoor Overture* in the Queensland Government's centenary music competition and won the first prize, of £150. In a congratulatory letter, David Felsman, ABC's Queensland manager and chairman of the Music and Arts Committee for the Centenary Celebrations, noted the 'high praise tendered by the adjudicators, whose musical integrity could never be questioned'. He informed her that it would be performed in Brisbane by the SSO in June 1959. It was well received by critics except for Roger Covell, who remarked that it 'was so brief and pointless that it might as well never have been composed'.[85] His offhand reception to this short, joyous work was not fully unjustified, since the competition's criteria called for a 'light' piece.

One of Margaret's finest orchestral achievements is arguably the *Concerto Grosso* (1958). In the traditional three-movement sequence of the classical concerto, Margaret borrowed the second theme of the third movement from 'The Jocund Dance' of her *Four Blake Songs* (1957). Scored for violin, viola, harpsichord (or piano), string orchestra and percussion (optional), it shows Margaret with the 'tauter tonal, modal and dissonant' approaches of neoclassically based music. Although it is not obviously technically simple, Margaret composed the concerto for groups that were amateur 'in the true sense—those who play for the love of it'. Its first performance was given by Melbourne amateur chamber music society Astra on 6 November 1959, with Margaret on piano, Sybil Copeland (violin) and John Glickman (viola). Another Astra performance on 10 June 1966 received the highest accolade from Melbourne *Advocate* critic Leon Noone. Margaret was 'a composer of highly-charged and sensitive imagination, whose musical inspiration is matched by technical skill'. He was elated to hear 'an Australian composition that had the distinguished mark and accent of the finest music'.[86]

Although the *Concerto Grosso* received a favourable ABC report in 1958, it was another twelve years before it was recorded by the MSO Strings under John Hopkins, with Copeland, Glickman and Max Cooke (harpsichord) as soloists. Hopkins, who became ABC federal director of music in 1963, was a 'great admirer' of all Margaret 'has done for music in this country'. He felt she was 'wrongly neglected both because she was a woman and a fairly acerbic type of person; she obviously had not got on with certain people'.[87]

In the mid to late 1960s, Margaret received a call from the ABC that Hopkins would like to see her larger orchestral scores. 'John came one morning', Margaret recalled, 'and stayed for lunch. He went steadily over and over, looking at everything, asking quite a few questions—apparently in no hurry. I became more and more astonished—I could not believe it'.

She had enormous respect for Hopkins as a musician; however, when she later discovered he was a Christian Scientist, she was disappointed by his having 'this strange obsession'. But this didn't stop her making a significant gift to him, a clear demonstration of her respect. 'She had called one day—she was quite elderly then', said Hopkins, 'and asked if she could come and see me'. She arrived in a government car with Lady Maie Casey, 'and when they emerged, they were carrying a parcel'. It was Rupert Bunny's portrait of her. 'She gave it to me', he added. Painted circa 1939, the work was the artist's gesture of appreciation for Margaret's help when he started composing music.[88]

In late 1958, Margaret was urgently admitted to hospital to have her gall bladder and appendix removed. She recovered well, though was frustrated by being unable to do much over the Christmas period. On a brighter note, the end of the decade saw an exciting development for the arts centre. In December 1959, Roy Grounds was appointed architect in charge of the project, and his master plan was approved in 1960.[89] This was a positive start to a decade that was to present further health and family issues for Margaret, but some interesting musical challenges too.

CHAPTER 12

KABBARLI, COMMISSIONS AND A-ROOM-AND-A-BIT (1960–1968)

I have had my very first commission! A work of chamber music, and it is wonderful to be ***asked*** *to write something! [Everything to date has had to be (not too) immaculate conception.]*

Margaret Sutherland[1]

THE DECADE STARTED well, with regular musical commitments in 1960. As a member of the Australian UNESCO Committee for Music, Margaret participated in a working party organising the UNESCO Seminar for Composers in Adelaide in March. This presented challenges, since two members were not her favourite people—the former and current Ormond Professors of Music, Sir Bernard Heinze and Professor George Loughlin.[2]

Although not everybody agreed about Heinze's abilities as a violinist or conductor, it was generally accepted that he had guided the conservatorium, and Australia's musical life, into the twentieth century. He predicted changes in cultural attitudes, believed in technological progress, and networked cleverly to secure his ambitions for the conservatorium and his professional orchestra. George Loughlin was quiet—even timid. His tastes favoured romantic church music, and he supported a traditional curriculum. If Margaret did not always admire Heinze's methods, she found Loughlin's conservatism abhorrent. He did not have an innovative and progressive vision for the conservatorium or for music in general, she thought. 'All he values is power', she complained to Don Banks.[3]

Fortunately, Margaret respected the UNESCO Seminar working party chair, Professor John Bishop. He led the development of a five-day seminar packed with lectures, study groups, readings of new works, concerts and an exhibition of Australian compositions. Apart from her administrative duties, Margaret facilitated a panel session on 'Problems facing the composer and how to resolve them'. She played piano for her *Concerto Grosso* (1958) and had the score of her *Quartet for Cor Anglais, Violin, Viola and Cello* (1956) reproduced for study during the seminar.[4]

The next month, Margaret took on another project. She knew US composer Aaron Copland was to visit Melbourne with the Boston Symphony Orchestra in June and invited him to meet Melbourne musicians. 'It was very kind of you indeed to write and invite me to meet musicians informally during my stay in Melbourne', he replied. 'I look forward with great interest, as you can imagine, to my first visit to Australia.' In typical fashion, Margaret stirred her musical colleagues into action to prepare lunch at her house on Sunday 12 June, followed by a Lyceum Club gathering. One was pianist Margaret Schofield, who had an ambivalent relationship with Margaret. She [Sutherland] was 'Mother Bird' at the Lyceum Club, Schofield said, and could be 'a venomous, horrible creature' who 'expected the whole world to wait on her'. Schofield was sometimes on the receiving end of Margaret's orders. 'She asked me to make a casserole for I don't know how many people.' When the Lyceum gathering concluded, Margaret directed Schofield to drive Copland to the airport and wait with him until his plane departed. Margaret sometimes hurt Schofield with her criticism of the pianist's interpretation of her music. Nevertheless, she acknowledged that

Margaret 'had original gifts', and regularly played her music, particularly at BMS concerts.[5]

By late November 1960, Margaret was again troubled about her son Mark. This made her ruminate on her marriage, and write an account for her son-in-law, Dean Bunney. 'A post-mortem such as this would be valueless and would never have been undertaken had it not been for Mark's recent behaviour', she wrote. At nearly thirty-two, he was again exhibiting his 'unhappy, fruitless egotism'. The details are unclear, but Margaret highlighted an infatuation with an actress. This 'plunged me back into the past, and the nightmares have loomed up again, lifesized'. Mark was still married to his first wife, Moya, and the couple had three children and little income.[6]

There is sadness embedded in Margaret's observations of Mark's character. As any parent would, she worried about him, and reflected on his early years, 'where the seeds of behaviour are sewn'. Mark resembled his father in being married three times, and a 'womaniser' who had extramarital liaisons. In 1970, Mark married his second wife, artist Astrid Dahl. Their union lasted just over four years, producing one daughter, Jasmine. For Dahl, it was an extremely unhappy marriage. She remembered him as emotionally and physically abusive, and wondered whether he 'needed to come out of the closet'—he had admitted an attraction to men.[7]

Mark was forging a precarious career as an actor. He worked in Australian television productions (including the well-known series *Bellbird*) and in live theatre from the 1950s to the 1980s. He had a role in Mart Crowley's controversial play *The Boys in the Band*, which was staged in Sydney, Melbourne and Canberra in 1968–69. Although composer Helen Gifford thought 'he was the only straight one' in the cast, Dahl wondered otherwise.[8] Sometimes Mark struggled to find acting work, but Margaret didn't have the means to offer financial support, and he took various jobs, including as a taxi driver.

Margaret's state of mind in November 1960 was reflected in a letter to the ABC acting director of music, Joseph Post. Disappointed in the ABC's slow response to submissions of her orchestral works, particularly the *Four Symphonic Concepts* (mid-1940s), the *Concerto Grosso* (1958) and *Concerto for Violin and Orchestra* (1960), she aired her frustration:

> You will appreciate, I feel sure, how difficult it is for 'freelancers' such as myself to get a hearing. If one writes chamber music one goes into the chamber music category, and so one's orchestral pieces have no chance. I understand how conductors must like and seek out 'conductors' pieces', i.e. the ones that come off brilliantly, but there is another vein of writing which belongs to this country but might be called, perhaps, more introverted. This falls by the way, though it may reflect more truly the age and the tempo of life. Excuse this outpouring. Composers have to live! And it's awfully difficult.[9]

Other unpleasant memories were rekindled at this vulnerable time. The letter to Post suggests she felt her music was misunderstood, as it was in 1926 after her return from abroad. She knew her compositions were sometimes considered intellectual, introverted and lacking in emotion. But these were not the only reasons for the ABC's lack of urgency in programming her orchestral music. Despite Post's reassurance that Margaret had not been 'labelled Chamber Music', that he would mention her music to conductors 'whenever the opportunity presents itself' and that he considered her *Concerto* a 'fine work', systemic sexism may have been at play.[10]

Margaret's observation that she was in the 'chamber music category' is in keeping with the historic perception that smaller forms inhabited the private, non-professional sphere, as women mostly still did in the early 1960s. Even by the 1990s, women tended to avoid orchestral writing. At the end of the twentieth century, around 20 per cent of composers represented by the Australian Music Centre were women, but their music comprised only about 10.6 per cent of orchestral writing. A survey of performances by mainstream music institutions in Sydney during the decade 1985–95 showed that 98 per cent of the compositions were by men, and musicologist Sally Macarthur postulated that these results could be generalised to Australia as a whole.[11]

These statistics highlight just how determined Margaret had to be in the 1950s and early 1960s. She was still puzzling over the issue of women's orchestral writing in 1968, when she commented to James Murdoch that women were less likely than men to want to engage in 'this symphonic business', 'but their contribution is no less important'.[12] Margaret was more confident writing orchestral music later in her career, and her competence increased, but perhaps her 1968 statement reflected fatigue from the constant battle for orchestral performances and led her to recognise anew the value of chamber music, and her love of it.

Amid other commitments and concerns, Margaret composed three works in 1960. Two were chamber works—her setting of Judith Wright's 'The World and the Child' and *Little Suite for Wind Trio*. Scored for flute, clarinet and bassoon, the *Little Suite* was written for bassoonist and composer George Dreyfus and his New Music Ensemble.

The third was her violin concerto, her only solo concerto. She had wanted to write a violin concerto for some time—an expansive one that showcased the instrument's tonal qualities and capabilities. In a demonstration of her intent, she commented that 'immense contrasts, together with the peculiarly poignant loneliness of an individual voice in the midst of overwhelmingly larger forces, are significant features of most concertos'.[13] This could be a metaphor for Margaret's experience of fighting lonely battles in both public and private life. Her admission that the work was more extrovert and passionate than usual reinforces the impression of this music as a profound expression of her inner self.

Romantic and lyrical in its intent and gestures, the concerto was, and is, contemporary, characterised by striking tensions, and bold rhythms, harmonies and orchestration. Its florid passages and extended double-stopping figures demand virtuosity, and the violinist for whom it was composed was more than capable. Hobart-based English violinist and conductor Thomas Matthews thought highly of the work and travelled from Hobart to rehearse with Margaret. The double-stopping 'called for enormous concentration and control', while 'the running passages lay more easily', he said.[14]

Margaret was dogged in her attempts to achieve a performance. In one letter to Post, she pointed out—tongue in cheek—that the concerto was 'even catchy'. It was premiered with the VSO conducted by French-born chief conductor (1960–65) Georges Tzipine on 11 October 1961. Margaret was delighted with Thomas's rendition. 'I can't tell you how enthusiastically he threw himself into my violin concerto, and how magnificently he played it. It just took my breath away.'[15]

The concerto was a triumph. Margaret had tackled a large orchestral form with success, was happy with Matthews' performance, and reviews were positive. *Herald* critic John Sinclair pronounced it a 'fine new concerto', with 'a tautly constructed first movement, a subtle and distinguished "adagio" and a lively last movement in which the material of the adagio is treated satirically'. 'There are no romantic cliches to describe the very personal spirit of the music', he continued. The 'writing is lean, economical, but intricate enough to make accurate (and of course, affectionate) playing an essential'. 'There is a warm glow of spiritual elation and much genuine invention about the work of Margaret Sutherland', declared *Age* critic (and composer) Felix Werder. The *Sun's* John Gilfedder felt the concerto demonstrated her ability 'to construct from basic themes, and an increased enterprise in isolating individual timbres' such as her striking use of the xylophone.[16]

Matthews made an ABC studio recording of the concerto—never released—with the South Australian Symphony Orchestra (SASO, now the Adelaide Symphony Orchestra) under Henry Krips. The work was not programmed again for another eleven years, when Patrick Thomas conducted the MSO with soloist Leonard Dommett in an all-Sutherland concert at the National Gallery of Victoria (NGV) for the composer's seventy-fifth birthday in 1972. A few weeks later, this group recorded it for the ABC. After another long break, there has, deservedly, been a recent resurgence of interest in the work.

In early February 1961, Margaret wrote pointedly to the ABC that she was 'needing performances just now quite urgently', and was giving a recital on 20 February 'as other opportunities come so few and far between'. She gathered her friends to organise the concert in the Assembly Hall; Con was concert director, and Dorothy Miller ticket secretary.[17] Although her eyes were increasingly troublesome, she continued to perform, and participated in this recital with trusted colleagues Jiří Tancibudek (oboe), Sybil Copeland (violin), John Glickman (viola) and Henry Wenig (cello). The program included her *Sonata for Viola (or Clarinet) and Piano* (1947), *Fantasy for Violin and Piano* (pre-1947), *Trio for Oboe and Two Violins* (1955), *Six Bagatelles for Violin and Viola* (1956), *Sonatina for Oboe and Piano* (c. 1954) and *Divertimento for Violin, Viola and Cello* (1958).

Six months later, Margaret donned her impresario hat again and conceived the idea to stage an annual concert for 'largish chamber groups' in the Assembly Hall, now that 'more Australian things are coming forward'. She tried to enlist the ABC's assistance, presumably by providing orchestral musicians. 'The Camerata Society would do all management required, and get the audience—Melbourne loves string orchestras', she argued. Post referred her to the ABC's Victorian office, but the idea went no further.[18]

Margaret's teaching was by now limited to her grandchildren. In 1961, she taught seven-year-old granddaughter Anna, the oldest of Jenifer and Dean Bunney's four children. Later in the 1960s, teenaged grandson Michael took lessons. Both agreed that 'Gran' was a hard taskmistress. An exacting teacher with high expectations of her students, Margaret made no concessions for youth or family. She made it clear when their playing was not good enough, and 'mucking around' on the piano was forbidden.[19]

Jenny regularly took her children to see their gran and Con, and separately to see Norman, Val and Von at Templestowe—she ensured they had access to both grandparents. Home-made lemonade, art and magic tricks were features of visits to their grandfather, while calling on Gran would inevitably include her playing the piano. Sometimes Anna stayed with Margaret, and 'the house would fill with her playing and all the intensity and emotion of a concert performance'.[20]

Despite decreased compositional activity in 1962 and 1963, Margaret stayed involved in the musical world. In April 1962, she visited Hobart, where she gave a paper at a music seminar about the need for overseas composers to visit Australia. 'We are swamped with executive [performing] artists, yet denied any creative musicians', a 'crippling handicap', she lamented. She also attended a studio broadcast of a new work for oboe, strings and percussion (the identity of the composer is unclear) with Thomas Matthews conducting the Tasmanian Symphony Orchestra. Before heading to Hobart to 'learn things', she visited Peter Sculthorpe in Launceston.[21]

Although delighted by an exciting project for publishing Australian scores, funded by the Myer Foundation, including a new 'music writer' machine that had become available in Australia, Margaret was depressed by the state of Australian composition. 'Do you like my 3 pigeon-holes for Australian music to date?' she asked Sculthorpe: 'Strong (very limited); Weak (very prevalent): Banal (limitless) ... There's another sad orchestral malaise going on ... Will debilitating viruses never cease? So much of it, as I see it, is due to half-baked ABC operators, as well as unionism gone rank and rotten.' This was a strong statement from a woman who fundamentally favoured unions' protection of their members. Her criticism was probably attributable to the musicians' union's control over orchestral players' pay rates and availability for external engagements such as her chamber concerts. She also thought the union had too much power 'in artistic matters instead of keeping within their own province'.[22]

There was cause for increased optimism about ABC orchestras in 1963. John Hopkins became federal director of music, and Heinze's long association with the ABC ended. Margaret expressed her delight to Banks:

> It did me <u>so</u> much good to see in *The Age* that Bernard H. is giving it over <u>forever</u>, and that Hopkins will be in charge, with dear Bob Hughes and Richard Meale. What could be better? ... To me it has been a ghastly business ... Women can't go through these hoops—at least—I couldn't—I feel that light has come over things. We can now depend on decency. It has been a long long time.[23]

The temporary break from composing was partly due to renewed concern about Mark. After his early attempt to become a jazz musician, he had trained as a schoolteacher, to provide him with a secure income.

But he gave it up and 'determined to join the Elizabethan Theatre Trust touring company for this year'. 'To make a long story short', Margaret wrote to Sculthorpe, 'his wife and 3 children have come here for the period'. Although she enjoyed seeing her grandchildren, she had not anticipated having them live with her. Mark's wife Moya was working as secretary to the *Age* news editor, so Margaret was 'in the yoke with a 4-year-old and 2 school-agers'. 'I am not unaccustomed to stresses, which I think is a help', she quipped.[24]

Margaret's failing eyesight was an added burden. In September 1963, she went to hospital for a cataract operation. 'The oculist is fairly hopeful', she wrote to Sculthorpe, 'as the earlier trouble, which caused the cataracts, is static. So it's worth a trial'. It may have been after this surgery that Margaret was fitted for contact lenses, which she was 'struggling painfully' to use before finally mastering it. When Maureen White lived upstairs in the Studley Avenue house in the mid-1960s, Margaret sometimes called for help locating her contact lenses, and Maureen would assist her to find and reinsert them.[25]

In the same letter to Sculthorpe, she noted that composer Dorian Le Gallienne's premature death in July 1963 at the age of forty-eight 'was a shattering blow to many of us'. Margaret admired Le Gallienne as a person and as a composer, as she did Sculthorpe (at least until the mid-1960s), Banks, Hughes, Richard Meale and Nigel Butterley, among others.

Otherwise, life continued as normal. The BMS remained a useful outlet, and she wrote to it in November 1963, expressing her appreciation of the society's recognition of Australian composers. She delivered a paper, 'The Prodigy', to the Catalysts on 11 February 1963, and her music featured in the Lyceum Club's Jubilee (50-year) celebrations from March 1962 to March 1963.[26]

The Lyceum was the venue for an airing in late July 1964 of the first fruits of Margaret's creative partnership with her friend Lady Maie Casey. The collaboration began eight months earlier, when Casey gifted Margaret a volume of ten *Verses*, illustrated by Australian artist Frances Burke. Burke and Casey were fellow students at the George Bell School in the 1930s and became close friends.[27]

Margaret again made an original choice of instrumentation for these settings—spoken voice, flute, viola, bassoon, contrabassoon, piano and percussion, though another version dropped the contrabassoon and piano. The first performance was at a National Trust fundraising concert in early March 1964 in the ballroom at Como House, an elegant nineteenth-century mansion in Melbourne's South Yarra. Although the score is lost, the National Film and Sound Archive lists a 1967 recording, which shows that not all ten poems were musically accompanied.[28]

Later in March 1964, Margaret was back in Adelaide for the Sydney chapter of the International Society of Contemporary Music's (ISCM) new music series at the biennial Festival of the Arts. In the final of three concerts, she enjoyed conducting her *Concerto Grosso* (1958) with SASO concertmaster violinist Robert Cooper leading the orchestra. Sadly, the festival's artistic director, John Bishop, who had suffered health problems since 1961, was confined to bed with laryngitis. By December, he was dead at sixty-one, having collapsed in the Australia House foyer in London with a heart attack. Bishop had earned Margaret's respect and affection, and she was shocked and saddened by his death. 'The void is going to be desperately serious', she wrote to Banks. 'He was a great man', with 'the right kind of visions'.[29]

Another orchestral work, *Three Temperaments for Orchestra* (1964), was premiered by the VSO in its Celebrity Concert Series in May 1964 under Georges Tzipine. 'I've always been interested in people', Margaret said, 'and I feel that music offers a great deal of scope for imaginary portraiture of them'. In her *Six Profiles* for piano (c. 1946), she represented individuals. On this occasion, it was 'types': 'cool and detached, warm-hearted and very humanly frail, and optimistically extroverted'. The three movements were originally written for two pianos in the 1950s or earlier, and Margaret orchestrated the third movement. Robert Hughes subsequently orchestrated all three, and they were relabelled 'Pavan', 'Air' and 'Canon'. In a program note for the VSO, Margaret acknowledged Hughes's input: 'The composer wishes to express her deep appreciation of the generosity of Mr Robert Hughes who has given outstanding help in the preparation of the scores'. Her assessment of the performance was qualified. The VSO played 'quite well', but she again criticised the ABC's orchestral management. 'The poor old orchestra is sadly depleted, especially in the wind section, owing fundamentally to the deputy conductor who reigns supreme for 7 months of the year and the union.'[30]

On a brighter note, Margaret found a solution to the problem of printing music. She expressed excitement to Banks about her acquisition of a Van Dyke music writer, 'invented by a German'. 'It's fabulous—a typewriter which prints music every bit as well as Boosey & Hawkes', whom she never forgave for their decision not to publish her *Concerto for Strings* because 'M. Sutherland' was a woman.[31]

Con Duncan's memory had been fading for some years, and by the end of 1964, aged sixty-eight, she needed more care than Margaret could provide. Con inherited atherosclerosis from her father, and although she was physically robust, this condition increases the risk of vascular dementia, which appears to have been her fate. Con's family were members of the Canterbury Baptist Church, and Con moved to a Baptist facility, the Hedley Sutton Aged Care Home. Characteristically, Margaret expressed little of the grief one would feel for an ailing friend, and about the gap in her life, though as Con deteriorated, she admitted to Banks in her understated way that 'the news of Con is sad'.[32]

Margaret was now in her late sixties. With Con no longer living there, and the upkeep of the large Studley Avenue house becoming too demanding, it was time to 'down-size'. A letter in November 1964 from her Adelaide cousin Kathleen Kyffin Thomas sympathised with Margaret for the 'impossible number of decisions' facing her.[33] The search took another year.

During 1964, Margaret worked on an ambitious collaboration with Lady Casey: her only chamber opera, *The Young Kabbarli*. The plot recalls an incident in the life of Irish–Australian self-taught ethnologist Daisy Bates, a welfare worker among Aboriginal communities in South and Western Australia. Casey had long been fascinated by Bates, having shared a train journey with the elderly woman in 1934. She probably also read the autobiographical work covering the latter part of her life, *The Passing of the Aborigines* (1939). While in London in 1964, the opera-loving

Casey realised the dramatic possibilities in Bates's story. The vignette that appealed painted Bates—nicknamed Kabbarli (grandmother) by her Aboriginal friends—in a positive light, though her interactions with Aboriginal people are now seen as controversial. Margaret first thought she could do nothing with the libretto, 'but then it got me in, and I had the piano score down in a couple of months', she said. She sent it to Casey, and the two met several times to fashion it.[34]

The events on which the libretto is based occurred at a Trappist mission in Beagle Bay on the northwest coast of Western Australia. Kabbarli and a Spanish Trappist Brother urge three hesitant young Aboriginal girls to ready themselves for their confirmation ceremony. Outside the chapel, a young man, Goondowell, watches the service through the chapel window while his wife Yoolbian lies sick in the shade of a bush. He mistrusts the 'white fella', whom he blames for his wife's illness. When the girls emerge from the chapel, Goondowell chases them, and mockingly imitates the confirmation, a tormented outcry against the white man's church. To heal Yoolbian, he and the girls perform an angular ritual dance to exorcise the Christian God. She awakens and gradually recovers. The Brother wants to bring the girls to God, but Kabbarli wonders whether Aboriginal people should ever join the white race. She explains Goondowell's distrust and the girls' fear to the Brother, telling him they have an intuitive understanding, but only of their own kind, as with animals and birds.

The Aboriginal theme may suggest a link with 'Jindyworobakism', which in Aboriginal Woiwurrung language, formerly spoken around modern-day Melbourne, means 'to annex' or 'join'. Jindyworobakism emerged as a nationalist literary movement of the 1930s–40s. In music, the term refers to composers' attempts 'to establish a uniquely Australian identity through the evocation of the Australian landscape and environment and through the use of Aboriginal elements in their music, text or subjects'. Aspects of Jindyworobakism have been observed in several Australian composers' work.[35] *The Young Kabbarli* could be linked with the movement, since Margaret used a European post-tonal musical idiom as a framework to incorporate Aboriginal melodic and rhythmic structures (as interpreted by a Western musician). There is also an optional didgeridoo solo (not included in the score), and the use of what would now be deemed inappropriate imitation of 'Aboriginal' English in Goondowell's diatribe against the white man.

But Margaret never referred to Jindyworobakism and is unlikely to have identified herself with its philosophies (or those of any other movement). Driven by her sympathy for Aboriginal people's plight, her principal attraction to *Kabbarli*'s libretto was its exploration of the uneasy relationship between Aboriginal and European peoples. The Australian theme also appealed, as did that of closeness to nature, the nurturing role implied in the character of Kabbarli, and the inherent criticism of Christian dogma.

The opera has a small cast of seven—Kabbarli (mezzo soprano), the Trappist Brother (bass), Goondowell (tenor), Yoolbian (soprano) and three Aboriginal girls (non-singing roles). The orchestra comprises two flutes (one doubling on piccolo), two clarinets (one doubling bass clarinet), bassoon (doubling contrabassoon), horn, percussion, piano, viola and double bass. Unlike traditional opera, where the action is driven by recitative interwoven with arias, choruses and ensembles, *Kabbarli* consists of a series of set pieces for its characters, with the action carried out through dance or mime.[36]

The Young Kabbarli was premiered during a three-day Festival of Contemporary Opera in Hobart, one of three one-act Australian operas performed on 19 August 1965 at the Theatre Royal. Margaret's music was well received, with the *Australian*'s Kenneth Hince describing it as 'serious, pleasant, and of some density and substance'. There is a consensus, however, that Casey's trite libretto is the reason the opera hasn't remained in the repertoire. She boasted that she had dashed it off in one day, which may account for its weaknesses. Margaret was 'hindered by a particularly inept libretto' observed Roger Covell.[37]

Two years later, James Murdoch, then editor-in-chief of the World Record Club Australia, suggested that producer Marissa Brumby stage the work at the Opera Group Workshop she had established with her composer husband Colin Brumby in Brisbane in 1964. She was reluctant.

'I looked at Margaret Sutherland's score deeply, and, although I want to do it because I simply love producing, it is lacking in real drama. It will always be half-baked. The music is nice, but the libretto very non-operatic.'[38]

Although its intentions were laudable, *Kabbarli* was of its time. Its attempt to evoke Aboriginal culture through a European art form would now be seen as morally objectional cultural appropriation. As early as 1972, when the opera was performed in Melbourne to honour Margaret's seventy-fifth birthday, Kenneth Hince called it 'a piece of chauvinism, well-intentioned, but with pasteboard solutions for the real problems of displacement of race'.[39]

If *Kabbarli* achieved anything, it cemented Margaret's friendship with Lady Casey. Their different political persuasions did not get in the way—perhaps there was an unspoken pact not to discuss them. 'My dear and all-important Safety Valve', Margaret began a letter to Casey in September 1965. She visited her several times at Government House in Canberra while Lord Casey was governor-general (1965–69). Although Lady Casey was not musical, she introduced musical evenings at Government House, and Margaret's assistance was likely welcomed.[40]

While working on *Kabbarli*, Margaret was approached in late 1964 by *Meanjin* founder and editor Clem Christesen regarding the HC Coombs Creative Arts Fellowship at Australian National University (ANU). Instigated in 1964 by Nugget Coombs, ANU pro-chancellor, the fellowship is awarded by invitation to a creative artist who spends a year working at ANU. Initially musicians/composers and architects were excluded, and Christesen was probably an independent adviser regarding whether music should be added to the list of approved creative arts. He sought Margaret's opinion and, naturally, she had a view, and interrupted her work to provide some 'jottings'. 'Forgive my not making a good copy—I am immersed in an intimate opera!' she wrote to Christesen.[41]

Margaret's 'jottings' were typed up, and their substance carries no surprises. While she conceded that creative music in Australia desperately needed help, it should be the right kind. The idea that one young composer should be singled out 'has nothing to recommend it—Such a scheme has never been sought by composers', she emphasised. It was wrong to isolate a composer in Canberra 'with an embarrassingly large amount of time on his hands'. It would be 'far more interesting, stimulating and more steadying if there are 3 (or any small group). We need many composers to find a Titan'. Her other suggestion was that the award be a commission for a large-scale work that would otherwise not be possible.

Nevertheless, the third fellowship (delayed from 1966 to 1967) was offered to bassoonist and composer George Dreyfus, who was privy to Margaret's comments, and wrote a long report detailing his counter-arguments.[42] Margaret and Dreyfus were always at other ends of the spectrum in their views on the creative process. According to the pragmatic Dreyfus, Margaret had a 'romanticised outlook', with no idea of the reality of being a 'full-time composer'. In contrast, Margaret was an idealist unwilling to cut corners to produce 'commercial' music to make money. She may have been financially better off if she had relaxed her principles, but that was out of the question. The aim of composition was not only to please audiences, she argued, but also to create original works that challenged listeners and broadened their musical horizons.

Unsurprisingly, Margaret was critical of the premier of Dreyfus's *Symphony No. 1*, the outcome of his fellowship. 'On Saturday night George Dreyfus's Symphony stepped out', she told Banks in March 1968. 'It is an unashamed pastiche. Felix Werder flays it in the *Age* this morning, mentioning most of its derivations by name.' 'Having more observation of historical antecedents than creative imagination', Werder wrote, 'he is forced to depend on his aural memory. He unashamedly aims to please, so he has put together an audience-hungry work rather than a serious contribution to symphonic literature'.[43]

The arts centre was not forgotten. Margaret was watching it grow from a 'scene of enormous underground activity … all unseen by the casual-passer-by. But little by little the above-ground activity grew and developed, giving promise of quite unbelievable things to come'. In mid to late 1965, 'one could now recognise the design, and get an idea of the vastness'. She thought of Gwenda Lloyd, whose husband John had died the year before, and on an impulse rang to ask if she would like to see the progress that had been made. They 'walked all over and around it, envisaging the possibilities, and picturing the ultimate end'. Margaret didn't imagine that this was the last time she would see her friend, but Gwenda died in October that year. 'This momentous morning, when we walked about, unmolested, and were deeply moved by the result of so many people's endeavours. It all had meaning', Margaret said.[44]

At the end of 1965, she finally purchased a property—a tiny one-bedroom flat in a simple brick two-storey horseshoe-shaped block set back off the road at 146 Power Street, Hawthorn. The sale of 20 Studley Avenue would take another year, and she scraped the money together to buy the new abode. Friends noted a stark difference in size and wondered how Margaret would cope, but she was contented enough, and relieved by the relative ease of maintaining it. 'This is a dear little flat with a roof garden [above the adjoining carport] and suits me exactly', she told Banks. She kept her sense of humour regarding the challenges. In a note headed 'How to Live in a Room-and-a-Bit (and still keep your reason—and your piano)', she wrote of needing to trade a baby grand piano for an upright, but 'you still must have a formidable array of etceteras, that is if you are one of those Mad Musicians'. The grand piano was moved to Jenny and Dean's Donvale property, and Margaret had to be 'fearfully clever about arranging the [smaller] piano' so that it took up 'the least possible amount of room', and 'leaving just enough room to squeeze yourself, painfully, onto the chair that unfortunately is necessary'. She had to find room for her stereo record player, tape recorder, prized 'music writer', and for the all-important 'Telly!' 'Whatever would we do without it? Like the dog, it surely is man's best friend.'[45]

After her move to Hawthorn, Margaret befriended leading left-wing politician Dr Jim Cairns, federal member of parliament for her electorate of Yarra, who lived close by in Wattle Road. She did not officially join the Labor Party, but was a passionate Labor supporter, and assisted Cairns in his successful campaign leading up to the federal election on 26 November 1966. 'She equated herself with the poor—she was poor', Helen Gifford confirmed.[46]

Coincidentally, Mark became involved with Cairns and Junie Morosi's countercultural, socially experimental 'Down to Earth' movement in the 1970s.[47] He went to the movement's haven of Nimbin in New South Wales, so-called drug capital of Australia, and saw a vision that changed his life. 'I found God', he wrote to his uncle, Norman's brother Harold. It seems plausible this was drug induced, or a psychotic symptom.[48]

Although none of her works were programmed in the Adelaide Festival in March 1966, Margaret wanted to attend. Instead, she went into hospital to have a kidney stone removed. These can be extremely painful, but she took it in her stride—or did not want to make a fuss. It was 'not serious—but bothersome', she told Banks.[49]

The recovery was slow, she admitted in May 1966 to Ella Grainger, Australian composer Percy Grainger's wife. 'I am very much better: but still rather *piano—adagio—poco andante*! It taxes one's patience, the long pull-up. But I am so thankful to be this side of it'. Margaret's first connection with Percy Grainger was in 1938, when he asked if she would donate manuscripts to the Grainger Museum at Melbourne University (opened in December 1938). Ella wrote to Margaret in late March 1966 to wish her well with her convalescence, and to thank her for recommending Robert Hyner, who became curator at the museum, assisted by his wife, composer Meta Overman.[50]

Margaret may also have been corresponding with Ella regarding a paper she wrote entitled 'The Strange Story of Percy Grainger: A Visionary Ahead of His Time', delivered to the Catalysts on 13 February 1967. Addressed primarily to music students, the paper discusses Grainger's musical career and paints him as a groundbreaking composer. Margaret was unaware at the time just how strange Grainger's story was. She had sent the article to James Murdoch, who had started an artist management company in London and was researching his book *Australia's Contemporary Composers* (1972). In early 1970, Margaret asked him to return the article, as Grainger's biographer, John Bird, was 'pushing' her for it. But when Bird 'uncorked' information regarding Grainger's odd private life, Margaret was concerned. '<u>Please</u> <u>Please</u> send me back the paper I wrote and <u>please</u> do no more about it', she begged

Murdoch. 'It must be changed regarding many matters.' She appreciated Murdoch's prompt attention to her 'somewhat agonised plea'. Grainger 'was a real Dr Jekyll and Mr Hyde', she concluded.[51]

Margaret wrote only two works in 1966, the first being a set of *Simple String Pieces*, and the other a further collaboration with Lady Casey. With friends Marnie Bassett, Rosemary Dobson and Joan Lindsay, Casey had produced the privately published set of five Australian carols *A Company of Carols*, which Margaret set charmingly to music for accompanied choir. As was her wont, Margaret visited Adelaide for the rehearsals. 'The breaking-of-ice with new musicians—and a previously unseen score—is always a lacerating experience', she confided to Casey. 'However, Patrick Thomas, the conductor, promises a really good performance, and many of the singers have lovely voices and are musical, alert and keen to make something of it all.'[52] The result went to air on the ABC on Christmas Day 1966.

In late 1966, Margaret was 'asked to write something!' At the age of sixty-nine, she was commissioned for the first time. As foundation chair of the Australian Performing Rights Association (APRA), Robert Hughes refused to end a meeting until they agreed to commission Margaret.[53] In early 1967, she began work on her three-movement *String Quartet No. 3*. Written for the Cremona Quartet, whose members she knew well (Leonard Dommett, violin 1; Sybil Copeland, violin 2; John Glickman, viola; and Henry Wenig, cello), Margaret was influenced by the emotional quality of intensity and rapport she noted in the group. The result was a confident exhibition of modernism that moved beyond her previous string quartets.

A second commission followed, this time by the Australian Musicians Overseas Scholarship Fund for a piano piece. *Extension* was one of three piano works written in 1967, the others being *Chiaroscuro I* and *II*. The title *Extension* refers to the thematic and tonal material extending from the basic shapes and pitch orders of the opening passages, as is also the case in the *Chiaroscuros*. As ever, Margaret was seeking new directions for her musical language, and in her last two years of composition, wanted to demonstrate her mastery of contemporary methods. If these pieces don't strictly adhere to the serialism of the Second Viennese School, they are the closest she came to it. They are unashamedly dissonant, ferocious and reflective. They were played at an ISCM contemporary music concert at the Adelaide Festival in 1968. Sadly, Margaret wasn't there, but heard that the festival was not up to standard. 'The contemporary music recitals are always left till the end', she grumbled, 'when players and listeners are fagged out. This should stop'.[54]

Margaret's music was featured in the ISCM's First Melbourne Festival of Contemporary Music (September–October 1967) organised by James Murdoch. To honour her forthcoming seventieth birthday and her many years as a champion of contemporary music, cultural activity and education in Australia, Murdoch, with Banks and composer/pianist Keith Humble, established 'The Margaret Sutherland Fund'. Donations were forthcoming from at least forty-three notable individuals and organisations both within and beyond the musical world in the UK and Australia. Among these were Australian conductor Richard Bonynge and soprano Joan Sutherland, and Lady Casey.[55] The fund contributed to a concert of a representative selection of her works at the Assembly Hall on 27 September as part of the festival, and to a commemorative program and yearbook presented to her at the concert. At Margaret's suggestion, any remaining funds were to be devoted to an annual concert of predominantly Australian contemporary music.

The concert's program was intended to survey over forty years of Margaret's output, starting with the *Sonata for Violin and Piano* (1925) and culminating in the premiers of two 1967 compositions *String Quartet No. 3*, performed by the Cremona Quartet, and *Extension*, played by Humble. 'At the age of 70', *Age* critic Felix Werder declared, 'composer Margaret Sutherland is the undisputed first lady of Australian music'. As did Werder, John Sinclair observed the great differences between the early *Sonata for Violin and Piano* and the third string quartet written forty-two years later, 'yet both works bear the composer's unmistakable thumbprints' of intelligence, discipline and consistency.[56]

At another festival event, the *Concertante for Oboe and Strings* (1961) and *Three Temperaments* (1958) were performed by the MSO conducted by John Hopkins at a studio workshop at the ABC's Waverley recording studios on 29 September. Sinclair viewed the *Concertante* as 'clear in design, transparent in texture and with a great deal of attractive musical character', played eloquently by the soloist for whom it was written, Jiří Tancibudek.[57]

Margaret was moved by the gesture of much-delayed recognition.

> But, dear Don [Banks], it gave me such a warm feeling—a feeling that had never happened to me in my life before that I was not <u>only</u> a poor frustrated female trying to do something she didn't ought, and battering her stupid head against brick walls, and just being tolerated because one doesn't hate animals, especially female ones![58]

This was not the last acknowledgement of Margaret's contribution to music; she was honoured publicly on several more occasions before her death.

The year 1968 was tougher. Margaret's declining eyesight, now obvious in her illegible handwriting, was making composition difficult. There was a retinal problem, meaning that removal of the second cataract was unlikely to improve the situation. She could focus on each individual note as she wrote it, her face right up against the manuscript, but reading many notes at once and making corrections was impossible because of 'blanks and distortions which plague one'. She had just learned that her blood count may have been low since the 1930s when she was a regular blood donor, which can apparently lead to retinal problems.[59]

Still disheartened by what she perceived as Professor Loughlin's ineptitude at the University of Melbourne Conservatorium, Margaret was encouraged by the imminent opening of the NGV building in August 1968. She was looking forward to the celebratory concert in the Great Hall on 27 August, where the MSO was to perform the final movement of *Four Symphonic Concepts*, 'Vistas' (mid-1940s). Even more exciting was the construction of the arts centre alongside it. This would 'afford miles more opportunity for expansion', she wrote to Banks. 'I think that is where the real musical life of Melbourne will develop.'[60]

Despite her deteriorating vision, Margaret composed two important piano works in early 1968—*Voices I* and *II*, which continued the more radical direction of *Extension* and *Chiaroscuro I* and *II*. These were her final works. Around mid-1968, aged seventy-one, she suffered a major stroke. Activity ceased from June to October, when she wrote to Murdoch that she had been 'out of things' and was just getting back.[61] It is tempting to interpret the title *Voices* as a metaphor for the musical 'voices' of her creative inner life that continued in her head long after she had to cease composing.

CHAPTER 13

I TERRIBLY LOVE AUSTRALIA (1969–1984)

You will smile when I tell you I have been awarded a Doctorate. I don't claim that I deserve it, but women have to take more of a part!

Margaret Sutherland[1]

MARGARET'S REPUTATION IN Australia's musical circles grew steadily, but it was in the last fifteen years of her life that the tributes flowed. The irony is that had this recognition started earlier, her renown—and her career—may have been enhanced. Nevertheless, these were heartening episodes in an otherwise disheartening decline in health, exacerbated by the traumatic death of her beloved daughter Jenny.

As Margaret recuperated from her stroke, she received news that the University of Melbourne was awarding her an honorary music doctorate in recognition of her wide-ranging contribution to Australia's artistic life. On 29 March 1969, she donned her regalia to be presented with her Degree *Honoris Causa*, the only one awarded that year. As dean of the conservatorium, Professor George Loughlin nominated Margaret for the doctorate, and it was he who read the citation at the ceremony.

Professor Richard Downing, chair of the professorial board, presented the doctorate—she likely preferred that division of duties. In his speech, Loughlin noted Margaret's strong character, acknowledged her work with the Combined Arts Centre Movement, and referred to her as an intelligent composer who was 'the mainspring of creative activity' in Australia. He emphasised Margaret's 'specifically Australian achievement' that had 'influenced the course of cultural developments in this country', while in her music, she 'remained true to herself'.[2] Margaret had little respect for Loughlin, but there is no evidence that the feeling was mutual. It wasn't his treatment of her as an individual that led to her misgivings, but her perception that he didn't share her broader vision for Australian music.

Although she didn't 'claim to deserve it', photographs show Margaret's comprehension of the momentous occasion. In one, she has a serious, regal expression that simultaneously suggests the mental fatigue from recovering from the stroke and her years of crusading for music. In another, she adopts a gentle smile for the photographer as she strolls through the university's Old Quadrangle alongside Loughlin. Margaret later accused him of 'always having TEA'.[3] At least on this occasion he was not, though he may have indulged in Union House afterwards.

Along with violinist Bertha Jorgensen, who was retiring from the MSO, the BMS honoured Margaret, by then an honorary life member, with a dinner on 14 August 1969.[4] Loyal supporter music critic John Sinclair wrote a glowing tribute:

> Now in her 73rd year [Margaret] is regarded no longer as an isolated non-conformist but as the first lady of Australian music and as the first resident Australian composer to write music reflecting the attitudes, and using the language, of her time. Posterity may well see her … as the key figure in Australian music in the first half of this century. On March 29 this year the University of Melbourne made her an honorary Doctor of Music in recognition of her great and uniquely varied contribution to the artistic life of this country—as a composer, a friend and adviser to young musicians, a crusader for intelligent and progressive attitudes to music and music education, and as a tireless fighter in the cause of the arts generally.[5]

Margaret exhibited behavioural changes following her illness. Personality changes often occur after a stroke, though symptoms usually improve with time. Emotions can be heightened, inhibitions relaxed and existing traits exaggerated. Depression and anxiety, to which Margaret was already prone, are common. Some patients also experience hallucinations.[6] Margaret was pricklier about issues that had always irritated her, and more forthright in her opinions. Poor vision and lack of energy made commitment to paper of the unceasing musical ideas floating through her head impossible. In her narrower world, the state of Australia's musical life exercised her more, and her sense of loneliness in the absence of regular contact with musical friends 'on her side' heightened her frustration.

Personal and musical exchanges with James Murdoch and Don Banks, both living in London, flesh out Margaret's story during this period. Her pleasure in 'getting a visible sign' from them is clear, as is the reciprocity of their relationships. To Murdoch in May 1969, she freely expressed her opinions about other composers. Sculthorpe had 'written himself out', and she was disappointed with Keith Humble, who was 'such a fine pianist, but NO composer'. It was 'misleading to the up-and-coming that he should write with no scruples'. Dreyfus was 'in America—perhaps he will stay? He has taken a backward path—very old hat'. Richard Meale and Nigel Butterley, on the contrary, were 'most interesting'. She added that she was feeling a lot better, but that her sight was not good. Murdoch echoed her consternation, and shared the good news that he might return to Australia to become music consultant to the first Music Board of the Australian Council of the Arts. This took three more years.[7]

The music board's predecessor as funding body for Australian composers carried the cumbersome title 'Commonwealth Assistance to Australian Composers (CAAC) scheme'. Established in 1966 by Liberal prime minister Harold Holt, its advisory board included Sir Bernard Heinze, Professor Frank Callaway (University of Western Australia) and John Hopkins. Its first major project was the survey *Musical Composition in Australia* (1969), largely executed by Professor Andrew McCredie (University of Adelaide). This comprised a concise history of

Australian composition, a catalogue of forty-six Australian composers and their works, a bibliography and a list of commercial recordings. There were recordings of music by ten composers—all male—together with scores and recorded talks. The survey was intended for overseas broadcasting stations, universities, colleges, music schools and other interested bodies.

The idea had merit, but its execution, according to *Herald* critic John Sinclair, was 'a first-class example of a third-class mess'. A year before its publication, he penned an article headed 'What a disgrace if they leave her out'.[8] Sinclair knew the advisory board had contacted Margaret, telling her she would be represented by a recording of her *Trio for Oboe and Two Violins* (1955). She had written back straightaway, expressing her pleasure at inclusion, but adding that the work was unsuitable, and the quality of the ten-year-old recording below standard. Heinze responded, regretting that she would be excluded, because the recording was unsatisfactory. They could not substitute another work, because other composers would expect similar treatment. It is hard to know whether Margaret's tense relationship with Heinze influenced this decision; her thoughts on Callaway and McCredie are not recorded.

Sinclair was outraged—first, that they would consider using an old mono recording when high-fidelity stereo recordings were available, and second, that they would consider omitting 'the doyen of Australian composers'. 'Well they did!', he headed an article in November 1969. In the publication's introduction, Heinze apologised for the survey's shortcomings that were due to lack of money and time. Sinclair criticised the publication and questioned the wisdom of allowing composers to talk about themselves. It was dangerous to let Dreyfus describe himself as 'a lone pioneer of Melbourne's avant garde' and Werder compare himself to 'a craftsman to the Greek sculptor Praxiteles'. 'I would be greatly surprised if [the publication] produced more than a yawn and a smile overseas.'[9]

Like other excluded composers, Margaret never forgave this affront. In its defence, the CAAC was under pressure to produce the survey for continued funding. Fortunately, when the ten-volume *Australian Festival of Music* (1972) was issued by Festival Records in collaboration with the ABC, APRA and the CAAC, Margaret's *Haunted Hills* (1950) was there.[10]

The repercussions of the stroke were still manifesting in September 1969—or it's possible Margaret had a second one. 'Have not been very well, hence my silence', she complained to Murdoch. 'After the wretched stroke (done to me!) I had a traumatic experience of my whole life lived again. Horrible! I am now at the [Lyceum] Club trying to forget it.' The next letter conveyed desperation. She had been 'hors-de combat' again but professed to be 'very nearly on top at last'. Hopkins was supportive, and Meale 'sincere', but she continued to be disappointed in Sculthorpe and Dreyfus. 'But do let me know if anything is cooking? Everything here lacks direction … We crave a touch of honesty.'[11]

Writing was 'a labour' now, 'on account of eyes', she told Banks in October. She was thrilled to hear that a work of his was being rehearsed. She commented on her growing grandchildren and imagined Banks's children were 'full of enterprise'. She was delighted that Murdoch had contacted Banks because they had 'something good in common'. 'The world is hard to take now, isn't it?' she asked. 'Everything moves too fast for me!'[12]

A surprising letter from Murdoch arrived on 20 December. He often addressed her as 'Dearest Margaret', but on this occasion, it was 'Beloved Margaret', and the letter ended with the words, 'Come to London and marry me!'[13] Murdoch never married and was thirty-three years Margaret's junior, so it is doubtful the offer was serious. He was experiencing challenges with health, finances and an expiring visa, and needed solace. Nevertheless, it showed his deep fondness for Margaret. Theirs was like a mother–son relationship, with Murdoch filling the role of the kind and caring son Mark never was.

Keen to repatriate, Murdoch would not do so without 'something concrete to return to'. Peggy Glanville-Hicks had visited him and promised to call on Margaret after her planned return to Australia the next year. Glanville-Hicks 'is nice, and honest, and a fighter', Murdoch observed. She must have read a draft of Murdoch's book *Australia's Contemporary Composers* (1972), since she told him she thought it 'very good and important'. The book was Murdoch's 'attempt to catch in passing a view of the contemporary music scene in Australia'.[14] It was 'a personal selection' that included thirty-three composers, of whom five were women, including Glanville-Hicks and Margaret.

Margaret's exchanges with Murdoch and Banks continued into 1970, though her letters were less frequent as it became harder to write. She interpreted Murdoch's marriage proposal in the manner in which it was offered and ignored it. She was, however, 'deeply concerned' at his other news. 'One is so devilishly at the mercy of irrelevant circumstances.' With no helpful suggestions, since 'everything is asleep at this time of year', she offered to write what truth she could find as soon as there were 'any pointers'.[15]

The outlook was brighter in February. Hopkins was conducting the MSO's Proms series. 'They are going with a BANG', Margaret told Murdoch, and there was 'an Australian work on each'. Her *Concerto Grosso* (1958) was to be performed on 24 February with Copeland, Glickman and Max Cooke (harpsichord) as soloists. 'I find Hopkins as straight as BH (Heinze) is crooked. He heeds your demands with extreme care and good nature.' And she could not resist a jibe: 'Things will go on improving as Heinze is obliged to leave the box seat'.[16]

Margaret delivered her paper 'The Struggle for the Arts Centre' to the Catalysts on 11 May 1970. 'Have got the Arts Centre well off my chest now', she wrote to Banks shortly after the talk.[17] Still following politics, she noted the 'great swing' in the UK (Tory leader Edward Heath easily defeated Labour's Harold Wilson in June 1970). 'Our politics are in a parlous state—one tears one's hair', she observed—possibly a reference to the Vietnam moratorium protests of 8 May 1970.

On 13 June 1970, Margaret officially became Dr Margaret Sutherland OBE, when she received an Order of the British Empire in the Queen's Birthday Honours Awards. Her only documented reaction was characteristically modest. 'I hoped it was for women in general, because I felt they hadn't had enough of that kind of existence.'[18]

The OBE was not mentioned in Margaret's next letter to Banks. Instead, she advised him regarding his decision whether to return to

Australia. He eventually did in 1972, initially to take up the creative arts fellowship at ANU, and in 1973 the role of head of composition studies at the relatively new Canberra School of Music (founded in 1965). The letter confirms her persisting commitment to her homeland:

> It is all a matter of concepts. Whether you want to live your life in a country that has antiquity (and all that covers), or whether you want one which still has to be moulded, where your children have scope (as indeed they would out here), whether you could not apply yourself in a creative sense to the exciting prospect of shaping a new field here for music, even if it means putting your own creative work temporarily into cold storage, to make something in another sense … Think of the new Conservatorium the way you would think of a new work for orchestra. This is my credo.[19]

On 13 September 1970, Con died in tragic circumstances. Duncan scholar Karen Pack discovered the details of her final days. Deteriorating senile dementia had necessitated her admission to Mont Park Mental Hospital in Macleod, Victoria, in late 1969. On 29 August 1970, Con had a serious fall during a violent, unprovoked attack by another patient. Initially nursed with a suspected broken leg, on 31 August she was admitted to the surgical unit at Willsmere Mental Hospital in Kew, where a fractured right femur was diagnosed. She died two weeks later of myocardial infarction and bronchopneumonia.[20] Margaret made no reference to Con's death—one imagines it was a loss she could not openly share.

Three months later, Margaret wrote to Banks about arts centre developments. She trusted in 'the serious, long-term and undeflectable nature of the men and women at the top', particularly the arts centre chairman, Melbourne businessman and arts patron Kenneth Myer. She remained disenchanted with the University of Melbourne Conservatorium under Loughlin's direction but was looking forward to spending Christmas at Jenny's home in Donvale, 'where the family would all gather', and to a surprise luncheon Mark's new wife Astrid Dahl was throwing for his birthday on 28 December. 'Things are going well', she concluded. 'I terribly love Australia.'[21]

In early January 1971, Banks was treated to another onslaught. Margaret criticised Keith Humble's work *Après le Légende* (1969) for piano and orchestra, scheduled for the Melbourne Proms concerts in February, and listed the Australian composers to be included. 'Felix [Werder] is off to Europe, to promote Felix', she added. In an appraisal of the global political situation that could refer to the present, she commented that she had 'faith in things righting themselves. China is coming up the strait and America is in for a very bad time'. Demonstrating her identification with the underprivileged, she felt in her bones that the 'too-rich nations will go under, and the poor, oppressed people of the East will come into their own'.[22]

This sentiment was reiterated in a letter to Murdoch in July. 'There are massive things to think about—as long as we are not rich—rich people are vermin!' This sweeping statement is attributable to Margaret's mental state after her stroke and should be interpreted as an overstatement of her distaste for people driven only by money. But the arts centre was doing marvellously, she reported. 'The 5 halls are starting off—and they are to be above-ground (a good thing). It's very exciting.'[23] Here she referred to the need to alter the original one-structure plan for the Concert Hall and Theatres Building, with much of it underground. The unstable foundations near the river necessitated serious revisions, including a division into two buildings.

In July 1971, a young Melbourne pianist Margaret admired, Stephen McIntyre, worked with her on her late piano compositions *Extension* and *Chiaroscuro I* and *II* (1967) and *Voices I* and *II* (1968). He recorded them for the ABC in early September. Back in March 1968, Margaret had written to Banks introducing McIntyre, who was based in Europe from 1963 to 1975. He possessed traits she appreciated: giftedness and humility. He was 'no hit-or-miss pianist—indeed quite the opposite', she wrote, 'and he can certainly hold his audience'. Although this was their only association, McIntyre remembered it well:

> Margaret was very intelligent, with a keen mind and a strong personality, and was most helpful when discussing the performance of her pieces. She had a great knowledge of piano-playing and took much time with

> me as I worked through them. I liked her very much, and don't know quite why we never met again. She had a great sense of humour, and we enjoyed our times together.[24]

The year 1971 ended in tragedy, when Margaret's 40-year-old daughter Jenny was killed in a car accident. On a stormy Sunday afternoon in early October, she was driving her VW Beetle to collect eldest daughter Anna from Presbyterian Ladies' College (PLC) following her return from a school camp. As she executed a right turn from Springvale Road onto Burwood Highway, a drunk driver hit the Beetle at great speed. Margaret's grandson, Anthony Bunney, recalled that Jenny had asked if he or his siblings wanted to accompany her on the drive. There were no takers.[25]

Little is recorded of Margaret's reaction—as a private person, she held her feelings of desolation close. She experienced many family deaths over the years, but mourning the death of one's child, regardless of cause or age, is usually intense, long lasting and complex. Parents do not expect to outlast their progeny. Such grief could only have exacerbated Margaret's inevitable decline. In January 1972, she managed a letter to Banks, in which she expressed pleasure at his imminent move to Canberra before saying that she had 'tragic news which I did not tell you during the brief time. My darling daughter Jenny was killed as she was going over to PLC, calling for her eldest, Anna. The wretched driver was drunk. Jenny was my greatest love'.[26]

According to Jenny's daughter, Kirsten Bunney, her mother was close to Margaret and Norman. Jenny did not emulate her mother in becoming a musician, but did continue in the family's artistic tradition. Sensitive, affectionate and loving, she trained as a teacher, but preferred the creative life, and a studio was built on the Donvale property for her use. She painted, and was always making something, Kirsten remembered, but 'there was a sadness about her', possibly attributable to the difficult home environment during her upbringing. At Jenny's funeral, a passage from Indian philosopher Jiddu Krishnamurti was recited from a book she was reading the night before she died. Kirsten felt her mother was still trying to find her voice, or a spiritual pathway, partly because she had married young.[27]

Jenny's husband, Dean Bunney, worked in public relations in the mining industry for Comalco and later for Conzinc Rio Tinto. He was driven and ambitious, and held high-powered positions that required regular overseas travel. But he was also kind and a good listener, who liked to grow vegetables on the Donvale property. Unlike Jenny, he had 'the gift of the gab'. Dean was fond of Margaret and very supportive, as was Jane, his second wife, whom he married in November 1973. He helped Margaret with her business affairs following the divorce, and continued to visit after Jenny's death, sometimes accompanying her to Lyceum Club functions. Composer Helen Gifford thought he was more like a son than a son-in-law. Like James Murdoch, he fulfilled a role that Mark, by then living in Nimbin, did not. Sadly, Dean died of cancer in 1990, aged sixty-five.[28]

Despite her daughter's tragic death hovering like a black cloud, several pleasurable events occurred in 1972. In the Lyceum's Diamond Jubilee year, Margaret accepted honorary life membership in recognition of her contribution to the music community and enjoyed the official jubilee dinner on 21 March. On 5 April, Mel Pratt interviewed her in her Power Street flat for the NLA's Oral History Programme. He was expecting her to be a difficult subject; her reputation for periodic intransigence, particularly following her strokes and Jenny's death, preceded her. Some guardedness—even peevishness—is apparent in Margaret's responses, and she admitted to Pratt that she was 'not a good person to get things out of'. This became more evident in later ABC interviews and letters.[29]

The celebrations for Margaret's seventy-fifth birthday on 20 November 1972 were the highlights of the year, with festivities in Adelaide and Melbourne. 'I find myself rather overwhelmed by the great kindnesses that so many of my old friends are showering on me', she wrote to Hopkins.[30] The extensive press coverage of her birthday and attendant festivities likely also heartened her, especially when she saw them collected in a booklet gifted by Melbourne literary and musical figure Nada Brozel. Coverage appeared in the newsletters of the National Trust of Australia and the National Gallery Society, *The Bulletin* and *Woman's Day*, and there were several articles in each of the *Age, Herald, Sun* and *Australian* newspapers, both before and after the festival.

To Margaret's delight, James Murdoch returned to Australia in 1972. In the same year, his book *Australia's Contemporary Composers* was published. His first generous (and time-consuming) gesture to his 'beloved' Margaret was, in conjunction with the ABC, to help plan and organise a festival of her works at the Great Hall of the National Gallery of Victoria (NGV) to honour her leading role in the Combined Arts Centre Movement and her seventy-fifth birthday. NGV director Eric Westbrook and his trustees agreed to sponsor the festival, which began with a formal dinner for eighty invited guests in the NGV restaurant on the evening of her birthday. The cake was not forgotten, and *Age* and *Sun* cameramen captured the moment she blew out the candle. Included on the guest list were members of the family, Hopkins and Lady Casey, whom Margaret referred to as one of her 'oldest and best friends-come-colleagues'. On the same evening, a program of her music was broadcast on ABC 3AR. She chose the music herself—Stephen McIntyre's renditions of her 1967 and 1968 piano works, and *Three Temperaments* performed by the MSO under Hopkins. A prerecorded interview was included.[31] Given the dinner started at 7 p.m., Margaret was too busy enjoying herself to be home in time for the broadcast's 9.15 p.m. timeslot.

Kabbarli was staged, and Australian artist Charles Blackman produced three drawings featuring Daisy Bates for the festival brochure. Also incorporated were forewords by Victorian premier Rupert Hamer, Nugget Coombs—chair of the Australian Council—and NGV director Eric Westbrook. The music began on Friday 24 November, with a recital of Margaret's chamber works written between 1946 and 1967. Among the performers was none other than Margaret Schofield—one hopes Margaret (Sutherland) kept any criticism of Schofield's interpretations to herself.

On Friday 28 November, the MSO under Patrick Thomas performed her orchestral compositions, including the *Concerto for Violin* (1960) with soloist MSO concertmaster Leonard Dommett, and the *Concertante for Oboe and Strings* (1961) with oboist Jiří Tancibudek. *Haunted Hills* (1950) and *Three Temperaments* (1958) completed the program. Margaret had hoped that Hopkins would be available to conduct. 'You have always given me my best performances', she wrote to him on 19 October, but she joked that in his very busy life he would not have 'time to conduct an old lady's music'. She also hoped he would be available to attend 'the little dinner they are giving me on my birthday'.[32] It is assumed he did.

Song settings of John Shaw Neilson and Judith Wright comprised the first half of the program on Wednesday 29 and Thursday 30 November. The second was reserved for Intimate Opera (SA)'s production of *The Young Kabbarli* (1964). A limited deluxe edition of the score was produced by J Albert & Son (Alberts) and the production was assisted by an Australia Council grant. The same program had been performed in Adelaide at the King's Music Hall on 13 and 14 November—Margaret and Lady Casey were probably present in the audience, with Margaret feted at the post-concert supper.

In early 1973, Banks assumed the position of chair of the Australia Council's Music Board and became an executive member of the Guild of Australian Composers. By then he had received his diagnosis of chronic lymphocytic leukaemia, which he battled for eight years until his death in 1980 at fifty-seven. Margaret never referred to this—perhaps she didn't know. In blissful ignorance of his health challenges, she was thrilled at his musical appointments. '<u>This</u> is what we need. We must have our own best to come back! It does a world of good', she wrote in a crooked scrawl in late January. She shared her pleasure at the result of the Australian federal election in December 1972, which brought the Labor Party under Gough Whitlam to power after twenty-three years of Coalition government (the Liberal and Country parties). 'What a new Government can do. I have great faith in them.'[33]

Margaret was understandably excited in early 1973, when, following publication of *The Young Kabbarli* the year before, Alberts purchased all the manuscripts in her possession—the exact number is unknown. It was the strangest thing she had ever experienced, she told Banks. 'I just can't take it in … I have always been very short of money', she confided, 'and I wanted to give as much as I could to some of my grandchildren who were short too'. Alberts published a total of six of her works.[34]

The *Kabbarli* performances in 1972 were followed in early 1973 with a history-making EMI recording in Adelaide by the same group of performers. Launched by Nugget Coombs in Sydney on 16 April, it marked four significant milestones: Margaret's seventy-fifth birthday, the seventy-fifth anniversary of the recording business, the first recording of an Australian opera, and the first commercially released Australian quadraphonic disc. The Blackman drawings were reproduced on the cover. Again, Murdoch played a role in the recording, and wrote the opera synopsis. Margaret was highly appreciative, as was Lady Casey. 'It could not have been better done', Margaret told him. Lyceum friend Aimée Wilkins was equally impressed. Margaret had spent a wonderful week with her at her farm in Merricks (Victoria) and had brought the record with her. 'I was expecting a lot, because of what we had read of the recording', Wilkins wrote to Murdoch, 'but it was so much more exciting than I had imagined. Margaret speaks of all your effort and energy and thought for her scores and of all you have done'.[35]

Murdoch further assisted Margaret by having a handwritten paper typed. Headed 'Difficulties', it is a series of vignettes from Margaret's life (quoted several times in this book). It was read to the Catalysts on 13 August 1973, 'written with such immediacy and vividness that the effect on her audience was spellbinding'. Helen Gifford was Margaret's guest, as was Madeline Williams, who delivered the paper—Margaret was no longer capable. She had known Williams and her companion, Madeline Crump, for many years, and the two, referred to as 'the Madelines', were extremely helpful to Margaret in her declining years. After Williams developed Alzheimer's disease, Crump continued to support Margaret, assisting her to find appropriate accommodation, writing letters for her and organising her musical affairs.[36]

Shortly after the Catalysts event, Margaret updated Banks regarding her recent adjudication of the three-year Ada Corder (née Freeman) piano scholarship at the conservatorium. 'I was with [Keith] Humble, and we got on really quite well!' she marvelled. Otherwise, she was feeling isolated and 'out of the loop' of musical life. Although she was pleased that Gordon Thomson was taking over from Eric Westbrook as NGV director, she did not 'know anything of what goes on!'[37] As frustration, isolation and poorer health set in, this sentiment became a trope.

Margaret's letters become increasingly difficult to read. She could no longer write in a straight line, and her cantankerousness was more marked. She was, however, thrilled when Murdoch formed the Australian Music Centre (AMC) in 1975, with the aim of documenting, coordinating, promoting and archiving Australian music. Murdoch enlisted German-born pianist, composer and Alberts editor Franz Holford to provide details of her works, recognising it would be difficult for Margaret to complete the necessary forms. Holford was charged with publication of Margaret's violin concerto, but the process was delayed, causing her great consternation. It finally appeared in print in 1978.[38]

In November 1975, the ABC's Norma Ferris invited Margaret to be interviewed about her life in music for the *Speaking Personally* program. This was not the first time Margaret had been featured on ABC radio programs. Four years earlier, she was interviewed by Ellis Blain for the network's *Portrait of a Composer* program. And in mid-1975, her music was featured in a program that included her in dialogue with Lydia Warren, along with brief tributes from Frances Lindsay, Aimée Wilkins, Canberra School of Music director Ernest Llewellyn, Margaret Schofield and John Hopkins.

In early 1976, the ABC's Ingrid Burke conducted the *Speaking Personally* interview over three sessions in January. A wide-ranging interview covering her whole life, the process was tiring for 78-year-old Margaret. In the unedited recording, the tape was stopped several times when she became fatigued or impatient. Her memory faltered on occasion, and she sometimes struggled to find the right words. Nevertheless, the interview is illuminating, at times confirming aspects of her story, and at others adding new insights. It was more evident to her at this stage of her life that her experience as a woman composer—especially in her early career—had been different from a man's. 'It was almost impossible as a woman. No-one would think that you would want to write music, and it was just accepted that you wouldn't, but I suppose if you were a man, they wouldn't feel that.' Her view endured that learning the rules of harmony and counterpoint was not sufficient to make a composer. 'They've got to have a quality to really express themselves … it must be something apart … Hard work is imperative, but if you haven't got that something, you can't write.' Her opinion about money had not softened with time. When asked what she considered the most important attribute for a composer, she replied, 'Not to make a lot of money … That's what is wrong with the world—money'.[39]

A major event in 1976 buoyed Margaret's spirits. Australian choreographer Graeme Murphy saw the potential of *Haunted Hills* (1950) as dance music for *Glimpses*, his interpretation of Norman Lindsay's drawings of voluptuous nymphs and satyrs. Well received when first aired at the Australian Ballet's 1976 Choreographic Workshop, the work won the *Canberra Times* Choreographic Award, and became Murphy's unwitting audition for the role of artistic director of the Dance Company of New South Wales (renamed the Sydney Dance Company in 1979). He remounted the work in March 1977 and toured it extensively around Australia. The score was used in its entirety, though Murphy added sound effects to lengthen it. Margaret was happy to grant permission to use the work and attended a performance, where she met Murphy. 'She was quite charming about the ballet but was already quite frail and aged', he said.[40]

Margaret was indeed becoming weaker, especially evident in her writing, and friends became her scribes. In early February 1977, Wilkins told Murdoch how 'interested and delighted' Margaret was to receive news from him that Murphy would restage *Glimpses* in March. 'Write again when you can and tell her of your plans for Australian music … Dear Margaret is not so strong or so able these days and I worry about her, but Margaret is a wonderful person and I know you know her worth.'[41] In the same month, Margaret was one of 6870 Australians to be awarded a Queen Elizabeth II Silver Jubilee Medal for contributions to the community; her reaction is unrecorded.

A few days later, Margaret wrote to Murdoch herself, agitated at the delay in the publication of her violin concerto. In her barely legible scrawl, she told him she would like Hopkins to conduct the concerto, 'because I need money'. She wanted a family history written, and 'It is going to cost quite a lot, and I must look ahead, being nearly eighty!!' Dean Bunney asked Australian historian Geoffrey Blainey for a recommendation, and Sydney academic Stuart Rosewarne was commissioned.[42]

Murdoch persisted with Holford and worked towards celebrations of another milestone—Margaret's eightieth birthday on 20 November 1977. An exhibition was planned at the Victorian College of the Arts (VCA) from 8 to 30 September of artwork by Jane and Ruth Sutherland, together with a collection of Margaret's scores, published material and facilities for listening to her music. At Hopkins' suggestion, VCA director Frances Lindsay wrote to Murdoch in July 1977, seeking his assistance with locating material relating to Margaret, and Murdoch set to work.

Margaret knew about the exhibition and dictated a letter to Crump for Murdoch. Still fixated on the publication of her violin concerto, she also mentioned 'an extremely nice girl [presumably Frances Lindsay]' who was arranging the exhibition. 'The paintings have to be re-furbished and the girl at the Gallery is good at that.' Hopkins was also helping, she said.[43]

But the momentous news in this letter was that Margaret had seen a doctor who advised her to move to the Old Colonists' Association retirement village in North Fitzroy. She hoped it would happen soon. 'Dear James, my dear love', she ended the letter. Recognising Margaret's increasing frailty, Crump had helped instigate the move to the Old Colonists', likely chosen because of its mission. Established in 1869 to care for Victorian-based retired and poor actors, it evolved into a facility for the aged and deserving poor. In early June, Margaret announced to Murdoch that she would soon relocate there.[44]

In his capacity as dean of the College of Music at the VCA, invitations to the opening of the exhibition were sent under Hopkins' signature. Sadly, Murdoch was overseas until mid-October and could not attend.

The catalogue attests to a comprehensive exhibition, with a foreword by Frances Lindsay and an essay on the Sutherland family by Stuart Rosewarne. Along with the collection of Margaret's scores and recordings, fifty-five artworks were shown: one by Margaret's grandfather, George Sutherland, twenty-eight by Jane Sutherland, twenty-five by Ruth Sutherland, and Rupert Bunny's portrait of Margaret. The exhibition, simply called *The Sutherlands*, was well received by press critics. The *Herald*'s Alan McCulloch found it 'of outstanding interest', and Sally White interviewed Margaret for the *Age*. 'For Dr Sutherland, the exhibition is a delight', she wrote. 'She sees the recognition as a sign that things are really changing for women at last', though she felt that attitudes towards women artists had always been marginally more tolerant than those towards women composers.[45]

As *The Sutherlands* came to a close, another ABC tribute was in the making. Producer Margaret Hetherington was compiling a program for Margaret's eightieth birthday. As well as playing her music, including the *Concerto for Violin and Orchestra*, the *Trio for Oboe and Two Violins*, and two of the *Company of Carols*, Hetherington gathered reminiscences and birthday greetings from Lady Casey, Madeline Crump, Helen Gifford, James Murdoch, Ernest Llewellyn, Frances Lindsay, Aimée Wilkins, Margaret Schofield and Mollie Turner Shaw. Interspersed were snippets of an interview with Margaret. Hetherington confided to Murdoch that she became 'quite emotionally involved over the whole thing'. Margaret was 'not at all happy in her present accommodation of one very tiny suite' but had taken an interest in helping with preparation of the program, Hetherington noted. The two-hour program aired on 18 November, with a shortened version broadcast on Radio Australia on the day of her birthday. Hetherington hoped Margaret would listen 'with friends in pleasant surroundings'.[46]

Exhausted after her birthday celebrations, Margaret asked Crump to write to Murdoch, thanking him for his telegram, flowers and contribution to the ABC broadcast. 'She is exceedingly frail now. All her close friends have noticed a great change in her over the past few months', Crump told Murdoch. This is evident in a picture published in the *Herald* with a short article marking the eightieth birthday. Her thin face reveals her as diminished, but a wry smile shows that her spirit remained.[47]

Murdoch was alarmed at Margaret's plight and wanted to help. To Crump, he confessed that 'As well as having a profound respect for her I also love her very much'. He continued to visit whenever he was in Melbourne, and 'observed her slow and valiant decline', though she still relished hearing news of the music world.[48] Dismayed at her acute distress in March 1978, Murdoch penned a letter to Australia Council CEO Dr Jean Battersby:

> [Life] has become a torment for her. She has only one kidney, is 90 per cent blind and so cannot read or watch television. She was in a tiny motel-type room surrounded by other old ladies whose radio and television sets (all at different stations) drove her demented. There is no common ground for communication with them … Surely this is only one of many elderly artists who through their life's work in artistic and intellectual activities have sensitivities and needs other than those who have led a 'normal' existence. Hypersensitive to sound, visual surroundings, relationships, the usual old people's homes are more than usually anathema to them. Has the Council given any thought to this problem?[49]

Murdoch alerted others to Margaret's plight, including Hopkins, who arranged for his students to visit her. He asked Dawn Westbrook (Eric Westbrook's wife) to check whether she would appreciate a cassette recorder. Wondering whether it would be possible to set Margaret up in a house with a caretaker, Westbrook asked Crump, who confirmed that Margaret was too ill to be moved, needed the attention provided at the Old Colonists', and seemed resigned to being there. Friends helped ensure she could still visit the Lyceum Club and the NGV. Distressingly, it appears that after his move to Nimbin in the early to mid 1970s, Mark was conspicuous by his absence in these final years of Margaret's life. He didn't visit her; nor did he attend her funeral.[50] Despite this apparent neglect, Margaret remembered him in her will, along with his first wife Moya.

In response to Murdoch's plea, Battersby contacted Dr Clive Pascoe, director of the council's music board, regarding a grant for a cassette recorder and music. The council obliged, on condition 'that the Music Board remains the arbiter in determining the ownership of the equipment purchased by the grant to a successor'.[51] Murdoch declined. Instead, he arranged for a Melbourne retailer to donate the equipment with no conditions attached. When it arrived in July 1979, Margaret dictated a letter thanking him for the wonderful present. But with her frailty, failing memory and bad eyesight, she couldn't operate it alone.

In late 1979, the AMC produced a brochure about Margaret with a biography, a list of works and discography. This gave her pleasure, and through Crump and Wilkins, she requested copies to send friends. In February 1980, she suddenly became much weaker, requiring investigation at a geriatric centre. After spending three weeks in Mount Royal Hospital for the Aged in Parkville, she was moved to the Princeton Private Nursing Home in Bellett Street, Camberwell, where more comprehensive nursing care was available than at the Old Colonists'. This was at least a 'temporary haven', Crump told Murdoch. A longer-term solution was soon found, and Margaret was transferred to the Aylesford aged care facility in Wattletree Road, Malvern.

The Madelines often visited Margaret at Aylesford and took her out. In August 1980, for example, they accompanied her to an exhibition of work by Australian artist Margaret Preston, followed by afternoon tea in the National Gallery Society lounge, where John Hopkins joined them.[52] Margaret's grandson Michael Bunney also collected his grandmother regularly for visits to the family home in Donvale. He remembers her complaining that—as at the Old Colonists'—there was no one at Aylesford like her.[53]

The last four years of Margaret's life were spent quietly as the inevitable deterioration escalated, but there were uplifting moments. On 13 June 1981, Margaret was awarded an Officer of the Order of Australia (AO) in the Queen's Birthday Honours for her services to music. It is unclear who nominated her. Predictably, she was unable to read the letter telling her of the honour. 'Someone read it to me', she told the *Age*. 'I just could not believe it. I already had the OBE; I didn't think there would be anything further.' Just as she had been when responding to previous honours, she was modest. 'I don't know that I did anything wonderful. I just loved music. And if you love music, you write it.'[54]

Needless to say, the most auspicious event of 1982, both for the arts in Melbourne and for Margaret, was the opening of the Melbourne Concert Hall (now Hamer Hall) on 6 November. Margaret had never ceased taking an interest in its progress. Before the opening, the Madelines took her for a tour, 'a private voyage of joy and wonderment' led by the theatre planning coordinator of the Victorian Arts Centre Building Committee, Bill Akers.[55] She is pictured in her wheelchair outside the Concert Hall in *Centre Stage*, the newsletter of the arts centre (now Arts Centre Melbourne) with general manager George Fairfax, and again with arts centre trust member John Hopkins. She managed a sweet smile for the camera.

In 1983, the documentary *Australian Women Composers* was produced. Adele Sztar was inspired to make it after observing that all the scores she studied at the University of Melbourne Conservatorium were by men, and very few were Australian. She conducted research that revealed the existence of women composers. In 1981, she received a grant from the Women's Film Fund and embarked on her project to raise awareness about ten mostly unknown female composers. Margaret was one, though she would not have been able to watch it and was probably too frail to absorb it. We are left to wonder what her reaction would have been to a film that showed 'music could be female too'.[56]

In April 1984, after an absence from Melbourne of eighteen months, Murdoch visited Margaret to discover she had suffered a fall the week before and cut her head. 'She was breathtakingly small and translucent like a mermaid in a silver-blue satin skin, beached on a bed of white seaweed. After a dawning recognition, she fell silent, and with the blazing gaze of the sightless, she looked at me and said, "It is time to go. I have waited too long".'[57]

Four months later, Margaret got her wish. On 12 August 1984, music's 'grand old lady', the 'tireless composer who tilled the musical desert', died peacefully at Lynn Private Nursing Home, Armadale, aged eighty-six. As Margaret had not adhered to any orthodox religion and wanted a simple funeral, friends and family organised a secular gathering at Tobin Brothers Chapel in Malvern on Tuesday 14 August. Appropriately, her music was played. George Fairfax, John Sinclair and Helen Gifford spoke.[58] A private cremation followed.

By coincidence, on the day of Margaret's death, mezzo soprano Elizabeth Campbell and pianist Anthony Fogg performed a concert of Australian song in the Sydney Opera House Recording Hall. Margaret's *Six Songs*, settings of Judith Wright's poetry, were first on the program. There could have been nothing more apt than the first stanza of one of the poems, 'Midnight':

> Darkness where I find my sight,
> shadowless and burning night
> here where death and life are met
> is the fire of being set.

CODA

There has been a passing. The kind that Kabbarli—Daisy Bates—would have marked, as for a tribal elder. Let us note it, and think on the life's work and person of an exceptional woman, with some love and gratitude for her gifts to us.

James Murdoch[1]

MARGARET DID NOT die a wealthy woman. Probate documents reveal she had enough to get by—she wouldn't have wished for more. Her real legacy was musical and cultural, immeasurable in monetary terms. She was a pioneer of Australian musical modernism, an unrelenting crusader for progressive attitudes to music and music education, and against apathy and ignorance. She dared to be a 'difficult' woman who commanded respect. During her lifetime, she contributed to Australia's development from culturally unrefined beginnings into a more artistically aware country, and to Melbourne's evolution from a city with few dedicated cultural venues into a civilised metropolis with a world-class arts centre.

Margaret's creative and intellectual family insulated her from the restrictions imposed on women by the wider society. Here the ground was laid for the talented child to pursue music, but when she embarked on composition, she had only one role model of a career-minded female composer—Mona McBurney, her first composition teacher.

Margaret's formative years taught her to fight for causes dear to her heart, and she never gave up hope despite a string of family traumas, an unhappy marriage and a society not quite ready for her. She is unlikely to have called herself a feminist, but she modelled a feminist existence. She exercised agency and choice in her domestic and professional life, trying to do justice to both, and played an active role in musical and public life.

It is fair to say that Margaret has been a source of creative drive for subsequent generations of musical women. Nowadays, the numbers of male and female composers in Australia are by no means equal—in 2017, only 26 per cent of composers were female—and the *Living Music Report 2020* suggests that women composers remain significantly under-represented in Australian concert programs.[2] Although a creative career is still financially precarious for both men and women, Australian women composers are no longer considered oddities.

As time progresses, we hear more music by women composers. Since 2019, ABC Classic FM has celebrated them with an annual four-day festival around International Women's Day, in which Margaret's music has been featured. Melbourne's 3MBS Fine Music radio station is also working to encourage the programming of women's music, including Margaret's.

Until recently, Margaret's works appeared only occasionally on concert programs, but there has been an encouraging resurgence of interest. In 2011, three distinguished Melbourne musicians, Caroline Almonte (piano), Elizabeth Sellars (violin) and Molly Kadarauch (cello), formed the Sutherland Trio. 'We wanted to find a name that reflected Melbourne in a significant way', Sellars explained. 'We knew the Sutherland family and its persevering women who contributed so much to the visual and musical arts when women were not expected or able to do so. Their pioneering example and strong artistic vision inspired us.'[3] The Sutherland Trio has regularly performed Margaret's music and that by other women composers. Sellars was soloist in the *Concerto for Violin and Orchestra* (1960) with the Monash Academy Orchestra in 2016, and the Canberra Symphony Orchestra played it in 2022 with soloist Courtenay

Cleary and conductor Fabian Russell. (CSO chief conductor Jessica Cottis was ill with Covid-19.)

In March 2021, the violin concerto was featured by the MSO with soloist Sophie Rowell. Conductor Benjamin Northey saw this as 'an opportunity to honour the talents and legacy of one of Australia's great composers. It is a work of tremendous quality, noted by all performers, and was vividly brought to life by our soloist'.[4] In his *Limelight* review, Ben Wilkie described it as 'hefty, serious, cerebral music that retains raw emotional appeal', and acknowledged its humour and lyricism.[5] *Haunted Hills* (1950) was programmed for August 2021 by the MSO but was postponed to March 2023 due to the Covid-19 pandemic.

As part of the 2021 Adelaide Festival, Australian media executive and composer Kim Williams AM curated a chamber music series, 'Incredible Floridas', which included five of Margaret's vocal and chamber works and featured Melbourne's Flinders Quartet, which has embraced Margaret's chamber music. As well as playing it, they completed a major publishing and recording project in 2021 and 2022. They recorded the three string quartets for the ABC, along with the *Quartet for Cor Anglais, Violin, Viola and Cello* (1956), *Serenade for Oboe and String Quartet* (1950) and the *Quartet for Clarinet and String Trio* (1967). New sets of performance parts published by Wirripang are part of this undertaking.

In 2016, Flinders Quartet cellist Zoe Knighton was introduced by oboist and cor anglais player Ben Opie to Margaret's *Quartet for Cor Anglais, Violin, Viola and Cello*, and it spoke to her on an intense emotional level. The three string quartets were a further revelation. Zoe related how the group plotted to 'ensure the world was given the chance to fall in love with Margaret's music as we had':

> The musician's greatest privilege is conversing with deceased composers through playing their music. In my imagination, Margaret was witty and intelligent, and her kindness genuine. She had the knack of expressing a contrary view in the most straightforward way, and I would have walked over hot coals to hear her opinion on anything.

While the effort is 'worth it in every sense', Margaret's music is 'some of the most difficult we have tackled—a testament to her craft, sense of structure, harmonic ingenuity and her own voice—her music is unmistakably "Margaret"'.[6]

Melbourne composer Katy Abbott is among many who have been encouraged by Margaret's lead. As part of Flinders Quartet's commitment to Australian chamber music, Abbott was commissioned in 2021 to write a song cycle to honour her forebear. She is 'wholly inspired by Margaret's achievements as a pioneering composer, the heart with which she approached her work, her advocacy and her grit'. In conceiving her work *Splitting the Ambivalence,* Abbott wanted to 'get to know the real woman behind the action, one who deeply appreciated beauty, nature and the mystery and magic of neglected spaces'.[7]

Fortunately, Margaret was still alive when Melbourne's Hamer Hall opened, but not when the State Theatre opened in October 1984. As the finishing touches were applied to the Victorian Arts Centre (now Arts Centre Melbourne), in an appropriate gesture to its early instigator, George Fairfax AM, John Hopkins AM OBE and Dean Bunney conceived a memorial gathering to commemorate her life in music. Hopkins presided over the event in the Stalls Foyer of the Melbourne Concert Hall on 1 October 1984. A short excerpt from Sztar's film was incorporated, as were speeches by dear friends. The occasion would not have been complete without a concert of Margaret's chamber works, curated by violinist Paul McDermott, whose quartet premiered Margaret's *Discussion* string quartet in 1954.

Margaret's role in the early 'struggle for the Arts Centre' is acknowledged today by the previous CEO of Arts Centre Melbourne, Claire Spencer AM:

> Arts Centre Melbourne is indebted to Margaret Sutherland and the public support she garnered for its place at the heart of Melbourne's cultural centre. As one of our most celebrated composers, Sutherland's contribution to Australian music was prolific and far reaching. Her commitment to establishing broader recognition for the arts in this country continues to be felt today, a creative spirit that guides our own endeavours for the future of Arts Centre Melbourne.[8]

Vicki Fairfax, author of *A Place across the River* and wife of the first general manager of the Victorian Arts Centre Trust, George Fairfax AM, similarly paid homage. 'We owe her a great debt for mobilising the Melbourne arts community in 1943 and petitioning the people of Victoria to create a first-class performing arts centre, where we witness wonders every night.'[9]

As if the Arts Centre Melbourne's (formerly the Victorian Arts Centre) existence were not enough, it was a beneficiary in Margaret's will, and the concertmaster's room backstage at the Concert Hall bears her name. The Victorian College of the Arts also received a small bequest for the education of its music students.

Margaret's beloved Lyceum Club was a vital source of friendship and intellectual stimulation for sixty years. 'When she wished to discuss something serious to her world, one would be invited to lunch with her at her club, the Lyceum', Murdoch wrote in his tribute. 'A Lyceum Club summons always meant something was afoot. The simple but elegant lunch would allow her time to expound with great persuasion a new thesis: a new book, a new artistic marriage. "What if we got X to meet Y"?'

The club was the beneficiary of a modest sum in Margaret's will, as were her descendants and a long list of dear friends. Among them were fellow Lyceum members Aimée Wilkins and Mollie Turner Shaw, who chose to preserve Margaret's name at the club rather than keep their bequests. In consultation with then Lyceum Club president Caroline Travers, they endowed the Margaret Sutherland Bursary Fund to acknowledge Margaret's interest in and support of young musicians. Every year since 1987, a competition has taken place at the club in which selected undergraduate students from Melbourne tertiary music institutions perform a recital, including (where possible) one of Margaret's compositions in their programs. Through Rupert Bunny's portrait, purchased by the Lyceum from John Hopkins' estate in 2014, Margaret lives on at the club, keeping an eye on musical events, and on the cultural and intellectual pursuits of subsequent generations of high-achieving women.

The many press tributes following Margaret's death acknowledge her stature, but no one encapsulated her legacy and personality more genuinely than James Murdoch:

> A woman has passed our way with gifts of love and of art. Let us at least recognise her passing in silence and most of all in music. She understood so well the value of both.
>
> Let there be hosannas and celebrations.[10]

Hear, hear! It is through her music that we listeners gain access to her humanity and her inner song. May she continue to inspire people—women, in particular—to listen to their own.

SELECTED REFERENCES

Abbreviations (Endnotes and References)

ADB — *Australian Dictionary of Biography*
AMC — Australian Music Centre
AMN — *Australian Musical News*
ASP — Australian Scholarly Publishing
MSO — Melbourne Symphony Orchestra
NAA — National Archives of Australia
NLA — National Library of Australia
OCAH — *Oxford Companion to Australian History*
OCAM — *Oxford Companion to Australian Music*
OUP — Oxford University Press
RCM — Royal College of Music, London
SCV — Supreme Court of Victoria
SLV — State Library of Victoria
UoM — University of Melbourne
VCAG — Victorian College of the Arts Gallery

Author Interviews/Discussions/Email Exchanges

Helen Gifford, interview, 16 September 1999
Margaret Schofield, interview, 4 October 1999
Elizabeth Von Rompaey, interview, 7 October 1999
Pamela Bloom, interview, 12 October 1999
Barbara Taylor, interview, 18 October 2019
Jane Bunney, interview, 20 January 2000
Valerie Cohen, interview, 25 January 2000
Maureen White, interview, 14 June 2000
Suzanne McWha, telephone conversation, 1 June 2020
Diane Langmore, telephone conversation, 30 July 2021
Beryl Kimber Leske, email exchange, 7 August 2021
Michael Bunney, interview, 5 August 2021

Astrid Dahl, email exchange, 5–9 August 2021
Paul Mishura, Scotch College Archivist, email exchange, 9 August 2021
Kirsten Bunney, interview, 11 August 2021
Stephen McIntyre, email exchange, 24 August 2021
Desley Deacon, email exchange, 10 September 2021
John Spicer, email exchange, 10 September 2021
Elizabeth Campbell, email exchange, 4 October 2021
Vicki Fairfax, email exchange, 2 November 2021
Zoe Knighton, email exchange, 4 November 2021
Claire Spencer AM, email exchange, 8 November 2021
Katy Abbott, email exchange, 9 November 2021
Elizabeth Sellars, email exchange, 10 November 2021
Benjamin Northey, email exchange, 23 November 2021
Kerry Murphy, email exchanges November–December 2021
Karen Pack, meeting, 3 December 2021; email exchanges, December 2021–January 2022

Manuscripts and Records

National Archives of Australia (NAA), Sydney

ABC Archives: Correspondence with Margaret Sutherland in SP827/2, SP1558/2, C2327, SP1101/1

National Library of Australia (NLA)

Donald Banks Papers, MS 6830—correspondence
Herbert and Ivy Brookes Papers, MS 1924—correspondence
James Murdoch Papers, MS 8372—Murdoch–Sutherland interview transcripts; correspondence with Margaret Sutherland, Jean Battersby, Marissa Brumby, Madeline Crump, Margaret Hetherington, Clive Pascoe, Dawn and Eric Westbrook, Aimée Wilkins
Maie Casey Papers, MS 1840—correspondence
Margaret Sutherland Papers, MS 2967—notes, articles, photographs, scrapbook; correspondence with Yseult Bailey, Una Bourne, Jack Brymer, Doris Carey, Aaron Copland, Max Crawford, David Felsman, Percy and Ella Grainger, Kathleen Kyffin Thomas, Keith Macartney, Nell, John Shaw Neilson, Nina Verchinina
Norman Albiston Biographical Summary, MS 6415
Peter Sculthorpe Papers, MS 9676—correspondence

Public Records Office Victoria

Probates: Ada Sutherland, 18 October 1923; George Sutherland Snr, 4 June 1885
Sutherland Family Wills

State Library of Victoria (SLV)

British Music Society, MS 13548—minutes

Catalysts Club, MS 11233—minutes
Lorna Stirling Diary, MS 8584
Louise Hanson-Dyer, MS 10770
Lyceum Club Melbourne Records, MS 11270—membership records, correspondence
Margaret Sutherland Papers, MS 8739, 12310, 12311—notes, articles, concert programs, scrapbook, Arnold Bax letter to J&W Chester, correspondence with Louise Hanson-Dyer, Nellie Melba, David Oistrakh

University of Melbourne (UoM)
Éditions de l'Oiseau-Lyre Archive 2016.0035—Louise Hanson-Dyer correspondence
Grainger Museum Collection
Meanjin Archive—Clem Christesen correspondence

Margaret Sutherland Material
ABC Archives
Program note supplied Prom concert, March 1971, ABC Library, Sydney
Recordings of programs featuring Margaret Sutherland: 1971, 1975, 1976, 1977

Anthony Bunney Private Collection
Autobiographical note addressed to Dean Bunney, November 1960
'Bartók', undated typescript
'Changing Horses in Mid-Stream', undated handwritten note
Correspondence with Kenneth Myer, Judith Wright
'First Glimpses', undated handwritten note
'How to Live in a Room-and-a-Bit (and still keep your reason—and your piano)', undated handwritten note
'Loose Legs in Europe', lecture to the Catalysts, 16 February 1953
Notebook, 1966
'Occupational Hazards', undated typescript
'Several Episodes', undated handwritten note
'The Prodigy', paper delivered to the Catalysts, 11 February 1963
'The Struggle for the Arts Centre', paper delivered to the Catalysts, 11 May 1970
'These Things I Must Remember', travel diary, 1951–52

Australian Music Centre (AMC)
Concert programs
Press clippings
Thematic Index: 'Names, descriptions and principal themes of works by Margaret Sutherland. Mar. 1939'

Interviews with Sutherland
Blain, Ellis, ABC *Portrait of a Composer* program, 10 November 1971—ABC Archives

Burke, Ingrid, ABC *Speaking Personally* program, January 1976—ABC Archives
Hetherington, Margaret, ABC *Margaret Sutherland 80th Birthday Celebrations* program, 18 November 1977—ABC Archives
Murdoch, James, 'Perspective', 19 August 1967—MS 8372, NLA
Murdoch, James, Untitled, 3 April 1968—MS 8372, NLA
Pratt, Mel, 5 April 1972, Oral History Section, TRC 121/31, NLA
Warren, Lydia, ABC Radio *Coming Out Ready or Not* program, 10 June 1975—ABC Archives

NLA

'1920 and So On', undated autobiographical note, MS 2967
CACM draft, 1943, MS 2967
CACM letter re petition, 1944, MS 2967
'Concerts for Young People', undated note, MS 2967
'Difficulties', paper delivered to the Catalysts, 13 August 1973, MS 8372
'Adelaide', pp. 1–3
'An Alliance that had to Break', pp. 18–22
'Heronswood', pp. 7–9
'Melbourne University', pp. 4–6
'John Hopkins, James Murdoch and Don Banks', pp. 24–5
'School', pp. 15–17
'The Strange Story of Percy Grainger', MS 2967
'Three Universities in One', undated handwritten note, MS 2967

Press and Journals

'A New Musical-Box: Whither Will It Lead?', *Argus*, 4 February 1928, p. 8.
'Accent on Music-Making', *Meanjin*, vol. 2, no. 2, Winter 1943, p. 40.
Age, letters to Editor—4 September 1943, 8 September 1944, 18 November 1949
Argus, letters to Editor, 7 and 10 August 1926
'Musical Emancipation: New Works and Old Standards', *Argus*, 13 November 1926, p. 12.
'Our Musicians Abroad', *The ABC Weekly*, 21 February 1953, p. 23.
'The Composer's Lodestone', *Canon: Australian Music Journal*, vol. 11, no. 10, May 1958, p. 328.
'The Vogue of Bach: A Perfect Musical Balance', *Argus*, 22 May 1926, p. 12.
'Theatre Needed for Children', *Herald*, 2 March 1944, p. 4.
'Young Days in Music', *Overland* 40, December 1968, p. 24.

SLV

CACM Scrapbook, MS 8739
'Chant Intérieur', paper delivered to the Catalysts, May 1956, MS 11233
'One Lap Behind', paper delivered to the Catalysts, 1959, MS 11233

Supreme Court of Victoria (SCV)

Affidavit, Divorce and Matrimonial Causes Jurisdiction, 3 November 1950

Divorce Certificate, Margaret Ada Sutherland and Norman Arthur Albiston, 2 July 1951

Books, Articles, Dissertations

Reference

ADB—Melanie Nolan (ed.), National Centre of Biography, Australian National University

OCAH—John Hirst and Stuart Macintyre (eds), Oxford University Press, Melbourne, 1998

OCAM—Warren Bebbington (ed.), Oxford University Press, Melbourne, 1997

Other

Albiston, Norman 'The Importance of Habit', in *The Growing Child: A Series of Five Lectures on Child Management'*, Melbourne University Press, Carlton, 1932, pp. 38–55.

Anis, Rehnuma Bint, 'The Woman Question in the Novels by the Brontë Sisters', *IIUC Studies*, vol. 3, December 2007.

Barnard, Francis G, *The Jubilee History of Kew, Victoria, Its Origin and Progress 1803—1910*, EFG Hodges, 'Mercury Office', Kew, 1910.

Beaton, Lynn, 'The Importance of Women's Paid Labour – Women at Work in World War II', in *Worth Her Salt – Women at Work in Australia*, Margaret Bevege et al. (eds), Hale & Iremonger, Sydney, 1982, pp. 84–98.

Birns, Nicholas, '"This Piece of Hardwood, Cunningly Shaped": Rex Ingamells Kicks off the Jindyworobaks', in *Telling Stories: Australian Life and Literature 1935–2012*, pp. 23–30.

Blainey, Ann, *I am Melba*, Black Inc., Melbourne, 2008.

Blainey, Geoffrey, *Centenary History of the University of Melbourne*, Melbourne University Press, Parkville, 1957.

Bomford, Janette, *Circles of Friendship: The Centenary History of the Lyceum Club Melbourne*, Australian Scholarly Publishing Ltd, Melbourne, 2012.

Bowen, Stella, *Drawn from Life: A Memoir*, Collins Publishers, Sydney, 1941, reprinted Picador, Sydney, 1999.

Campo, Monica, 'Children's Exposure to Domestic and Family Violence', Australian Institute of Family Studies website.

Chodorow, Nancy, *The Reproduction of Mothering: Psychoanalysis and the Sociology of Gender*, University of California Press, Berkeley, 1978.

Citron, Marcia, 'Women and the Lied', in Jane M Bowers and Judith Tick (eds), *Women Making Music: The Western Art Tradition, 1150–1950*, University of Illinois Press, Chicago, 1987, pp. 224–48.

——'Gender, Professionalism and the Musical Canon', *Journal of Musicology*, vol. 8, no.1, Winter 1990.

——*Gender and the Musical Canon*, University of Illinois Press, Chicago, 1993.

Clarke, Patricia, 'Bailey, Editha Olga Yseult (1903–1980), *Australian Women's Register* website.

Covell, Roger, *Australia's Music: Themes of a New Society*, Second Edition, Lyrebird Press, Melbourne, 2016 (first edition 1967, Sun Books).

Crotty, Joel, 'From Balletic Binge to Cultural Cringe: Choreographic Music in Australia, 1936–56', *One Hand on the Manuscript: Music in Australian Cultural History 1930–1960*, Nicholas Brown et al. (eds), Humanities Research Centre, ANU, Canberra, 1995, pp. 217–28.

——'Laurel Martyn and Her Composers, 1946–1956', *Brolga*, June 1996, pp. 47–51.

Damousi, Joy, *Freud in the Antipodes*, UNSW Press, Sydney, 2005.

Davidson, Jim, *Lyrebird Rising: Louise Hanson-Dyer of l'Oiseau Lyre 1884–1962*, Melbourne University Press, Carlton, Victoria, 1994.

Dawson, Sandra, 'Her career started with a guilt complex', *Australian*, 21 April 1965.

De Vries, Susanna, 'Jane Sutherland (1855–1928), Margaret Sutherland (1896–1984): Outstanding Women in Art and Music', in *Strength of Purpose: Australian Women of Achievement from Federation to the Mid-20th Century*, Harper Collins, Sydney, 1998.

Devaney, Beulah Maud, 'Anne Brontë: the Unsung Sister, who Turned the Gaze on Men', *Guardian*, 17 January 2014.

Excell, Richard, 'Unsung Lyrics: Recent Margaret Sutherland Discoveries', *University of Melbourne Collections*, Issue 9, December 2011, pp. 43–51.

Fairfax, Vicki, *A Place across the River: They Aspired to Create the Victorian Arts Centre*, Macmillan Australia, Melbourne, 2002.

Falk, Barbara, *D.J.: Dorothy Jean Ross 1891–1982*, Melbourne University Press, Carlton, 2000.

Fay, Amy, 'Women and Music', *Music*, vol. 18, October 1900, Chicago, p. 506.

Fitzpatrick, Kathleen, *Solid Bluestone Foundations and other memories of a Melbourne girlhood 1908–1928*, Macmillan, South Melbourne, 1983.

Foreman, Lewis, *Bax: A Composer and His Times*, Scolar Press, London, 1987.

Garretty, Joyce, 'Three Australian Composers', MA, University of Melbourne, 1963.

Gates, Eugene, 'Why Have There Been No Great Women Composers? Psychological Theories, past and Present', *Journal of Aesthetic Education*, vol. 28, no. 2, 1994, pp. 27–34.

Geitenbeek, Monique, 'Reaching a Public: Opportunities for Australian Women Composers 1930–1960', in *Repercussions: Australian Composing Women's Festival and Conference, 1994*, Thérèse Radic (ed.), National Centre for Australian Studies, Monash University, Clayton, 1995, pp. 30–4.

Ghandar, Ann, 'Condensed Clouds: Margaret Sutherland's *Sonata for Violin and Piano*', in *Repercussions: Australian Composing Women's Festival and Conference, 1994*, Thérèse Radic (ed.), National Centre for Australian Studies, Monash University, Clayton, 1995, pp. 66–71.

——'The Context of *Chiaroscuro* I by Margaret Sutherland', in *One Hand on the Manuscript: Music in Australian Cultural History 1930–1960*, Nicholas Brown et al (eds), Humanities Research Centre, ANU, Canberra, 1995, pp. 126–7.

Gifford, Helen, 'Recalling a Lost Voice: Margaret Sutherland's Sonata for Violin and Piano (1925)', in *One Hand on the Manuscript: Music in Australian Cultural History 1930–1960*, Nicholas Brown et al. (eds), Humanities Research Centre, ANU, Canberra, 1995, pp. 107–21.

Gillison, Joan, *A History of the Lyceum Club (Melbourne)*, McKellar, Melbourne, 1975.

Graham, Jillian, 'Composer, Wife and Mother: Margaret Sutherland as Conflicted Subject', MMus, University of Melbourne, 2001.

——'Composing Biographies of Four Australian Women: Feminism, Motherhood and Music', PhD, University of Melbourne, 2009.

Gray, Cecil, *A Survey of Contemporary Music*, Oxford University Press, London, 1924.

Green, Clinton, 'The International Society for Contemporary Music in Melbourne: Forerunners, Foundation, and Decline', *Musicology Australia*, vol. 32, no. 2, December 2010, pp. 243–63.

Greer, Germaine, *The Obstacle Race: The Fortunes of Women Painters and their Work*, Secker & Warburg, London, 1979.

Grimshaw, Patricia et al. (eds), *Creating a Nation*, Penguin, Melbourne, 1996.

Hain, Gladys, 'Margaret Sutherland: An Australian Composer', *Illustrated Tasmanian Mail*, 28 April 1926.

Halstead, Jill, *The Woman Composer: Creativity and the Gendered Politics of Musical Composition*, Ashgate, London, 1997.

Hammond, Victoria and Juliet Peers, *Completing the Picture: Women Artists and the Heidelberg Era*, Artmoves Incorporated, Hawthorn East, 1992.

Heilbrun, Carolyn, *Writing a Woman's Life*, Ballantine Books, New York, 1988.

Hill, Jess, *See What You Made Me Do*, Black Inc., Melbourne, 2019.

Hopkins, John (with William Cottam), *The Point of the Baton: Memoir of a Conductor*, Lyrebird Press, Melbourne, 2009.

Hyslop, Anthea, 'Agents and Objects—Women and Social Reform in Melbourne 1900 to 1914', in *Worth Her Salt—Women at Work in Australia*, Margaret Bevege et al. (eds), Hale & Iremonger, Sydney 1982, pp. 230–43.

Jenkins, Cyril, 'Celebrity Concert & Richard Crooks' Season, *Table Talk*, 15 June 1939, p. 8.

——'Music of the Week', *Table Talk*, 6 July 1939, p. 12.

——'Music of the Week', *Table Talk*, 1 September 1939, p. 8.

Jennings, Rebecca, 'Sandra Willson: A Case Study in Lesbian Identities in 1950s and 1970s Australia', *History Australia*, vol. 19, no. 1, 2013, pp. 99–124.

Kincaid, James R, *Tennyson's Major Poems: The Comic and Ironic Patterns*, West Virginia University Press, Morgantown, WV, 1976.

Langmore, Diane, *Glittering Surfaces: A Life of Maie Casey*, Allen & Unwin, St Leonards, NSW, 1997.

Lee Martin, Ruth, 'The Dark Corner: A Study of the Dynamic Dialectic between Women Composers and the Australian Orchestral Milieu', PhD, Australian National University, Canberra, 2000.

Longmire, Anne, *The Catalysts: Change and Continuity 1910–2010*, Anne Longmire and the Catalysts, Melbourne, 2011.

Lorenz, Andrew, 'The Australian Violin Concerto', MPhil, University of Southern Queensland, 2010.

Macarthur, Sally, 'Feminist Aesthetics in Music', PhD, University of Sydney, 1997, p. 130.

McCalman Janet, *Journeyings: The Biography of a Middle-Class Generation 1920–1990*, Melbourne University Press, Carlton, Vic, 1993.

McCarthy, Erica, 'Ship Carvers in eighteenth- and nineteenth-century Britain', *Sculpture Journal*, vol. 24, no. 2, 2015.

McWha, Suzanne, 'Baldur and the Art of Female "Muscle Culture"', *Kew Historical Society Newsletter*, March 2016, no. 114, p. 9.

Manzie, Keith, 'New Approach to Shakespeare: Tin Alley Players', *Argus*, 28 April 1941, p. 6.

Mike, Celia, 'Howell, Dorothy', *The New Grove Dictionary of Women Composers*, Julie Anne Sadie and Rhian Samuel (eds), Norton, New York, 1994, p. 231.

Modjeska, Drusilla, 'Rooms of their Own: The Domestic Situation of Australian Women Writers between the Wars', in *Women, Class and History: Feminist Perspectives on Australia 1788–1978*, Elizabeth Windschuttle (ed.), Fontana/Collins, Melbourne, 1980, pp. 330–52.

——*Stravinsky's Lunch*, Pan Macmillan, Sydney, 1999.

Moresby, Isabelle, *Australia Makes Music*, Longmans Green, Melbourne, 1948.

Murdoch, James, *Australia's Contemporary Composers*, Macmillan, Melbourne, 1972.

——'Margaret Sutherland–Tribute to a Music Elder', *24 Hours*, October 1984, p. 10.

Nemet, *History of The Musical Society of Victoria: 1861–1981*, Musical Society of Victoria, Melbourne, 1981.

Neuls-Bates, Carol (ed.), *Women in Music: An Anthology of Source Readings from the Middle Ages to the Present*, Harper & Row, New York, 1982

Nochlin, Linda, 'Why Have There Been No Great Women Artists?', *Woman in Sexist Society: Studies in Power and Powerlessness*, Basic Books, New York, 1971.

Oldaker, Max, 'Two Australian Composers', *The London Magazine*, vol. 2, no. 6, 1962, pp. 75–8.

Osborne, WA, *William Sutherland: A Biography*, Lothian Book Publishing, Melbourne, 1920.

Pack, Karen, 'Singularly Engaged: How and Why Unmarried, Evangelical Christian Women in Australia Engaged in Activism Outside the Church from the Late Nineteenth to the mid-Twentieth Centuries', PhD, Macquarie University, Sydney, 2022.

Petrus, Pauline, 'Esther Rofe: Theatre Musician', in *One Hand on the Manuscript: Music in Australian Cultural History 1930–1960*, Nicholas Brown et al. (eds), Humanities Research Centre, ANU, Canberra, pp. 75–94.

Prentis, Malcolm, *Scots in Australia: A Study of New South Wales, Victoria and Queensland, 1788–1900*, UNSW Press, Sydney, 2008.

Radic, Thérèse, 'Margaret Sutherland: Composer', *Double Time: Women in Victoria – 150 Years*, Marilyn Lake and Farley Kelly (eds), Penguin, Melbourne, 1985.

——*Bernard Heinze*, Macmillan, South Melbourne, 1986.

——'Adelaide Women Composers' Festival 1991', *Sounds Australian*, vol. 32, Summer 1991–1992, pp. 5–8.

Robinson, Suzanne, *Peggy Glanville-Hicks: Composer and Critic* (e-book), University of Illinois Press, Chicago, 2019.

Rosewarne, Stuart, 'Sutherland Family History', unpublished draft typescript, 14 November 1978, Bunney collection.

——'The Sutherland Family', catalogue of The Sutherlands exhibition, Victorian College of the Arts Gallery, 8–30 September 1977, Bunney collection.

Sculthorpe, Peter, *Sun Music: Journeys and Reflections from a Composer's Life*, ABC Books/Griffin Press, 1999.

Sinclair, John, 'Margaret Sutherland: Australian Composer', *The Australian Journal of Music Education*, vol. 4, 1969, pp. 57–8.

Slaughter, Peta Sheridan, 'Aspects of Margaret Sutherland's Vocal Style', BMus (Hons), University of Queensland, Brisbane, 1976.

Smyth, Ethel, 'Female Pipings in Eden', Peter Davies, London, 1933.

Southcott, Jane, 'The Melbourne UNESCO Seminar, 1956: A Watershed in Australian Music Education', in *Musical Dimensions: A Festschrift for Doreen Bridges*, Martin Comte (ed.), Australian Scholarly Publishing, Melbourne, pp. 80–98.

Stephen, Sarah, 'A Quest for Collegiate Identity: Women in Ormond 1885 to 1910', in *Ormond College Centenary Essays*, Stuart Macintyre (ed.), Melbourne University Press, Parkville, 1984.

Stockigt, Janice B, 'Conversations with Jiří Tancibudek', 2002, pp. 38–40.

Summy, Hilary, 'From Missionary to Ministerial Adviser: Constance Duncan and Australia–Japan Relations 1922–1947', *Australian Journal of Politics and History*, vol. 54, no. 1, 2008, pp. 28–43.

Sutherland, John, *The Bonds of Society*, Heath, Cranton & Ouseley Ltd, London, 1931.

Symons, Christopher, *The Melbourne Symphony Orchestra*, MSO, 1987.

Symons, David, *The Music of Margaret Sutherland*, Currency Press, Sydney, 1997.

——'"The Jindyworobak Connection" in Australian Music, c. 1940–1960', *Context* 23, Autumn 2002, pp. 33–47.

Tan, Eril, *The Musical Society of Victoria: Celebrating 150 years 1861–2011*, Musical Society of Victoria, Melbourne, 2011.

Thomas, Adrian, '"Beware of Snakes, Spiders and Sinclair." John Sinclair (1919–1991), Music Critic for the *Melbourne Herald*: The Early Years', *Context*, vols 15, 16, 1998, pp. 79–90.

——'The Climate of Change: The ABC as Patron of Australian Music During the Hopkins Era', *Australasian Music Research*, vol. 7, 2002, pp. 47–54.

Thomas, David, *The Life and Art of Rupert Bunny*, Thames & Hudson, Port Melbourne, Victoria, 2017.

Thompson, Thelma Rae Payne, 'Algernon Charles Swinburne: No Other God—a Vision of Life', PhD, University of Oklahoma, Norman, OK, 1968.

Topliss, Helen, *Modernism and Feminism: Australian Women Artists 1900–1940*, Craftsman House, Sydney, 1996.

Tregear, Peter, *The Conservatorium of Music, University of Melbourne: An Historical Essay to Mark Its Centenary 1895–1995*, CSAM, University of Melbourne, 1993.

Tremearne, J E, 'Australian Works at Concert', *Herald*, 30 May 1939, p. 16.

——'Orchestra Plays Music by Australians', *Herald*, 24 November 1941, p. 11.

——'Virility in New String Quartet', *Herald*, 27 August 1938, p. 39.

Turner, Henry Gyles, *Alexander Sutherland: his life and work*, Lothian, Melbourne, 1908.

Turner Shaw, Mollie, Transcription of talk given at Margaret Sutherland Memorial Recital, Melbourne Concert Hall Foyer, 1 October 1984, MS 12311, SLV.

——'Education of a Squatter's Daughter', in *The Half-Open Door: Sixteen modern Australian women look at professional life and achievement'*, Patricia Grimshaw and Lynne Strahan (eds), Southwood Press, Sydney, 1982, pp. 278–303.

Unger, Rhoda and Mary Crawford, *Women and Gender: A Feminist Psychology*, McGraw Hill, New York, 1992.

'University Honours Composer', *University Gazette*, vol. XXV, no. 3, 26 May 1969, p. 10.

Van der Kolk, Bessel, *The Body Keeps the Score: Mind, brain and body in the transformation of trauma*, Penguin, 2015 (e-book).

Warren, John. 'David Josef Bach and the "Musik-Und Theaterfest" of 1924', *Austrian Studies*, vol. 14, 2006, pp. 119–42.

Waters, Thorold, 'Bach to Bax: Two-Piano Transition', *Sun*, 15 March 1927.

——'Brahms's Requiem: Tribute to Zelman, *Sun*, 28 June 1927.

——'Musical Moderns: Some First Performances', *Sun*, 19 March 1927.

——'One-Composer Programme: Australian Woman Gives Concert', *Sun*, 30 March 1938.

——'Women in the Creation of Music': An Australian Legislator Starts Something', *Australian Musical News*, 1 July 1938, pp. 3–4.

Watters-Cowan, Cherie, 'Reconstructing the Creative Life of Australian Composer Margaret Sutherland: The Evidence of Primary Source Documents', PhD, University of New South Wales, Sydney, 2006.

Wilkinson, Kenneth, 'Tin Alley Players', *Herald*, 28 April 1941, p. 11.

Wilson, Catherine, 'Opportunity and Success: The Music of the Women's Work Exhibition (1907)', in *Aflame with Music: 100 Years of Music at the University of Melbourne*, Brenton Broadstock et al. (eds), Centre for Studies in Australian Music, University of Melbourne, 1996, pp. 441–9.

Woolf, Virginia, 'A Room of One's Own', in *A Room of One's Own (1929), Three Guineas (1938)*, Morag Shiach (ed.), Oxford University Press, Oxford, 1992, pp. 3–149.

Zemgulys, Andrea P, '"*Night and Day* is Dead": Virginia Woolf in London "Literary and Historic"', *Twentieth Century Literature*, vol. 46, no. 1, Spring 2000, pp. 56–77.

Newspapers/Magazines Consulted

Advertiser (Adelaide)

Advocate (Melbourne)

Age (Melbourne)

Albury Banner and Wodonga Express (Albury, NSW, and Wodonga, Victoria)

Argus (Melbourne)
Australasian (Melbourne)
Australian (Sydney)
Australian Musical News (AMN, Melbourne)
Australian Women's Weekly
Canberra Times
Corowa Chronicle (NSW)
Corowa Free Press (NSW)
Critic (Adelaide)
Daily Mirror (Sydney)
Geelong Advertiser
Guardian—Australian online edition
Herald (Melbourne)
Illustrated Tasmanian Mail
Leader (Melbourne)
Limelight
Mail (Adelaide)
Morning Post (Cairns)
News (Adelaide)
Observer (Adelaide)
Punch (Melbourne)
Register (Adelaide)
Sun (Melbourne)
Sydney Morning Herald
Sydney Sun
Table Talk (Melbourne)
The Reporter (Box Hill)

Commercial Recordings Available

'100 Years: Melbourne Symphony Orchestra', vol. 4, 2020, John Hopkins (conductor), Jiri Tancibudek (oboe), Patrick Thomas (conductor); CD compilation released 2020: *Haunted Hills* (1950), *Concertante for Oboe and Strings* (1961)

'A Piano Odyssey', Trevor Barnard (piano), Divine Art, 2008: *Two Chorale Preludes* (pre-1934)

'Australian Composers', vol. 1, MSO, Patrick Thomas (conductor), 1995: *Concerto for Strings* (1948–49), *Haunted Hills* (1950), *Concerto Grosso* (1958), *Concerto for Violin and Orchestra* (1960)

'Australian Song Cycles', Wendy Dixon (soprano), David Miller (piano), Wirripang, 2010: *Four Blake Songs* (1957)

'Bach Transcriptions and Modern Australian Piano Music', Trevor Barnard (piano), Divine Art, 2013: *Two Chorale Preludes* (pre-1934), *First and Second Suites* (1937)

'Chamber Music Made and Played in Australia, 1945–1952', Thomas White (clarinet), Roy White (horn), William Krasnik (viola), Margaret Sutherland (piano), remastered 1996, Canberra School of Music: *House Quartet* (1942), *Contrasts* (1953), *Six Bagatelles* (1956), *Divertimento for String Trio* (1958)

'Crimson Songs', Perihelion: Margaret Schindler (soprano), Philippa Robinson (clarinet), Carson Druon (piano), Artworks, 2002: *Orange Tree* (1938)

'Margaret Sutherland: The Chamber Music with Strings', Marina Marsden and Colleagues, Tall Poppies, 1997: *Sonata for Violin and Piano* (1925), *Contrasts* (1953), *Six Bagatelles* (1956), *Divertimento* (1958), *World and the Child* (1960)

'Margaret Sutherland: The Piano Music', David Lockett (piano), ABC Classics, 1997: *Two Chorale Preludes* (pre-1934), *First and Second Suites* (1937), *Miniature Sonata* (c. 1939), *Valse Descant* (1941), *Six Profiles* (c. 1946), *Sonatina* (1956), *Extension* (1967), *Chiaroscuro I & II* (1967)

'Monday's Child', Katja Webb (soprano), David Wickham (piano), Allan Meyer (clarinet) and Peter Facer (oboe), Stone Records, 2015: *Cradle Song* (pre-1930), *September* (1930s), *Five Songs* (1934), *Arab Love Song* (pre-1938), *Orange Tree* (1938), *Gentle Water Bird* (c. 1954), *Four Blake Songs* (1957)

'O for a Muse of Fire: Shakespeare Settings by Australian Composers', Michael Halliwell (baritone), David Miller (piano), Australian Music Centre, 2012: *You Spotted Snakes* (1940), *O Mistress Mine* (1942)

'Nostalgia: Piano Music by Australian Women', Jeanelle Carrigan (piano), Wirripang, 2016: *Dithyramb* (c. 1939)

'Retrospect', Larry Sitsky (piano), Tall Poppies, 1995: *Two Chorale Preludes* (pre-1934)

'Rush: The Adventures of Sebastian the Fox and Other Goodies', George Dreyfus (bassoon), Diane Ridell (flute), Marla Swift (clarinet), Move Records, 1988: *Little Suite for Wind Trio* (1960)

'Six Profiles of Women Composers', Katie Zhukov (piano), Wirripang, 2015: *Six Profiles* (c. 1946)

'Songs of Sea and Sky', Nigel Westlake (clarinet), David Bollard (piano), Tall Poppies, 1991: *Sonata for Clarinet (or Viola) and Piano* (1947)

'Spirit Dances', Marina Marsden (violin), Clemens Leske (piano), Wirripang, 2009: *Sonatina* (1954)

'Tall Trees', Canberra New Music Ensemble, Angela Giblin (mezzo soprano), Margaret Legge-Wilson (piano), 2000: *Five Songs* (1934), *Six Songs* (1949)

'The Red of a Woman's Heart', Lisa Harper-Brown (soprano) and David Wickham (piano), Stone Records, 2014: *Silence, Beautiful Voice* (1913), *The Night Wind* (1914), *I Who am Dead a Thousand Years* (c. 1939), *Jenny Kiss'd Me* (1939), *O Mistress Mine* (1942), *Tom O'Bedlam's Song* (1946), *Six Songs* (1949), *Four Blake Songs* (1957)

'Viva Sax', Margery Smith (saxophone), Daniel Herscovitch (piano), Tall Poppies, 1996: *Sonata for Cello (or Saxophone) and Piano* (pre-1937).

'Woman's Song', Elizabeth Campbell (mezzo soprano), Ian Munro (piano), Tall Poppies, 2003, 2005: *Six Songs* (1949), *World and the Child* (1960)

ENDNOTES

Prelude

1 Radic, 'Margaret Sutherland: Composer', p. 398.
2 Sinclair, *Herald*, 8 November 1982.
3 Hamer, Concert Hall Opening Speech, Australian Performing Arts Collection, Arts Centre Melbourne; Sinclair, *Herald*, 8 November 1982.
4 Garretty, p. 59.
5 Covell, p. 152; Murdoch, *Australia's Contemporary Composers*, p. 181.
6 Susan Gubar, 'Blank Page', *Critical Inquiry* 8, 1981, p. 244.
7 Rousseau, quoted in Citron, 'Gender, Professionalism and the Musical Canon', p. 111.
8 Rousseau, quoted in Halstead, p. 98.
9 Upton, quoted in Neuls-Bates, p. 207.
10 Van der Kolk.
11 Heilbrun, pp. 17, 20, 22–3, 48.
12 Halstead p. 7; Gates, pp. 27–34.
13 The Catalysts women's group formed in 1910. They meet monthly for dinner and a lecture, and inspired the establishment of the Lyceum Club, Melbourne, in 1912.

Chapter One: The Gala Days (1897–1901)

1 Sutherland, 'Prodigy', p. 2.
2 Sutherland, 'Young Days', p. 24.
3 Sutherland, 'Three Universities in One'.
4 ibid.
5 ibid.
6 'Prodigy', p. 1.
7 ibid.
8 ibid. The birth certificate states Margaret's birth year as 1896, but Margaret believed it was 1897; major life events were celebrated based on 1897; Prentis,

pp. 67, 77, 140, 142, 231; McCarthy, p. 192; Burke ABC program; Rosewarne, VCAG catalogue.

9 Prentis, pp. 32–3; Alexander (1852–1901), Jane (1853–1928), George (1855–1905), William (1859–1911), Julia (1861–1930), James (1863–1916), John (1867–1914), Jessie (1869–1934). The city was dubbed 'Marvellous Melbourne' by British journalist George Augustus Sala in 1885. 'Marvellous Melbourne', SLV website.

10 Rosewarne, VCAG catalogue.

11 Scotch College 'History', Scotch College website.

12 Turner, p. 7. Designed by architects Henderson & Smart, the building is heritage listed by the National Trust.

13 'Young Days', p. 25. The Australian Church's first minister, Dr Charles Strong, was a progressive cleric who broke away from the Presbyterian Church. He perceived compatibility between belief in God and acceptance of Darwin's theories. His advocacy for the underprivileged and social reform was condemned by his colleagues, and caused a schism in the Presbyterian Church, leading to the formation of the Australian Church. Badger, 'Strong', *ADB*, 1976.

14 Rosewarne, 'Sutherland Family History', p. 1.

15 Examples of other children's stories: *Sixteen Stories of Australian Exploration and Settlement*, with titles including 'Captain Cook's Landing Place', 'Captain Sturt's Black Friend', 'The Burke and Wills Expedition', 'The Roof of Australia', 'A Story of Queensland'.

16 Rosewarne, 'Sutherland Family History', pp. 1–2.

17 ibid., p. 7. Other major works are *Australia or England in the South* (London, 1886) and *The South Australian Company: A Study of Colonisation* (London, 1898).

18 Rosewarne, 'Sutherland Family History', p. 4.

19 Bourne, *OCAM*, pp. 11–14; Rosewarne, 'Sutherland Family History', p. 4.

20 'Sutherland Family History', p. 5.

21 Bowen, p. 13; Rosewarne, 'Sutherland Family History', p. 5.

22 Bowen, p. 19.

23 Rosewarne, 'Sutherland Family History', p. 9.

24 'Young Days', p. 23; ibid.; Burke program; Rosewarne, 'Sutherland Family History', p. 8.

25 Sutherland, 'Adelaide', p. 3; 'Young Days', p. 23.

26 'Adelaide', pp. 1–2.

27 ibid., pp. 2–3.

28 ibid., p. 3.

29 Rosewarne, 'Sutherland Family History', p. 10; 'Young Days', p. 24. Family ties evidenced in Fitzpatrick.

30 Rosewarne, 'Sutherland Family History', p. 11; Tregear, pp. 20–1; RMP formed in 1853; MSV in 1861. Liedertafel groups were brought to Adelaide by German immigrants in the early to mid nineteenth century and spread to Melbourne and elsewhere. Wilmott, 'Liedertafel', *OCAM*, pp. 341–3.

31 Sutherland, notebook, 1966, p. 23.

Chapter Two: The First Memorable Jolt (1901–1903)

1 'Young Days', pp. 24–5.
2 ibid., p. 23; notebook, 1966, p. 23; Burke program; Pratt interview, p. 4.
3 'Young Days', p. 25.
4 ibid.
5 Burke program.
6 De Vries, pp. 196–7.
7 ibid., p. 196; Lindsay, 'Sutherland, Jane', *ADB*, 1990. The Buonarotti Club was established in the 1880s and became a force in Melbourne's art world, advocating for artistic professionalism and expounding bohemian ideas.
8 Hammond and Peers, p. 70.
9 'Young Days', p. 24.
10 Burke program.
11 Osborne, pp. 19–51.
12 Notebook, 1966, p. 8; Home, 'Sutherland, William', *ADB*, 1990.
13 'Young Days', p. 25; Osborne, p. 92.
14 'Young Days', p. 25.
15 ibid., p. 23.
16 Murdoch interview, 1968, p. 8; De Vries, p. 199.
17 Notebook, 1966, p. 27; Sutherland, 'Difficulties', p. 10.
18 'Young Days', p. 25.
19 Alexander's publications included *Victoria and Its Metropolis* (1888, vol. 1), and articles for the *Melbourne Review*, which he founded and coedited. He wrote biographies of Australian author Henry Kendall and poet Adam Lindsay Gordon for *The Development of Australian Literature* (1898), coedited with Henry Gyles Turner, and memoirs of Sir Redmond Barry and Edward Hearn. Northcott, 'Sutherland, Alexander', *ADB*, 1976.
20 The university was the subject of the Fink Royal Commission into University Affairs after embezzlement by its accountant, and was forced to adopt stringent financial measures.
21 'Three Universities'.
22 ibid.
23 ibid.
24 Sutherland, 'Heronswood', p. 7.
25 ibid.
26 ibid., p. 8.
27 Rosewarne, 'Sutherland Family History', p. 12.
28 Barnard.
29 'Difficulties', p.10.
30 Burke program; 'Difficulties', p. 11.
31 Rosewarne, 'Sutherland Family History', p. 13.
32 A memorial fund was established at the university for the Alexander Sutherland Prize, awarded annually to the most outstanding third-year English literature student. 'Heronswood', p. 9.

33 Rosewarne, 'Sutherland Family History', p. 17.
34 Notebook, 1966, p. 10.
35 Burke program; 'Difficulties', pp. 12–13.
36 ibid., pp. 13–14.
37 ibid., p. 14.

Chapter Three: Educated in the True Sense (1904–1913)

1 Sutherland, 'Changing Horses'.
2 McWha, p. 9.
3 Barnard, *Jubilee History* advertisement; 'Baldur', *Australasian*, 1907, p. 53; *Reporter*, 3 January 1908, p. 4; McWah.
4 Radic, 'Adelaide Women Composers' Festival 1991'.
5 Halstead, pp. 108–9; McCalman, pp. 182–3.
6 Gifford, pp. 112–13. The full work was first performed in 1926; Patton, 'McBurney', *ADB*, 1986; *Table Talk*, 24 June 1926, p. 8.
7 'Young Days', p. 25; Burke program.
8 'Young Days', p. 25; Sutherland, quoted in Gillison, p. 49.
9 Sutherland, 'First Glimpses'.
10 'Young Days', p. 24.
11 *Age*, 4 December 1905.
12 'Difficulties', p. 11; 'Young Days', p. 24; Notebook, 1966, p. 29.
13 Burke program; 'Young Days', p. 24; 'Difficulties', p. 11.
14 'Difficulties', p. 12; Rosewarne, 'Sutherland Family History', p. 17.
15 Kingston, *OCAH*, pp. 192–3; Notebook, 1966, p. 29.
16 Sutherland, 'An Alliance', p. 18.
17 ibid.
18 Wilson, p. 441.
19 Radic, 'Margaret Sutherland: Composer', p. 401; Rosewarne, 'Sutherland Family History', pp. 17–18.
20 Wilson, p. 441; Rosewarne, 'Sutherland Family History', pp. 17–19.
21 'Young Days', p. 24.
22 Notebook, 1966, p. 33; Burke program.
23 'Young Days', p. 25.
24 ibid.
25 Moresby, pp. 127–8; Garretty, p. 62; *Advertiser*, 11 August 1926, p. 18. The concert was at Adelaide's Liberal Hall on Friday 13 August 1926. *Register*, 14 August 1926, p. 13.
26 Kincaid. The score is lost, though it was previously thought to be in the Grainger Collection at the University of Melbourne.
27 The school was sold in 1908, following Andrea Tuxen's death. The headmistress was probably Mary Slight Mills. Warren ABC program; Burke program.
28 Unger and Crawford, p. 265.
29 Family background has been equally important for women artists. Nochlin, pp. 352, 360; Greer, p. 12. Fay, 'Women and Music', *Music* 18, 1900, p. 506;

Halstead, p. 86; Citron, 'Women and the Lied', p. 228; Citron, *Gender and the Musical Canon*, p. 61.
30 'Young Days', p. 25.

Chapter Four: To Strike out Somehow (1914–1923)

1 'Young Days', p. 25.
2 ibid.; Rosewarne, 'Sutherland Family History', p. 28.
3 Radic, 'Marshall-Hall', *ADB*, 1986; Tregear, p. 13. Marshall-Hall befriended Heidelberg School painters. These may have included Jane Sutherland.
4 For a while, there were two orchestras in Melbourne. The amateur MSO was formed in 1906 by violinist Alberto Zelman. Until 1902, when a committee took over, Marshall-Hall met his orchestra's expenses himself. In 1908, Sir James Barrett organised the Permanent Orchestra Trust Fund under Lady Northcote's patronage. Radic, 'Marshall-Hall', *ADB*; Tregear, p. 70.
5 Radic, 'Marshall-Hall', *ADB;* Tregear, p. 26.
6 'Young Days', p. 26; Tregear, p. 31.
7 Tregear, pp. 27–8, 57–8; Rosewarne, 'Sutherland Family History', p. 27; 'Young Days', p. 25. Goll arrived in Melbourne in 1911 as Welsh tenor Ben Davies' accompanist. He met a wealthy 45-year-old Australian widow, Julia O'Brien (née Walsh), whom he married in February 1912. 'Goll', *OCAM*, p. 242.
8 'Three Universities'.
9 Watters-Cowan, p. 219.
10 'Young Days', p. 25; 'Three Universities'.
11 Robinson, Chapter 2; Radic, 'Hart', *ADB*, 1983.
12 Watters-Cowan, p. 217; 'Order of Studies', 1915, p. 7, quoted in Watters-Cowan, p. 218.
13 The Celtic 'twilight' was the aesthetic movement in British culture that developed out of the Irish Literary Revival. Symons, p. 6; Sutherland, 'One Lap Behind', p. 14; 'Young Days', p. 25.
14 Rosewarne, 'Sutherland Family History', p. 26; Tregear, 'Hart', *OCAM*, p. 260.
15 The Musical Association of Victoria, formed in 1861, and the Musical Artists and Organists Society of Victoria, formed in 1877, amalgamated in 1892 under the name of 'The Musical Society of Victoria'. Margaret and peers had works performed there. Nemet, 1981, pp. 7, 27; Tan, pp. 11, 37.
16 'Three Universities'. Alfred was at the Gallipoli landing. He was badly injured by a mine and hospitalised for some time. His war experience dogged his postwar life and, like his father and uncles, he died young of heart failure. Despite his asthma, Douglas was permitted to enrol and was shipped to France. In early 1915, he was invalided to England, where he remained until the war ended. He resumed his journalistic career with the *Western Australian*, where he was a subeditor for many years. Cousin Keith survived but, tragically, Dallas was killed in action in France on 19 August 1916. Notebook, 1966, pp. 40–1.
17 'Three Universities'; 'Young Days', p. 25.
18 'Young Days', p. 25; 'One Lap Behind', p. 14.

19 Robinson, Chapter 2; Watters-Cowan, p. 43.
20 Garretty, p. 54; Devaney; Anis, p. 22.
21 McCalman, p. 185; Fitzpatrick, p. 149; Blainey, p. 141.
22 'Young Days', p. 25; Grimshaw et al., *Creating a Nation*, pp. 215, 218; Tregear, p. 54.
23 'One Lap Behind', p. 11.
24 'Young Days', p. 26.
25 'Three Universities'; Rosewarne, 'Sutherland Family History', p. 33.
26 Sutherland, 'School', p. 15.
27 'Young Days', p. 26.
28 Tregear, p. 56; 'Young Days', p. 26.
29 'Young Days', p. 26.
30 ibid.
31 ibid. Julia died in 1930 at sixty-nine; Jessie in 1934 aged sixty-five. These deaths, and Dorothy's in 1937, occurred as Margaret was preoccupied raising children in a hapless marriage, accounting for the absence of reference to these bereavements.
32 Verbrugghen founded this string quartet in Scotland in 1903. He played first violin with Scots Jenny Cullan (second violin) and David Nichols (viola), and Dane James Messeas (cello). 'One Lap Behind', p. 13; 'Young Days', p. 26; Covell, p. 118.
33 Rosewarne, 'Sutherland Family History', p. 36; Davidson, p. 29; Hetherington program.
34 Rosewarne, 'Sutherland Family History', p. 31; 'Young Days', p. 26.
35 Burke program.
36 Margaret probably encountered Dame Nellie Melba at the Lyceum Club, which she joined in 1922. Melba was made an honorary life member in 1916. Bomford, p. 43; Blainey, *I am Melba*, pp. 306–11.
37 'One Lap Behind', p. 4.
38 ibid.
39 ibid., pp. 4–5.
40 ibid., p. 5.
41 ibid.
42 Melba, letter to Sutherland, undated.
43 Rita Stang was educated at PLC from 1905. She graduated in medicine from the University of Melbourne in 1918 and completed a Diploma of Public Health in 1927. When she met Norman, she was practising in Port Fairy, and was resident medical officer at Melbourne public hospitals. She and Norman married in 1919 and divorced in 1927. Tamblyn, 'Stang', *ADB*, 1990; Sutherland, autobiographical note, 1960.
44 *Herald*, 29 October 1918. This is the only reference to Ada's involvement in charity events. *Australasian*, 25 December 1920; *Table Talk*, 30 August 1923.
45 Clarke was well regarded for her softly focused impressionistic style and was the only woman to be included in the First Exhibition of the Australian Salon on Photography in 1924. 'Clarke, Pegg', Australian Women's Register website.

Margaret's lifelong friend and fellow Lyceum member harpsichordist Mancell Kirby told Gifford in 1993 that Margaret was Goll's favourite student, and that he favoured her as his concert page-turner. Gifford, p. 121; Gifford interview.

46 *Register*, 17 May 1920; *Critic*, 19 May 1920.

47 *Age*, 3 May 1921; *Argus*, 3 May 1921.

48 *Herald*, 13 June 1918, p. 5; *Argus*, 19 July 1917, p. 9; *Age*, 6 November 1919, p. 8; AMN, 1 December 1919, p. 170.

49 *Sydney Morning Herald*, 8 December 1919, p. 5; *Sydney Sun*, 7 December 1919, p. 2.

50 'Young Days', p. 27.

51 ibid.

52 ibid.

53 Topliss, p. 110; 'One Lap Behind', p. 12.

54 Bowen, p. 27.

55 'Young Days', p. 27.

56 Gifford interview; Rosewarne, 'Sutherland Family History', p. 50; 'Young Days', p. 27.

57 'Young Days', p. 27.

58 ibid. Ada Sutherland's estate was worth £1370, bequeathed equally to her five children. The Studley Park Road property, valued at £1300 when Ada died, was sold in 1927. Rate records show Margaret boarded in Milton Street, Caulfield, in a house owned by a woman named Susie Ellis. *Rate Books, Victoria*.

Chapter Five: No Props (1924–1925)

1 'Young Days', p. 27.

2 Sutherland, '1920'; *Herald*, 11 February 1924, p. 14; Passenger Departure Records, February 1924, NAA.

3 Gifford, p. 109. Australian citizenship was created through the *Nationality and Citizenship Act 1948* of 26 January 1949. Prior to this, Australians were British subjects.

4 Bowen, p. 6

5 Fitzpatrick, p. 179; Robinson, Introduction; Bowen, pp. 19, 25–6.

6 Rosewarne, 'Sutherland Family History', p. 38.

7 Zemgulys, p. 56. A reference to 'A Room of One's Own', Virginia Woolf's essay arguing for literal and figurative spaces for women writers.

8 Hetherington program; Turner Shaw, Sutherland Memorial talk, p. 2.

9 '1920'; Autobiographical note, 1960, p. 1; Rosewarne, 'Sutherland Family History', p. 38.

10 Autobiographical note, 1960, p. 1; Rosewarne, 'Sutherland Family History', pp. 38–9.

11 Sutherland, quoted in Dawson.

12 Petrus, pp. 79–80, 83–5; Pratt interview, p. 6.

13 Halstead, pp. 108–9; Gray, pp. 245–6. Gray adapted Samuel Johnson's quote 'A woman's preaching is like a dog's walking on his hind legs. It is not done well,

but you are surprised to find it done at all.' Quoted in James Boswell's *The Life of Samuel Johnson LLD* (1791).

14 'Young Days', p. 27.

15 *Argus*, 27 November 1925, p. 22; *Australasian*, 16 August 1924, p. 48; '1920'; 'An Alliance', p. 22.

16 Burke program; Pratt interview, p. 6; '1920'; Mike, p. 231; Gifford, p. 114.

17 *Australasian*, 5 July 1924, p. 46 and 16 August 1924, p. 48; Foreman, p. 410; Symons, p. 13.

18 'Young Days', p. 27; 'Difficulties', p. 23. Margaret's respect for Bax may have been influenced by Goll's enthusiasm for his music. Symons, p. 30; *AMN*, vol. 13, March 1924, pp. 26–7.

19 Burke program; Foreman, p. 219.

20 Oldaker, p. 76; Hain; Pratt interview, p. 6.

21 'Difficulties', p. 23; Foreman, p. 219.

22 Murdoch interview, 1968, p. 7.

23 *Australasian*, 16 August 1924, p. 48; 'An Alliance', pp. 18–21.

24 *Australasian*, 27 September 1924, p.57; Pratt interview, p. 6.

25 Symons, p. 14; Burke program; '1920'; Radic, 'Margaret Sutherland: Composer', p. 401. Les Six included composers Darius Milhaud, Francis Poulenc, Arthur Honegger, Georges Auric, Louis Durey and Germaine Tailleferre.

26 *Argus*, 27 November 1925; Warren, pp. 119–42; Hain.

27 *Listener In*, 16–22 August 1941; Hain.

28 Hain; Davidson, pp. 90, 136, 241. Hanson-Dyer founded Éditions de l'Oiseau-Lyre in 1932, to print historical editions of the music of Lully, Couperin, Jacopo da Bologna and Purcell. She established the BMS Melbourne branch in 1921, to foster music-making by Melbourne players and composers. *OCAM*, p. 75. The BMS became autonomous in 1933 after the demise of its parent body. In 1936, the James and Louise Dyer Trust endowed it with £10000, but its influence gradually waned after Hanson-Dyer left Melbourne for Europe in 1927. Radic, *Bernard Heinze*, p. 37. Hanson-Dyer joined the Lyceum Club in 1912.

29 Hain.

30 Using tone rows—orderings of the twelve pitch classes—this technique ensures the chromatic scale's twelve notes are sounded equally often, preventing emphasis on any one note.

31 Symons, p. 12.

32 Hain.

33 ibid.

34 'An Alliance', p. 22.

35 ibid.

36 The original handwritten score was found by Dr Ian Burk in 2002 in AE Floyd's papers in the Grainger Museum, the University of Melbourne. Lang, *The Swinburne Letters*, quoted in Thompson, p. 19. Melbourne choral director/

composer Daniel Brinsmead assessed 'Death and Birth' and produced a printed version.

37 Garretty, p. 79; Ghandar, *Repercussions*, p. 67.

38 Symons, p. 16. Neoclassicism refers to the trend of returning to aesthetic precepts associated with 'classicism': order, balance, clarity, economy and emotional restraint. It reacted against late romanticism and the experimentation of the twentieth century's first two decades. Although inspired by historical styles, neoclassical works are distinctly twentieth century. 'Neoclassical Music', *New World Encyclopedia*. Gifford, p. 108.

39 'Young Days', p. 27; Bax, letter to Chester, 6 September 1926, MS 12311, SLV.

40 Leila Doubleday spent time in London and studied in Vienna. With her husband, pianist Max Pirani, she toured widely with the Pirani Trio from 1923 to 1940. Elise Steele joined the Society of Women Musicians on 9 July 1923, and Lorna Stirling joined on 9 June 1926. SWM Archive, RCM, London.

41 Sophie Fuller, 'Society of Women Musicians', British Library website.

42 Rosewarne, 'Sutherland Family History', p. 40; *Herald*, Melbourne, 24 August 1925, p. 13; *Argus*, 27 November 1925.

43 Lady Evelyn Guinness (née Erskine), was the fourteenth Earl of Buchan's daughter, and married Walter Guinness, heir to the Guinness brewing fortune. This and the Society of Women Musicians performance were among the rare occasions Margaret performed while overseas.

44 Pratt interview, p. 7, *Argus*, 27 November 1925.

45 'Our History', RANZCP website; '1920'; Rosewarne, 'Sutherland Family History', p. 42.

46 *Australasian*, 16 August 1924, p. 48; *Argus*, 27 November 1925. The eight-week annual Proms were inaugurated in Queen's Hall in 1895 by impresario Robert Newman, to attract wider audiences through lower ticket prices and an informal atmosphere. Conductor Sir Henry Wood's name became the one most associated with them.

47 Sutherland, letter quoted in *Australasian*, 12 September 1925, p. 60. William Boosey, then managing director of Chappell & Co., the Proms proprietor, detested broadcasting.

48 Hain.

49 ibid.

50 'Young Days', p. 27.

Chapter Six: Return to an Uphill Journey (1926–1927)

1 'Young Days', p. 27.

2 *Australasian*, 20 June 1925, p. 48; *Argus*, 27 November 1925, p. 22; *Age*, 26 November 1925, p. 9; Rosewarne, 'Sutherland Family History', p. 44.

3 Rosewarne, 'Sutherland Family History', p. 44; Young Days', p. 27; Gifford, p. 110.

4 Murdoch, 'Perspective' interview; Tregear, pp. 62, 77.

5 Tregear, pp. 71–5; Radic, 'Heinze', *ADB*, 2007 and *Bernard Heinze*, pp. 33, 118, 122.

6 'Perspective' interview.

7 *Melbourne University Calendar, 1926*, p. 59, quoted in Watters-Cowan, p. 226; Tregear, p. 75. Margaret's brother Douglas boarded with the Heinze family in Ballarat after their father's death. Sutherland, 'Several Episodes'; 'Perspective' interview.

8 'Perspective' interview; 'Young Days', p. 27. Musician Ivy Brookes participated in the Lady Northcote Permanent Orchestra Trust Fund with her husband, the businessman, pastoralist, public official and philanthropist Herbert Brookes. She was foundation vice-president of the USO Ladies' Committee, which promoted the USO's concerts under Heinze. Patrick, 'Brookes', *ADB*, 1979. Letters to Brookes, 21 and 27 January 1926, MS 1924, NLA. Designed by architect Henry Kemp, the Assembly Hall, 156–60 Collins Street, was built for the Presbyterian Church (Scots' Church), on the site of the old manse, and opened in May 1915. The late Gothic Revival sandstone structure blends with the adjacent Scots' Church and is on the Victorian Heritage Register. The hall contains the Fincham organ (built in 1905, donated 1920) and a memorial stained-glass window by William Montgomery. 'Assembly Hall', e-Melbourne website.

9 Pavlova performed at His Majesty's Theatre 13 March–14 April 1926. The tour was sponsored by JC Williamson Theatres. Melita, Ausdance website.

10 *Argus*, 13 March 1926, p. 27; Several Episodes'; *Age*, 13 March 1926, p. 16; *AMN*, 1 April 1926, p. 29; *Register*, 14 August 1926, p. 13.

11 Sutherland returned to Martyr's poetry with her *Songs for Children* (1929) and *Two Blue Slippers* (1935).

12 *Argus*, 13 March 1926, p. 27; *Morning Post*, undated, Sutherland Scrapbook, MS 2967, NLA.

13 Citron, *Gender and the Musical Canon*, pp. 168, 180.

14 *Age*, 13 March 1926, p. 18.

15 *Australasian*, 20 March 1926, p. 43.

16 *Argus*, 13 March 1926, p. 27.

17 *AMN*, 1 April 1926, p. 29.

18 'Several Episodes'.

19 Sutherland, quoted in Dawson; 'Perspective' interview; 'Young Days', p. 27.

20 Sutherland, quoted in Garretty, p. 53; Sutherland, 'Occupational Hazards'.

21 Thomas, *Context*, p. 81; Sinclair, *Herald*, 14 May 1964.

22 Letter to Brookes, 14 March 1926.

23 Absolute music is composed simply as music, without attempting to represent anything. Program music is based on literary ideas or mental pictures.

24 Sutherland, 'The Vogue of Bach'.

25 Symons, p. 55.

26 Rosewarne, 'Sutherland Family History', p. 45; *Observer*, 24 April 1926, p. 52.

27 *Mail*, 7 August 1926, p. 16.

28 *Register*, 11 August 1926, p. 10.

29 ibid.
30 *Mail*, 14 August 1926, p. 16.
31 Probably organised by Margaret's cousin and Lyceum member Kathleen Kyffin Thomas. *News*, 12 August 1926, p. 6. The reviewer refers to the concert on 15 May 1920. *Mail*, 14 August 1926.
32 *Age*, 6 September 1926, p. 14. The work referred to may have been Henry Tate's *Bush Miniatures*. Performed in Melbourne in 1925, it contains transcriptions of Australian native birdsong. Carmody, 'Tate', *ADB*, 1990. Oldaker, p. 76.
33 *Age*, 6 September 1926, p. 14.
34 *Corowa Free Press*, 30 July 1926, p. 5; *Corowa Chronicle*, 31 July 1926, p. 3; *Albury Banner and Wodonga Express*, 6 August 1926, p. 32.
35 Blain program; Joan Lindsay, Chapter 2, *Time without Clocks* (e-book), Text, 2020. Daryl Lindsay was NGV director from 1942 to 1956.
36 Holst wrote the music and libretto of this one-act chamber opera, *Sāvitri*. The story is based on the episode of Sāvitri and Satyavan from the *Mahābhārata*. *Argus*, 11 August 1926, p. 16; 30 September 1926, p. 8.
37 The performance started with Holst's *Hymn to Travellers*. Three *Fantasias* for strings and a *Pavan and Galliard* by Orlando Gibbons were included, the latter performed by dancers in Elizabethan costume.
38 Davidson, pp. 115–16.
39 *Age*, 23 October 1926, p. 18; *AMN*, 1 November 1926, p. 22.
40 Sutherland, 'Musical Emancipation'.
41 *Australasian*, 19 March 1927, p. 54.
42 Waters, 15 March 1927; *Age*, 15 March 1927, p. 11; *Argus*, 15 March 1927, p. 13. The first three bars are in Margaret's 1939 thematic index.
43 Waters, 19 March 1927; *Argus*, 19 March 1927, p. 32.
44 *Sun*, 30 April 1927; *Herald*, 28 June 1927, p. 9; *Argus*, 28 June 1927, p. 16.
45 *Australasian*, 16 July 1927, p. 58; 'Young Days', p. 27.

Chapter Seven: The First Hideous Years of Marriage (1927–1933)

1 Sutherland, autobiographical note, 1960, p. 1.
2 Jenny Bunney told Helen Gifford this in the late 1960s, following Margaret's stroke in 1968. Gifford interview.
3 Turner Shaw, 'Education of a Squatter's Daughter', p. 298; Modjeska, 'Rooms of Their Own', pp. 346–7.
4 Von Rompaey interview; Gifford interview; Watters-Cowan, p. 381; Albiston biographical note; Kirsten Bunney interview.
5 Henrietta Dugdale, *A Few Hours in a Far-Off Age*, McCarron, Bird & Co, 1883, p. 11.
6 Osborn, 'Albiston', *ADB*, 1979; Rosewarne, 'Sutherland Family History', pp. 47–8; Affidavit, SCV.
7 Sutherland, 'How to Live in a Room-and-a-Bit'. Mora quoted in McGrath, *Australian*, 30 August 1978, p. 8; Rosewarne, 'Sutherland Family History', p. 49; Sutherland, p. 92.

8 Hyslop, p. 241; Chodorow, pp. 4–5.
9 Crump, quoted in Hetherington program; Turner Shaw, Sutherland Memorial talk, p. 6.
10 White interview. When White was growing up in the 1940s, she often visited Margaret in the family's house in Studley Avenue, Kew, and became a long-term friend. She and her sister lived upstairs in the Studley Avenue house for a period in the 1960s.
11 Sutherland, 'Chant Intérieur', pp. 1–2.
12 Garretty, p. 56.
13 Autobiographical note, 1960, p. 1; Moresby, p. 129.
14 Letter to Brookes, 19 February 1928, MS 1924, NLA.
15 White interview.
16 Autobiographical note, 1960, p. 3.
17 Modjeska, 'Rooms of Their Own', p. 343; Beaton, p. 85.
18 Murdoch interview, 1968, p. 3. Sutherland was invited to submit works to the 1932 AMEB syllabus, and possibly on other occasions. Geitenbeek, p. 32. Although Margaret's works have been listed, she disapproved of music exams and did not pursue inclusion.
19 Turner Shaw and Wilkins quoted in Hetherington program.
20 Fullard, January 1980, quoted in Watters-Cowan, p. 241.
21 Murdoch interview, 1968, p. 2.
22 Gifford, Jane Bunney, Von Rompaey interviews.
23 Bloom interview; Rosewarne, 'Sutherland Family History', pp. 36, 54–5. It is unclear how this edict was transmitted, since Arthur Albiston denied it, and the family valued music.
24 Radic, 'Margaret Sutherland: Composer', p. 404, and 'Adelaide Women Composers' Festival', p. 8; Autobiographical note, 1960, p. 2.
25 In August 1928, she wrote to the *Argus* editor, questioning a concert by British–Russian pianist Benno Moiseiwitsch, who was to perform Beethoven's popular *Appassionata Sonata*. Margaret felt it was selected by entrepreneurs with a low opinion of public taste. *Argus*, 7 and 10 August 1928. An example of an article is 'A New Musical-Box', *Argus*, 4 February 1928, p. 8, about the invention by Russian professor Leo Theremin of 'an amazing instrument', the theremin.
26 'Several Episodes'; Burke program. John Hopkins suggested the event took place at a different venue, the home of Sir David Hennessy. Heinze was apparently courting Hennessy's daughter Valerie (who later became his wife) at the time. See Hopkins (with William Cottam), p. 58.
27 Bomford, p. 11.
28 Turner Shaw, Sutherland Memorial talk, p. 2.
29 Rosewarne, 'Sutherland Family History', pp. 48, 52; Modjeska, 'Rooms', p. 332; Van Rompaey interview.
30 Rosewarne, 'Sutherland Family History', pp. 50–1.
31 'Piano and Vocal Recital', *Age*, 7 June 1928, p. 15.

32 Craft Robert, *Chronicle of a Friendship*, quoted in Modjeska, *Stravinsky's Lunch*, pp. 16–17; 'Chant Intérieur', p. 9.
33 Robinson, OCAM, pp. 475–6; Symons, p. 40. Poems: 'My Kewpie's Name Is Adelaide', 'The Frogs', 'The Black-Bird', 'The Canterbury Bell', 'The Grey Cat', 'Spiders', 'In the Grass', 'Willy Wagtail', 'Good-Night'.
34 Many of Margaret's clarinet works were written for friends Isobel Carter and Thomas White.
35 Yseult Bailey, later Lady Yseult Bailey OBE, was active in Victoria's Kindergarten Union and the Melbourne University Women's Wartime Nursery. She was founding president of the Canberra Nursery Kindergarten Society after moving to Canberra with her husband, Kenneth Bailey, during World War II. She furthered the interests of women and children through the National Council of Women (ACT), the YWCA and the Australian Pre-School Association, with periods as president of all three. Clarke, 'Bailey', Australian Women's Register website. Rosewarne, 'Sutherland Family History', p. 53.
36 Autobiographical note, 1960, p. 8.
37 Albiston, pp. 38–55; Autobiographical note, 1960, p. 8.
38 Albiston, pp. 50, 52; 'Parental Conflict and its Effect on Children', Family Court of Australia website.
39 Letter to Don Banks, 9 January 1972, MS 6830, NLA; Rosewarne, 'Sutherland Family History', p. 56; Kirsten Bunney interview.
40 '1920'.
41 Evan Stark quoted in Hill, Chapter 1.
42 Autobiographical note, 1960, p. 3.
43 Affidavit, SCV.
44 Michael Bunney interview; Letter to Banks, 23 February 1966; Campo.
45 Katie Wright, 'Help for Wayward Children', *History of Education Review* 41:1, 2012, p. 11. According to Rosewarne, Norman was employed briefly as a psychiatrist at the Royal Melbourne Hospital. Rosewarne, 'Sutherland Family History', p. 48; Damousi, p. 184; Albiston biographical note; Sutherland, Autobiographical note, 1960, p. 4.
46 Autobiographical note, 1960, p. 4.
47 ibid., p. 2.
48 For example, Phyllis Batchelor's career began when she appeared on ABC radio in *Young Australia*. She remained with the ABC until the 1970s. Much of her work was performed, broadcast and recorded; only 8 per cent has been published. Esther Rofe worked with the ABC as an arranger and balance officer. Dulcie Holland and Moneta Eagles enjoyed successful careers as film music composers with the NSW Department of the Interior Film Unit. Geitenbeek, p. 31.
49 AMN, August 1933, p. 21, 1 October 1935, p. 10. The Australian Performing Rights Association (APRA) also gave awards, provided a fund to assist composers with music copying and subsidised the commercial release of Australian compositions. Geitenbeek, p. 30.
50 Gifford, p. 118.

Chapter Eight: Breaking Out to Compose (1933–1939)

1 Pratt interview, p. 7.
2 Letter to William Cleary, 26 September 1935, ABC Archives, NAA.
3 *Argus*, 12 March 1938, p. 29.
4 Lee Martin, p. 193.
5 Letter to Robert McCall, 2 November 1938; McCall, memo to James, 19 November 1938, ABC Archives, NAA. Ballarat-born pianist/composer William James studied piano in Melbourne, London and Brussels. He joined the Australian Broadcasting Co. in the late 1920s. When the company was superseded in 1932, he became controller of programs in Victoria, and in 1935 was appointed federal controller, a position he held until 1957. He received an OBE in 1960. Hort, 'James', *ADB*, 1996.
6 Burke program; Radic, 'Margaret Sutherland: composer', p. 404; Hanson-Dyer also supported Australian composer Peggy Glanville-Hicks through publication. Radic, *Bernard Heinze*, p. 37.
7 Lee Martin, pp. 9–10, 189; Citron, 'Gender, Professionalism and the Musical Canon', p. 106.
8 *Age*, 12 December 1934, p. 17. The ABC recorded *Break of Day*, *Green Singer* and another work for two-part girls' voices, *Country Places* (pre-1935; text Eiluned Lewis) with the MLC Choir under Ruth Flockart in 1953. ABC Archives, NAA.
9 The figures for publication and recordings of Sutherland's music were gleaned from varied sources, mostly the latest full catalogue of her works appended to Cherie Watters-Cowan's thesis, pp. 460–669. The Australian Music Centre sells copies of these scores.
10 Murdoch, 'Perspective' interview.
11 Sutherland, quoted in Dawson.
12 Murdoch interview, 1968, p. 7.
13 ABC reports on Margaret's orchestral pieces show she found orchestration for large forces more challenging. Watters-Cowan, p. 283.
14 Smyth.
15 Halstead, p. 112.
16 Lee Martin, p. 25.
17 Waters, *AMN*, 1 July 1938, pp. 3–4.
18 Letter to Don Banks, 21 October (probably) 1975, MS 6830, NLA.
19 *Age*, 14 August 1934, p. 10.
20 *Age*, 2 November 1934, p. 14.
21 *Herald*, 12 March 1947, p. 7; Tregear, pp. 78–80; Radic, 'Heinze', *ADB*.
22 'Several Episodes'; Pratt interview, p. 20.
23 Other works performed included three pieces for unaccompanied cor anglais: these were likely to have been *Threesome (Walking Tune, Homage and Pastorale,* composed pre-1928); *Sonata for Violin and Piano* (1925), *String Quartet No. 1* (1937) and *The Orange Tree* (1938). BMS papers, SLV; Louise Hanson-Dyer/BMS papers, SLV.

24 *Airs* are from Couperin's *Les Goûts-réunis, ou, Nouveaux Concerts* (1724), intended for playing by a variety of musical instruments. They are in the Stockigt Collection at the University of Melbourne's Hanson-Dyer Library, donated by Dr Jim Stockigt, Isobel Carter's son, and catalogued by Dr Jennifer Hill, Dr Peggy Lais and Richard Excell. Original manuscripts of *Two Lyrics for Clarinet Solo*—presumably written for Carter—were also uncovered. These were not included in Margaret's 1939 thematic index. Excell, p. 47.

25 *Age*, 17 October 1935, p. 13; *Herald*, 17 October 1935.

26 Finlay, memo to James, 15 February 1939, ABC Archives, NAA; Gifford interview.

27 Choral works: *Break of Day* (1934), *Quietly as Rosebuds* (1934), *The Green Singer* (c. 1934), *Lament for Early Buttercups* (c. 1935), *Heart of Spring* (1950) and *Petticoat Green* (1953). Voice and instrumental works: *The Orange Tree* (1938) for voice, clarinet (or flute) and piano; *The Soldier* (1943) for spoken male voice or three female voices, wind quartet, celeste and percussion; and *The Gentle Water Bird* (1954) for mezzo soprano, violin or oboe or piano.

28 Slaughter, p. 27; Anderson, 'Neilson', *ADB*, 1986.

29 This appears to be the only work published by the Northcote Trust, though Margaret wrote to it in late 1941, seeking publication assistance. Letter to Herbert Brookes, 9 December 1941, MS 1924, NLA.

30 Symons, p. 50. Elsa Haas copied some of Margaret's works in the 1930s and 1940s.

31 Margaret submitted *The Orange Tree* with several other works to the ABC in July 1939. It recorded *The Orange Tree* (1949) with Swiss–British soprano Sophie Wyss, Thomas White (clarinet) and Margaret (piano). See Radio Supplement, *Age*, 6 October 1949.

32 Shaw Neilson, letter to Sutherland, 22 March 1938, MS 2967, NLA.

33 Shaw Neilson, letter to Sutherland, 30 March 1938.

34 *AMN*, 1 May 1938, p. 7; Waters, *Sun*, 30 March 1938; *AMN*, 1 May 1938, p. 7.

35 *Age*, 30 March 1938, p. 16; Jenkins, *Table Talk*, 6 July 1939; *AMN*, 1 May 1938, p. 7; Tremearne, *Herald*, 30 March 1938.

36 Covell, p. 155; Radic, 'Margaret Sutherland: Composer', p. 405; Woolf, p. 105.

37 Symons, p. 58.

38 Unidentified review, 27 August 1938, quoted in Symons, p. 58; *Argus*, 27 August 1938, p. 13; *AMN*, 1 October 1938, p. 13; Tremearne, *Herald*, 27 August 1938.

39 McCall, memo to James, 16 May 1938; Letter to James, 5 September 1938. The *String Quartet No. 1*, which Hubert Clifford (BBC Empire music supervisor) presumably procured from Hanson-Dyer in London, was one of the few compositions submitted to the BBC (1942); outcome unknown. Watters-Cowan, p. 265.

40 Letter to James, 26 May 1938.

41 Symons, pp. 63–5.

42 Margaret was paid ten guineas for one concert with two repeat performances. James, letter to Sutherland, 2 May 1939. Burke, ABC *Speaking Personally* interview.

43 Autobiographical note, 1960, p. 3.
44 ibid.
45 ibid., p. 4.
46 *Age*, 8 June 1939, p. 4.
47 Tremearne, *Herald*, 30 May 1939; Jenkins, *Table Talk*, 15 June 1939.
48 Autobiographical note, 1960, p. 2.
49 Affidavit; *Australian Women's Weekly*, 19 August 1939, p. 51.
50 Autobiographical note, 1960, p. 3.
51 Sutherland, quoted in Dawson.

Chapter Nine: Compelled to Make the Strongest Protest (1939–1942)

1 Letter to Keith Barry, 3 January 1940.
2 Letter to Chapple, 14 July 1939; Chapple, letter to Sutherland, 19 July 1939.
3 Letter to Chapple, 27 August 1939; Watters-Cowan, pp. 391, 416; Garretty, p. 54.
4 The cello sonata was substituted for Margaret's piano *Sonatina*, because of problems preparing parts. Letter to Chapple, 21 November 1939; Barry, memo to Chapple, 20 November 1939.
5 Letter to Barry, 3 January 1940.
6 Letter to Moses, 29 January 1940.
7 Redstone, memo to James, 18 January 1940; McCall, memo to Moses, 6 February 1940.
8 Barry, memo to Moses, 23 February 1940; James, memo to Moses, 28 February 1940; James, letter to Sutherland, 26 March 1940.
9 Letters to James, 17 February, 22 April 1940.
10 Letter to Barry, 12 March 1940.
11 Barry, letter to Sutherland, 14 March 1940; Letter to Barry, 17 March 1940.
12 Grant, memo to James, 4 April 1940.
13 Letter to James, 28 March 1940.
14 Cleary, letter to Sutherland, 9 April 1940.
15 Letter to Cleary, 10 April 1940.
16 Moses, letter to Sutherland, 29 April 1940.
17 Symons, p. 67.
18 Letter to Chapple, 28 July 1939; James, memo to Moses, 8 April 1940.
19 Collins, 'Post', *ADB*, 2002; Letter to James, 22 April 1940.
20 Kay Dreyfus, 'Ballet Russes in Australia', *Musicology Australia* 34:1, 2012, pp. 151–3.
21 *Listener In*, 16–22 August 1941; Garretty, p. 96.
22 Crotty, 'From Balletic Binge to Cultural Cringe', p. 218; *Age*, 10 May 1940, p. 12; *Sydney Morning Herald*, 20 September 1940, p. 4; Burdett, *Herald*, 10 May 1940; Verchinina, telegram to Sutherland, 20 September 1940.
23 *Herald*, 20 August 1941, p. 5; *Argus*, 20 August 1941, p. 5.
24 James, letter to Sutherland, 10 February 1942; BBC report, 22 July 1942, cited in Watters-Cowan, p, 273.

25 Crotty, *Brolga*, p. 47.
26 Langmore, *Glittering Surfaces*, p. 71; Rosewarne, 'Sutherland Family History', p. 63.
27 ibid. *Midsummer Night's Dream* program, Tin Alley Players Archives, Melbourne University Student Theatre website.
28 For example, *Lullaby* and *Cavatina*.
29 Wilkinson; Manzie; Rosewarne, 'Sutherland Family History', p. 63.
30 Crawford, letter to Sutherland, 2 May 1941, MS 2967, NLA.
31 Letter to James, 7 July 1941.
32 James, letter to Sutherland, 19 August 1941.
33 Letter to James, 27 July 1941.
34 ibid., 4 August 1941.
35 ibid., 3 October 1941.
36 Cardus, *Sydney Morning Herald*, 15 October 1941.
37 Radic, 'Heinze', *ADB*; Tremearne, *Herald*, 24 November 1941.
38 *Argus*, 24 November 1941, p. 2; *Age*, 24 November 1941, p. 6.
39 Rosewarne, 'Sutherland Family History', p. 61.
40 Letter to Don Banks, 21 October 1975. It may have been only the orchestral score that she burned, as she told James in late February 1942 that pianist Raymond Lambert wanted to play her *Concertino*, and that she had given him 'the part'.
41 Letter to James, 1 January 1942; Redstone, memo to James, 6 January 1942.
42 Letter to James, 21 January 1942.
43 Letter to James, 11 April 1942.
44 James, letter to Sutherland, 13 April 1942.
45 Letter to James, 1 January 1942.
46 James, letter to Sutherland, 6 January 1942.
47 *Listener In*, 13–19 December 1941, p. 13.
48 Austin Health website.

Chapter Ten: Something to Do with Unhappiness (1942–1947)

1 Sutherland, CACM draft, 1943, MS 2967, NLA.
2 Pratt interview, p. 8.
3 'Three Universities'.
4 Rosewarne, 'Sutherland Family History', p. 64; *Age*, 18 November 1940, p. 3.
5 Forbes, OCAM, p. 33.
6 Sutherland, 'Accent on Music-Making'.
7 *Age*, 14 September 1943.
8 Turner Shaw, Sutherland Memorial talk, p. 3.
9 Sutherland, 'Struggle', p. 13.
10 Radic, *Bernard Heinze*, p. 111.
11 Stirling diary, 22 January 1943.
12 ibid.
13 Burke program.

14 'Struggle', pp. 10–11. 'Nugget' Coombs was an Australian economist who advised the government on postwar reconstruction. He held governorships of the Commonwealth and Reserve Banks, and had a long relationship with Australian poet Judith Wright.
15 *Argus*, 17 September 1942, p. 5.
16 Stirling diary, 7, 8, 23 March 1943.
17 ibid., 9 January 1943.
18 Sutherland, *Age*, 8 September 1944.
19 Stirling diary, 27 January 1943.
20 Clifford, Report on *The Soldier*, 1945.
21 *Argus*, 17 June 1943, p. 6.
22 According to Dr Ian Burk, the *House Quartet* was broadcast on Dr AE Floyd's *Music Lover's Hour* on 6 May 1951. Watters-Cowan, p. 94; *Argus*, 3 and 8 May 1944, p. 6.
23 Cardus, *Sydney Morning Herald*, 22 October 1945; Kelly, *Sun*, 22 October 1945; *Daily Mirror*, 22 and 25 October 1945.
24 *Canberra Times*, 22 October 1945, p. 2.
25 Symons, p. 84; Murdoch interview, 1968, p. 3.
26 Sutherland, 'Concerts for Young People'.
27 Stirling diary, 20 March 1943.
28 Murdoch interview, 1968, p. 5.
29 Fairfax, p. 18.
30 The Technological Museum became Scienceworks (Newport) in 1992. The Melbourne Museum opened in its premises near the Exhibition Building in 2000.
31 Fairfax, pp. 29–31.
32 ibid., p. 26.
33 Pratt interview, p. 9; 'Struggle', p. 1.
34 Sutherland, CACM letter re petition, 1944, MS 2967, NLA; Fairfax, pp. 27–8.
35 CACM draft, 1943.
36 There were also literary and dramatic societies, the Melbourne Ballet Club, the NGV, the Contemporary Art Society, Twenty Melbourne Painters, Victorian Housewives' Association and several subsidiary groups. 'Struggle', pp. 6–7.
37 Sutherland, note, CACM Scrapbook; 'Struggle', p. 2.
38 'Struggle', pp. 3–5.
39 CACM draft, 1943.
40 'Struggle', p. 10; 'Arts Centre', *Age*, 13 April 1944; Sutherland, *Herald*, 2 March 1944.
41 Turnbull, *Herald*, 10 February 1944.
42 Lloyd, *Herald*, 5 June 1944.
43 ibid., 26 July 1944.
44 Rosewarne, 'Sutherland Family History', p. 82; *Herald*, 2 September 1944.
45 *Argus*, 10 November 1944.

46 *Herald*, 9 November 1944; *Argus*, 10 November 1944.
47 *Argus*, 10 November 1944.
48 Sutherland, Autobiographical note, 1960, p. 5; Mishura email, 9 August 2021; Dahl emails, 5–9 August 2021.
49 Sutherland, note, CACM Scrapbook.
50 CEMA Autumn Program, MS 12311, SLV; note, CACM Scrapbook; Text for ABC Broadcast, ABC Archives, NAA, April 1945.
51 After a concert at the Royal Albert Hall in London, Bernard Heinze introduced Hephzibah and her brother Yehudi to Australian brother and sister Lindsay and Nola Nicholas, heirs to the Australian 'Aspro' pharmaceutical fortune. Yehudi married Nola and, aged seventeen, Hephzibah married Lindsay. Hephzibah Menuhin, letter to Sutherland, 5 December 1944; see 'Struggle', p. 15.
52 Rosewarne, 'Sutherland Family History', p. 84.
53 Autobiographical note, 1960, p. 5.
54 'Struggle', p. 17; Graham, 'Tiriki Onus awarded Harold Blair Scholarship', UoM VCA/MCM Blog, 2012.
55 'Struggle', pp. 17–23; Jenny Crew (John and Gwenda Lloyd's daughter) quoted in Jillian Graham, 'Tiriki Onus'; *Maryborough Chronicle*, 26 April 1948, p. 3; *Herald*, 17 February 1948, p. 1.
56 *Advertiser*, 13 May 1949, p. 9; *Age*, 1 March 1948, p. 2; *Age*, 15 March 1949, p. 4; *Advertiser*, 24 May 1949, p. 1.
57 Sutherland, letter to the *Age*, 18 November 1949, p. 2.
58 Burke program.
59 'Struggle', pp. 23–6.
60 ibid., p. 27.
61 Divorce was still fault based. This changed in 1975 with the Commonwealth Family Law Act. Grimshaw & Nelson, *OCAH*, p. 191. Autobiographical note, 1960, p. 6; Affidavit, SCV.
62 Bomford, p. 115.
63 Gillison, p. 72.
64 Turner Shaw, Sutherland Memorial talk, p. 3.
65 Bomford, p. 135.
66 Langmore, *Glittering Surfaces*, p. 289.
67 Until Ross required large-print books herself, she regularly read to near-blind Margaret in the 1970s. Falk, p. 159.
68 Catalysts Minutes.
69 Rosewarne, 'Sutherland Family History', p. 91; Summy, p. 28; Langmore, 'Duncan', *ADB*, 1996.
70 Sutherland, 'Bartók'; 'Dunera Boys', National Museum of Australia website.
71 Rosewarne, 'Sutherland Family History', p. 93; Langmore, 'Duncan', *ADB*.
72 Rosewarne, 'Sutherland Family History', p. 91; Pratt interview, p. 8.
73 Affidavit, SCV; Autobiographical note, 1960, pp. 6–7.
74 Autobiographical note, p. 7.

75 Gifford interview; Hill, Chapter 3; Modjeska, 'Rooms of their Own', p. 332; Pratt interview, p. 8.
76 Margaret's cousin Sheila, Alexander Sutherland's eldest daughter and a trained librarian, also had marital problems. Aged forty-three, she married a widower, who expected her to give up her Melbourne Book Club job to have children. The marriage being barren contributed to the couple's separation. Rosewarne, 'Sutherland Family History', pp. 22, 50–2, 57.
77 Bailey, letter to Sutherland, 8 October 1947; Macartney, letter to Sutherland, 19 November 1947.
78 Carey, letter to Sutherland, 23 November 1947.
79 Autobiographical note, 1960, p. 5.
80 Hanson-Dyer, letter to Hewett, 29 March 1943.
81 Symons, p. 86.
82 ibid., p. 88; Sutherland, 'Composer's Lodestone', p. 328; Redstone, memo to James, 10 November 1947.
83 Crotty, 'Laurel Martyn', p. 48; Watters-Cowan, p. 416.
84 James, memo to Charlton, 21 July 1948.
85 Turner Shaw, quoted in Hetherington program; Sutherland Memorial talk, p. 4.
86 Albiston, Divorce Certificate, SCV.
87 Alistair Knox, *A Middle Class Man*, Alistair Knox website; 'Stella Park', Family Recollections website; Schofield interview.
88 Cohen interview, Kirsten and Anthony Bunney interviews: the oldest sibling, Anna, died of cancer in 2014, aged sixty; Dahl email; Jane Bunney, Helen Gifford interviews.
89 Barbara Taylor interview.
90 Autobiographical note, 1960, p. 5.

Chapter Eleven: Life Enthralls One (1948–1959)

1 Sutherland, '1920'.
2 Michael and Anthony Bunney interviews; Turner Shaw, Sutherland Memorial talk, p. 6; Rosewarne, 'Sutherland Family History', p. 92.
3 White interview; Jennings, 'Sandra Willson', p. 99. Howe, p. 237. See also Jennings, 'From "Woman-Loving Woman" to "Queer"', *History Compass* 5/6, 2007, pp. 1901–20.
4 Nell (surname unknown), letter to Sutherland, 6 December 1955.
5 Gifford interview.
6 Langmore, 'Duncan', *ADB*.
7 *Argus*, 9 January 1948, p. 5; ABC Program Summaries, 1948, NAA.
8 Letter to Boyer, 24 July 1951.
9 Boyer letter to Sutherland, 2 August 1951.
10 Letter to Boyer, 10 August 1951.
11 *Argus*, 25 August 1948. p. 7; *Advertiser*, 24 August 1948, p. 5.
12 Sinclair, *Herald*, 12 May 1948, p. 5.

13 *Sydney Morning Herald*, 25 June 1949, p. 7.
14 The Victorian State Government insisted on the name 'Victorian State Orchestra' to reflect the orchestra's responsibility to the state. In 1965, Sir Charles Moses persuaded Victorian premier Sir Henry Bolte to revert to 'Melbourne Symphony Orchestra' to conform with overseas practice. By this time, the University of Melbourne was willing to cede its copyright in the title. Radic, *Bernard Heinze*, p. 144; Symons, *The MSO*, pp. 64, 78.
15 Kimber Leske email.
16 Glickman, quoted in Watters-Cowan, p. 410; Turner Shaw, Sutherland Memorial talk, p. 6.
17 Rosewarne, 'Sutherland Family History', pp. 93–4.
18 Murdoch interview, 1968, p. 3.
19 ibid.
20 Radic, *Bernard Heinze*, p. 163.
21 Murdoch interview, 1968, p. 4.
22 Symons, p. 91.
23 Palmer, preface. The songs are: 'Ballad of Ben Hall', 'Broken Down Squatter', 'Flash Jack from Gundagai', 'Old Bullock Dray', 'Old Keg of Rum', 'Road to Gundagai', 'Song of Ballarat', 'Song of the Free Selector', 'The Stockman's Last Bed', 'Wild Colonial Boy', 'Ballad of Jack Lefroy', 'The Banks of Condamine' and 'Overlander'. The ABC recorded the last three in 1955.
24 Redstone, memo to James, 2 September 1947; Symons, p. 82.
25 Garretty, p. 74; Sutherland scrapbook, Bunney collection; Symons, p. 106.
26 Judith Wright, letter to Sutherland, 15 June 1950.
27 Slaughter, p. 41; Garretty, p. 71.
28 *Advertiser*, 21 April 1950, p. 13.
29 Sinclair, *Herald*, 6 May 1950, p. 11.
30 Tidemann, *Advertiser*, 5 May 1950, p. 17.
31 ibid., 8 May 1950, p. 5; Penalurick, *News*, 8 May 1960, p. 5.
32 *News*, 9 May 1960, p. 19.
33 Watters-Cowan, p. 105; Symons, p. 137.
34 'Composer's Lodestone'; Sutherland, program note, March 1971.
35 Pratt interview, p. 16; letter to Murdoch, April 1976; Oldaker, p. 76.
36 James, letter to Sutherland, 20 October 1950; *Sydney Morning Herald*, 24 March 1951, p. 2; Allen, *Argus*, 15 October 1951, p. 6; Sinclair, *Herald*, 15 October 1951, p.2; Antill, ABC Report, 6 May 1955.
37 Robertson, *Advertiser*, 27 August 1951, p. 6.
38 Murdoch interview, 1968, p. 6; letter to Banks, 22 February 1975.
39 *Argus*, 18 August 1951, p. 18; Symons, p. 95.
40 *Canon*, December 1951, p. 227.
41 Letter to James, 8 November 1951; James, letter to Sutherland, 13 November 1951.
42 Sutherland, 'These Things'.

43 ibid.; Pratt interview, p. 14.
44 Murdoch interview, 1968, p. 6.
45 Refer Symons, p. 72.
46 Letter to James, 6 February 1953; Joseph Post (ABC acting director of music), letter to Sutherland, 14 March 1958; James, letter to Moses, 24 May 1955; Badger, letter to James, 11 April 1955; 1955 ISCM Festival, ISCM website. One of Margaret's works (probably *Trio for Clarinet, Viola and Piano*, 1935) was submitted to the ISCM Festival in Barcelona in 1936, held despite the Spanish Civil War (1936–39). Margaret's work was not programmed, and the score went missing during its return. She was unwilling to submit another until 1955. *Herald*, 3 July 1937; Gifford, p. 118; Kerry Murphy email, 8 December 2021.
47 Bourne, letter to Sutherland, c. 1956.
48 Sculthorpe, p. 32; O'Connell, *Age*, 27 November 2012, p. 15.
49 Symons, p. 18; Watters-Cowan, p. 276.
50 ABC Archives, NAA; Watters-Cowan, pp. 257, 260, 263–4, 267.
51 Sutherland, 'Our Musicians Abroad', p. 22.
52 ibid., p. 23.
53 *Advertiser*, 22 February 1952.
54 'These Things'; Anthony Bunney interview.
55 'These Things'.
56 ibid.; Brymer, letter to Sutherland, 28 August 1952.
57 Sutherland, 'Loose Legs'.
58 ibid., Sutherland, letter to Hanson-Dyer, 15 June 1951.
59 'Loose Legs'.
60 'These Things'.
61 ibid.
62 Langmore, 'Duncan', *ADB*.
63 Fairfax, p. 57; Letter to Banks, 21 April 1953.
64 Sutherland, letters to the *Age*, 27 March 1953, p. 2; 2 May 1953, p. 2.
65 Green, p. 246; Symons, pp. 22, 166.
66 Symons, p. 168; *Argus*, 10 September 1954; Dorian Le Gallienne, *Argus*, 17 July 1956, p. 7; Symons, pp, 168–70; Sinclair, *Herald*, 10 August 1954, p. 7; *Age*, 10 August 1954, p. 2; Badger, letter to James, 11 April 1955.
67 Watters-Cowan, p. 135; Garretty, p. 96.; 'Lodestone'.
68 Symons, pp. 142–3; Murdoch interview, 1968, p. 7.
69 Pratt interview, p. 17; Sutherland, 'John Hopkins, James Murdoch and Don Banks'.
70 *Age*, 2 August 1954; Sinclair, *Herald*, 2 August 1954.
71 Stockigt, pp. 38–40; Graham, 'Kogan', *ADB*, 2007.
72 Letter to Banks, 19 December 1958.
73 Oistrakh, letter to Sutherland, 6 July 1959.
74 Myer, letter to FG Nicholls, 4 October 1957; Letter to Sculthorpe, 14 August 1957.
75 Murdoch interview, 1968, p. 9; Pratt interview, p. 18.

76 Fairfax, pp. 55–8.
77 Hopkins, p. 58. The CAAC is explained further in Chapter 13.
78 Radic, 'Heinze' *ADB*; *Bernard Heinze*, 1986; Fairfax, p. 25; Heinze, telex to James, 6 July 1956, ABC Archives, NAA.
79 Quoted in Radic, *Bernard Heinze*, p. 177.
80 Radic, *Bernard Heinze*, p. 122.
81 Heinze chaired the working party. Other members were John Bishop and singer/arts administrator Dorothy Helmrich. Southcott, pp. 81–2.
82 Symons, p. 174; Lorna Stirling Memorial program, Bunney collection, 1 April 1957; Garretty, p. 92.
83 Sutherland, quoted in Garretty, p. 72; Symons, p. 108; Antill, ABC report, 10 April 1958.
84 Letter to Sculthorpe, 2 June 1958. Prokofiev originally composed this sonata for flute, but Oistrakh persuaded him to arrange it for violin. 'In Honour of David Oistrakh' program, MS 2967, NLA; 'Beryl Kimber, Clemens Leske', Adelaide A–Z website.
85 Felsman, letter to Sutherland, 1 June 1959; Covell, 'The Music of Centenary Year', *Music and Dance* 50:6, 1959, p. 9.
86 Symons, p. 153; Quoted in *Herald*, 31 October 1959; Noone, *Advocate*, 16 June 1966.
87 Antill, ABC Report, 5 September 1958; Hetherington program; Hopkins, p. 56.
88 'Hopkins, Murdoch and Banks', p. 24; Letter to Murdoch, 20 July 1975; Hopkins, p. 56. The painting was first shown at the Twenty Melbourne Painters Society Exhibition, 1939. David Thomas, p. 247.
89 Letter to Banks, 29 December 1958; Fairfax, pp. 63, 67.

Chapter Twelve: Kabbarli, Commissions and a-Room-and-a-Bit (1960–1968)

1 Letter to Banks, 4 December 1966.
2 Heinze departed for the New South Wales State Conservatorium in 1957; Loughlin replaced him. He was Ormond Professor of Music from 1958 to 1979, and director until 1974.
3 Tregear, pp. 101, 112; Letters to Banks, 1 October 1967, 1 January 1968.
4 UNESCO Seminar Program, 1960, Bunney collection.
5 Copland, letter to Sutherland, 22 April 1960; Schofield interview.
6 Sutherland, Autobiographical note, 1960, p. 8.
7 ibid.; Dahl email.
8 Gifford interview.
9 Letter to Post, 20 November 1960.
10 Post, letter to Sutherland, 5 December 1960.
11 Figures provided by Judith Foster, AMC, 15 February 2008; Macarthur, p. 130.
12 Murdoch interview, 1968, p. 7.
13 Sutherland, quoted in Garretty, p. 97.
14 Letter to Murdoch, 19 April 1976; Matthews, quoted in Garretty, p. 100.

15 Letter to Post, 7 February 1961; Letter to Sculthorpe, 30 October 1961.
16 Sinclair, *Herald*, 11 October 1961; Werder, *Age*, 12 October 1961; Gilfedder, *Sun*, 12 October 1961.
17 Concert flier, 20 February 1961, ABC Archives, NAA.
18 Letter to Post, 8 August 1961; Post, letter to Sutherland, 14 November 1961.
19 Michael Bunney interview.
20 Anthony Bunney interview; Anna Davies, quoted in Watters-Cowan, pp. 226–7.
21 Letter to Sculthorpe, 29 March 1962.
22 Letters to Sculthorpe, 29 March 1962, 5 June 1963; Letter to Banks, 9 June 1964.
23 Letter to Banks, 1963.
24 Letter to Sculthorpe, 10 February 1963.
25 ibid., 1 September 1963; Letter to Banks, 6 March 1965; White interview.
26 BMS minutes, 16 May 1962, 28 November 1962, BMS Annual Report 1962–3; Bomford, p. 186.
27 Bomford, p. 191; Langmore, *Glittering Surfaces*, p. 148. The poems are 'Australia', 'Awaking', 'Wind and Places', 'For a Birthday Book', 'Flight', 'To Any Human Body', 'For a Birthday Book 2', 'Kyoto', 'My Mother's Garment' and 'Incantation'.
28 Langmore, *Glittering Surfaces*, p. 181; Watters-Cowan, p. 91. The musicians were George Dreyfus (bassoon), Vincent Edwards (viola), Peter Richardson (flute) and Sutherland (either percussion or piano).
29 Melbourne chapter formed by James Murdoch in 1965. Green, p. 248; Adelaide Festival program, 1964, p. 20; Murdoch interview, 1968, p. 7; Brissenden, 'Bishop', *ADB*, 1993; Letter to Banks, 7 January 1965.
30 Jillett, *Age*, 9 May 1964; Sutherland, VSO Celebrity Concerts program note, May 1964, quoted in Watters-Cowan, p. 120; Letter to Banks, 9 June 1964. The 'deputy conductor' may have been Heinze.
31 Letter to Banks, 9 June 1964.
32 'Vascular Dementia', Johns Hopkins Medicine website. Professor John Spicer, a member of the Canterbury Baptist Church, remembers the Duncan family and suggested it was the Hedley Sutton facility, then at 2 Gascoigne Street, Camberwell, where Con moved. This was confirmed by an electoral record search by Constance Duncan scholar Karen Pack. Spicer email, 3 September 2021; Pack email, 10 December 2021; Letter to Banks, 23 February 1966.
33 Kyffin Thomas, letter to Sutherland, 12 November 1964.
34 Langmore, *Glittering Surfaces*, p. 181; Symons, p. 114; *Sydney Morning Herald*, 5 August 1965.
35 Birns, p. 23; Symons, 'Jindyworobak Connection', *Context* 23, 2002, pp. 33–5. Composers include Alfred and Mirrie Hill, Clive Douglas, John Antill, James Penberthy and Peter Sculthorpe.
36 Symons, *Music of Margaret Sutherland*, p. 122.
37 Hince, *Australian*, 23 August 1965; Langmore, *Glittering Surfaces*, p. 181; Covell, p. 260.
38 Brumby, letter to Murdoch, August 1967.

39 Hince, *Australian*, 9 December 1972, p. 21.
40 Letter to Casey, 27 September 1965; Langmore, *Glittering Surfaces*, p. 201.
41 HC Coombes Creative Arts Fellowship website; Letter to Christesen, 1 October 1964.
42 Dreyfus, Comments on Memorandum, 29 January 1966, Christesen Archive, UoM.
43 Letter to Banks, 24 March 1968; Werder, *Age*, 25 March 1968, p. 4.
44 'Struggle', pp. 28–9.
45 Letter to Banks, 23 February 1966; Sutherland, 'How to Live in a Room-and-a-Bit'.
46 Gifford interview.
47 Cairns was an economist and left-wing politician. Briefly deputy prime minister in the Whitlam government, he was prominent in the anti-Vietnam war movement. Through Junie Morosi, with whom he had an affair that caused public controversy, he became involved in the counterculture movement.
48 Taylor interview.
49 Letter to Banks, 23 February 1966.
50 Letter to Ella Grainger, 5 May 1966; Ella Grainger, letter to Sutherland, 24 March 1966.
51 Sutherland, 'Strange Story of Percy Grainger'; Letters to Murdoch, 1 January 1970, 3 February 1970, 22 February 1970. Murdoch may have planned to use the Grainger article for *Australia's Contemporary Composers*, but Grainger isn't featured.
52 Letter to Casey, 13 December 1966.
53 Letter to Banks, 4 December 1966; Williams, 'Hermit of Green Light', concert introduction, Adelaide Festival, 6 March 2021.
54 Scholarship founded by pianists Ada Corder and Nancy Weir in 1965. Until 1976, it commissioned original piano works by Australian composers and enabled Australian pianists to study abroad. Matthews, 'Corder', *ADB*, 2007. Gifford, quoted in Ghandar, 'The Context of *Chiaroscuro* I', pp. 126–7; Letter to Banks, 24 March 1968.
55 'Concert of Works by Margaret Sutherland' program, 27 September 1967.
56 Werder, *Age*, 26 and 28 September 1967; Sinclair, *Herald*, 28 September 1967.
57 Sinclair, *Herald*, 30 September 1967.
58 Letter to Banks, 1 October 1967.
59 White interview; Letter to Banks, 1 January 1968; Shah, p. 30.
60 Letter to Banks, 1 January 1968.
61 Letter to Murdoch, postmarked 28 October 1968.

Chapter Thirteen: I Terribly Love Australia (1969–1984)

1 Letter to Banks, 4 May 1969.
2 UoM commencement booklet, 29 March 1969; George Loughlin, *Cities of Departure*, self-published, 1984; *University Gazette*, May 1969, p. 10.
3 Letter to Murdoch, 24 July 1971.

4 BMS minutes, 22 April 1969.
5 Sinclair, 'Margaret Sutherland', p. 57.
6 'Emotional and Personality Changes after Stroke', Australian Stroke Foundation (ASF) website. 'Depression and Anxiety after Stroke', ASF website; 'Hallucinations and Delusions', UK Stroke Association website.
7 Letter to Murdoch, 27 May 1969; Murdoch, letter to Sutherland, 5 June 1969.
8 Sinclair, *Herald*, 26 February 1968.
9 ibid.,14 November 1969.
10 Radic, *Bernard Heinze*, pp. 199–200.
11 Letters to Murdoch, 15 September 1969, 6 October 1969.
12 Letter to Banks, 15 October 1969.
13 Murdoch, letter to Sutherland, 20 December 1969.
14 ibid.; Murdoch, *Australia's Contemporary Composers*, p. xii.
15 Letter to Murdoch, 11 January 1970.
16 The same musicians recorded it for the ABC. See Chapter 11; Letter to Murdoch, 22 February 1970.
17 Letter to Banks, 16 May 1970.
18 Burke program.
19 Letter to Banks, postmarked 28 June 1970.
20 Pack, Chapter 44.
21 Letter to Banks, 21 December 1970.
22 ibid., 1 January 1971.
23 Letter to Murdoch, 24 July 1971.
24 McIntyre email, 24 August 2021.
25 Kirsten and Anthony Bunney interviews.
26 Letter to Banks, 9 January 1972.
27 Kirsten Bunney interview.
28 Kirsten, Michael and Anthony Bunney interviews, August 2021; Gifford interview; Ryerson Index.
29 Bomford, p. 216; Lyceum Archives, SLV; Pratt interview, pp. 1, 15.
30 Letter to Hopkins, 19 October 1972.
31 Westbrook, letter to 'Mr and Miss Bunney', 3 November 1972; *Age*, 21 November 1972; *Listener In*, 18–24 November 1972, p. 9.
32 Letter to Hopkins, 19 October 1972.
33 Letter to Banks, 30 January 1973.
34 Symons, p. 26; Sitsky, 'Banks', *ADB*, 1993; Letter to Banks, 22 February 1973; Watters-Cowan, pp. 460–669.
35 Stevens, *Age*, 7 July 1973; Letter to Murdoch, 26 April 1973; Wilkins, letter to Murdoch, 14 June 1973.
36 Catalysts minutes, 13 August 1973; Jane Bunney interview.
37 Ada Corder was a student of Edward Goll at the Melbourne University Conservatorium. She was a concert pianist but was best known as a teacher. Her pupils included Stephen McIntyre. Letter to Banks, 16 August 1973.

38 Lorenz, p. 74.
39 Burke program.
40 *Canberra Times*, 1 November 1976, p. 1; *Age*, 2 July 2001; Murphy, letter to Watters-Cowan, 11 March 2002; reproduced in Watters-Cowan, p. 392.
41 Wilkins, letter to Murdoch, 11 February 1977.
42 Letter to Murdoch, 17 February 1977. The history was not completed, but the draft is a useful source. Jane Bunney interview.
43 Letter to Murdoch, 20 May 1977.
44 'Our History', Old Colonists' website; Letter to Murdoch, 5 June 1977.
45 McCulloch, *Herald*, 15 September 1977; White, *Age*, 12 September 1977.
46 Hetherington, letter to Murdoch, 15 November 1977.
47 Crump, letter to Murdoch, 25 November 1977; Sinclair, *Herald*, 21 November 1977.
48 Murdoch, letter to Crump, 1 December 1977; Murdoch, 'Tribute', October 1984, p. 10.
49 Murdoch, letter to Battersby, 15 March 1978.
50 Murdoch, letter to Westbrook, 10 April 1978; Westbrook, letter to Murdoch, 12 April 1978; Gifford interview.
51 Battersby, letter to Murdoch, 20 March 1978; Pascoe, letter to Murdoch, 16 February 1979.
52 Crump, letters to Murdoch, 13 March 1980, 11 August 1980.
53 Michael Bunney interview.
54 *Age*, 13 June 1981, p. 14.
55 Murdoch, 'Tribute', p. 11.
56 Anna Murdoch, *Age*, 9 April 1984.
57 Murdoch, 'Tribute', p. 10.
58 Sinclair, *Herald*, 14 August 1984; Mitchell, *Australian*, 5 September 1984; Gifford interview.

Coda

1 Murdoch, 'Tribute', p. 10.
2 Ciaran Frame, *Living Music Report 2020*.
3 Sellars email, 10 November 2021.
4 Northey email, 23 November 2021.
5 Wilkie, *Limelight*, 31 March 2021.
6 Knighton email, 4 November 2021.
7 Abbott email, 9 November 2021.
8 Spencer email, 8 November 2021.
9 Fairfax email, 2 November 2021.
10 Murdoch, 'Tribute', p. 11.

INDEX

'MS' means Margaret Sutherland. Endnotes are indicated by page number followed by note number, for example '268n54'.

THE MIEGUNYAH PRESS

This book was designed and
typeset by Cannon Typesetting
The text was set in 11 point Albertina
with 15¾ points of leading
The text was printed on 80gsm uncoated woodfree
This book was edited by Sarina Rowell

THE
MIEGUNYAH
PRESS